THE HISTORICAL ATLAS OF THE BIBLE

A Quantum Book

ISBN: 978-1-84573-566-1

This book is produced by
Quantum Publishing
6 Blundell Street
London, N7 9BH

This edition printed in 2014
QUBMED

Publisher: Kerry Enzor
Quantum editorial: Sam Kennedy and Hazel Eriksson
Production manager: Rohana Yusof

Edited & designed by 3REDCARS
www.3redcars.co.uk

Manufactured by 1010 Printing International Ltd.
Printed in China

THE HISTORICAL ATLAS OF THE BIBLE

BY
DR IAN BARNES

Quantum Books

CONTENTS

INTRODUCTION

THE WORD 'Bible' comes, through Latin, from the Greek word biblia, *meaning 'books', which in its turn comes from* byblos, *meaning 'papyrus', the material from which books were made.*

We are used to speaking of the Bible as a single book, but, in fact, it is a collection of works, of different authorship and written at different times, and selected from a wider range of writings to make up the Bible as we know it. The books of the Old Testament were written over centuries, and some of them were added to or changed their form over many years. None of the original manuscripts has survived, but by the 2nd Century BC the Old Testament had been organized into the 24 books that make up the Hebrew Bible.

The earliest translation of the Hebrew scriptures was the Septuagint, a Greek translation of all the Old Testament canonical books and some of those that are regarded by many as apocryphal. The Jewish translators started work on the Pentateuch (Genesis, Exodus, Leviticus, Numbers and Deuteronomy) in Alexandria in the first half of the 3rd Century BC. The other canonical books appear to have been translated by the end of the 2nd Century BC. The Septuagint forms the basis for several subsequent translations. In AD 382, St Jerome made a Latin translation, called the Vulgate, which is still used by the Roman Catholic Church.

Where translations of the Old Testament books are taken from the Hebrew, the source is generally what is known as the Masoretic text or Masorah. The Masoretes (transmitters) probably started their work around AD 500 and did not finish it until the 10th Century.

Most biblical texts have come down to us as a result of repeated copying in a perishable medium, such as leather or papyrus. The latter was made from the pith of the papyrus plant, cut into strips and glued together cross-wise like plywood. The single sheets of papyrus were normally joined together to form rolls up to 9 metres (30 ft) long. These were inscribed on the inner side only, where the fibres ran lengthwise. The text was written in narrow parallel columns, with a reed pen trimmed at the top, which was dipped into ink made from soot or gall. Another form of book commonly chosen by biblical scribes was the codex, which in its basic form corresponds to a modern book. Four or more double-size sheets were laid on top of each other and folded in the middle, forming a 'codex' that then needed binding. The page of a codex was written in one to four parallel columns.

After AD 200, the more expensive, but much harder wearing, parchment gradually supplanted papyrus. Parchment is animal skin (from sheep, goats, calves or antelopes) with hair and grease removed, and then smoothed and bleached. In the late Middle Ages, parchment was gradually replaced by paper.

The greatest breakthrough in finding old texts was the discovery of the Dead Sea Scrolls in 1947. The Scrolls were found in a cave near the Dead Sea and finally identified as Hebrew texts. One of them was a copy of the Book of Isaiah. When compared with the Masoretic texts, various differences were found, but on the whole there were no major changes and the discovery tended to give greater authority to the accuracy of the Jewish copyists. The books of the New Testament were written in Greek in the 1st Century AD, but the earliest manuscripts date from the 3rd and 4th Centuries AD. There are about 175 manuscripts dating from this period, written on papyrus or parchment, most of them well preserved.

ILLUMINATED MANUSCRIPTS
This decorated initial to the Gospel of Matthew comes from the richly illustrated Lindisfarne Gospels. The manuscript dates back to the 8th Century.

Two developments stimulated the reading of the Bible: the printing press and the rediscovery in the Renaissance of classical authors. The scholarly study of Greek and Latin was then extended to Hebrew and Aramaic. As early as 1477, the Psalms were printed in Hebrew in Italy; the complete Old Testament followed in 1488. An early scholarly edition is the Bombergiana (1516–17), edited by Felix Pratensis and named after its Antwerp printer, Daniel Bomberg, who had set up his Venetian printing house in 1515. The Bombergiana is what is known as a rabbinical Bible, because each page has a Hebrew text of the Old Testament with its Aramaic translation, and commentaries by Jewish scholars above, below and alongside the Bible text. The text of its second edition of 1524–25 has remained the basis of all printings of the Hebrew Bible.

Equally important is the Complutensian Polyglot, which appeared in Alcalá, in Spain, around 1520. This opus has Hebrew, Aramaic, Latin and Greek text and marginal notes on each page of the Old Testament. The printing of the New Testament was complete in 1514, but the Papal imprimatur did not arrive until 1520, so the Basel printer Froben preceded the publication of the Complutensian Polyglot with a less thorough edition of the Greek New Testament in 1516, the work of Erasmus of Rotterdam.

In the history of the Greek New Testament, the most significant edition is the Editio Regia of the Paris printer Robert Stephanus. It contains the Erasmus text corrected in accordance with the Complutensian Polyglot and other manuscripts and is the first edition to possess a critical apparatus. The next edition of this publication in 1551 originated the division of the text into the verses we use today. The traditional division into chapters had appeared soon after 1200 and is attributed to Archbishop Stephen Langton of Canterbury, England.

The Renaissance made a highly dramatic contribution to Bible study – the Reformation. The reformers thought the Bible had been closed to far too many Christians and claimed that people should learn to live again by the Bible, *sola scriptura* – 'by the scriptures alone'. Hence, the Bible was translated into English by John Wycliffe (c. 1382), William Tyndale (1525) and Miles Coverdale (1535).

The Bible is the bestselling and most widely distributed book in the world. In 1988, the United Bible Society reported that the number of languages and dialects into which complete books of the Bible had been translated had reached 1,907. This includes Bibles in 310 languages and New Testaments in 695 languages.

Why has the Bible, a collection of ancient and diverse writings, achieved such a status in the modern world? There is no single answer, just as there is no single attitude to the Bible. To some, it is the supreme holy book, the inspired word of God, still relevant as a guide to faith and conduct. To others, it is primarily of great historical interest, charting the history of the Jewish people over centuries and the origins and growth of the Christian Church. To some, it is essentially a myth, a collection of stories that evolved to explain natural phenomena and events.

For many people, the Bible has no particular significance. It is a book they own but never read, believing it to be of little interest or relevance. They are missing out on a wealth of information and entertainment. Whatever the reader's religious views, the Bible remains an important record of ancient history and ideas, whose significance on Western culture, language and thought is incalculable. It is also a considerable work of literature, containing beautiful poetry, exciting stories and inspirational characters.

TIMELINES

In this book, the story of the Bible is covered thematically, which can make relating one event to another problematic. The charts on these pages give some background into the chronology of these turbulent times. The first chart, below, locates the history of states of Israel and Judah alongside other major ancient civilizations mentioned in the Bible, such as the Egyptians, Syrians and Romans.

The second chart, on the opposite page, represents a slice through a mound or 'tel', to use the Hebrew word that appears in many place-names, including Tel Aviv. The chart reveals the different layers of human culture that would be found from the Stone Age through to the most recent Islamic period. On this chart the beginning of the Bronze Age is referred to as the transitionary Chalcolithic (Copper-Stone) Age.

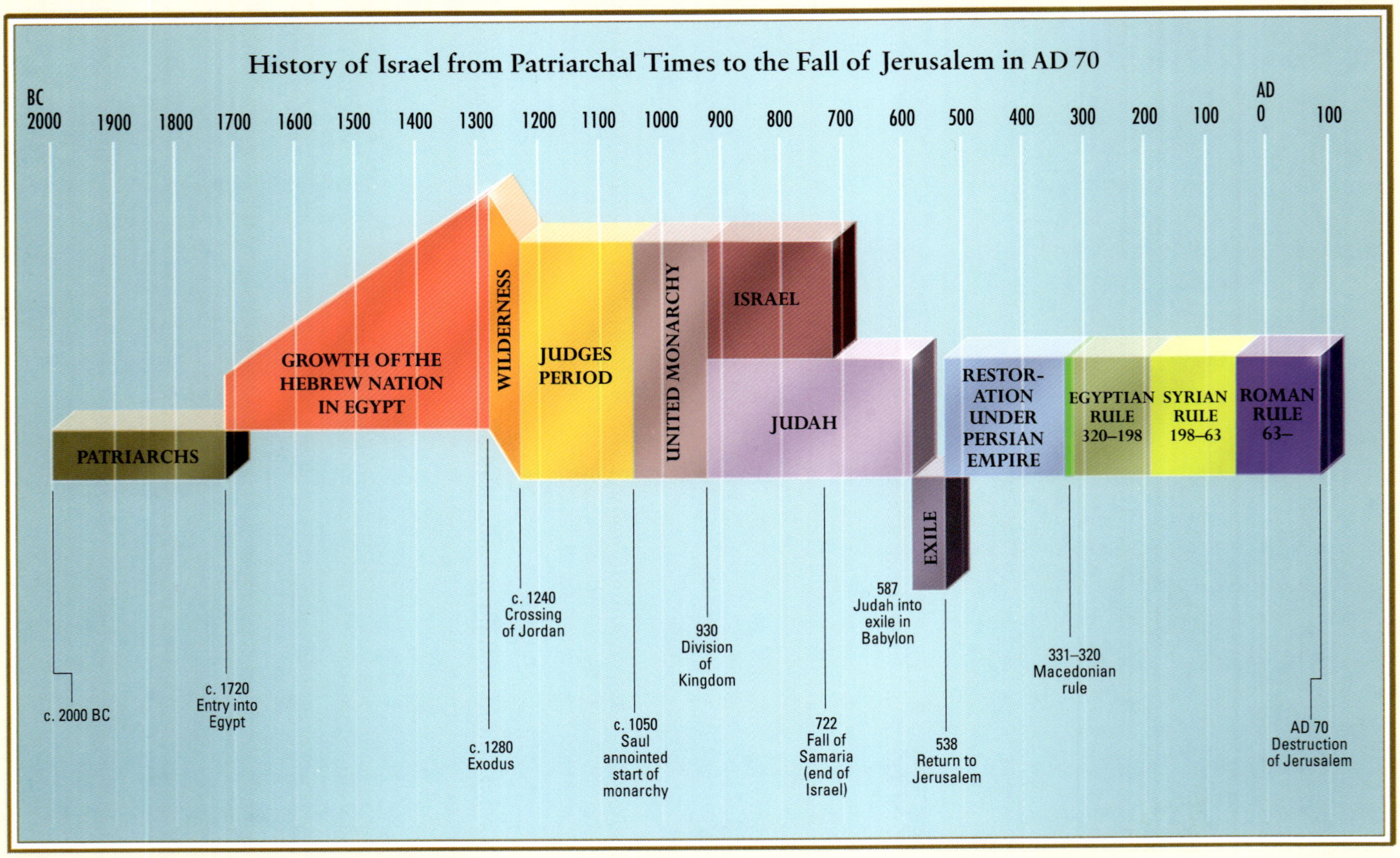

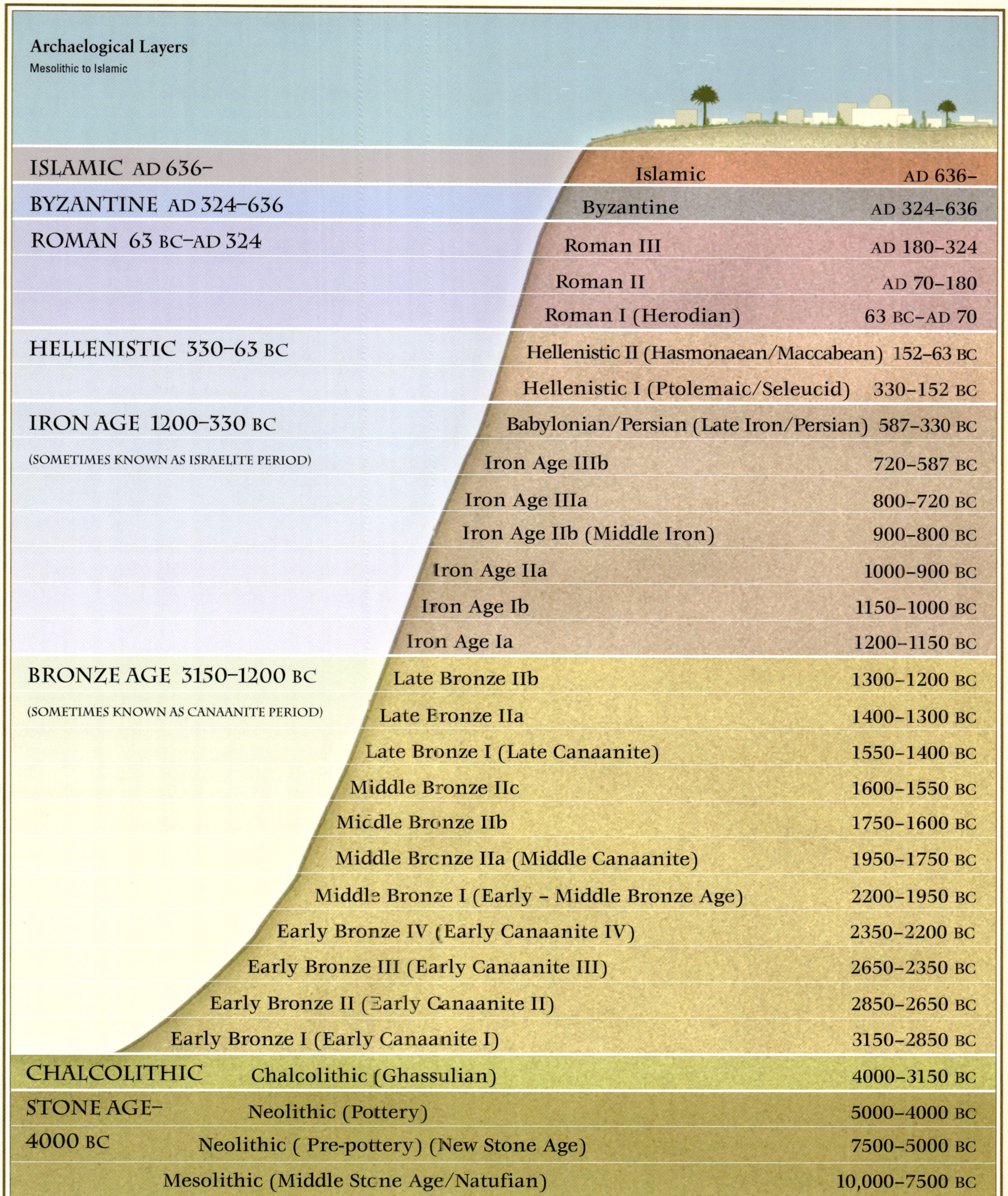
Archaelogical Layers
Mesolithic to Islamic
ISLAMIC AD 636–
BYZANTINE AD 324–636
ROMAN 63 BC–AD 324
HELLENISTIC 330–63 BC
IRON AGE 1200–330 BC
(SOMETIMES KNOWN AS ISRAELITE PERIOD)
BRONZE AGE 3150–1200 BC
(SOMETIMES KNOWN AS CANAANITE PERIOD)
CHALCOLITHIC
STONE AGE–4000 BC
Islamic AD 636–
Byzantine AD 324–636
Roman III AD 180–324
Roman II AD 70–180
Roman I (Herodian) 63 BC–AD 70
Hellenistic II (Hasmonaean/Maccabean) 152–63 BC
Hellenistic I (Ptolemaic/Seleucid) 330–152 BC
Babylonian/Persian (Late Iron/Persian) 587–330 BC
Iron Age IIIb 720–587 BC
Iron Age IIIa 800–720 BC
Iron Age IIb (Middle Iron) 900–800 BC
Iron Age IIa 1000–900 BC
Iron Age Ib 1150–1000 BC
Iron Age Ia 1200–1150 BC
Late Bronze IIb 1300–1200 BC
Late Bronze IIa 1400–1300 BC
Late Bronze I (Late Canaanite) 1550–1400 BC
Middle Bronze IIc 1600–1550 BC
Middle Bronze IIb 1750–1600 BC
Middle Bronze IIa (Middle Canaanite) 1950–1750 BC
Middle Bronze I (Early – Middle Bronze Age) 2200–1950 BC
Early Bronze IV (Early Canaanite IV) 2350–2200 BC
Early Bronze III (Early Canaanite III) 2650–2350 BC
Early Bronze II (Early Canaanite II) 2850–2650 BC
Early Bronze I (Early Canaanite I) 3150–2850 BC
Chalcolithic (Ghassulian) 4000–3150 BC
Neolithic (Pottery) 5000–4000 BC
Neolithic (Pre-pottery) (New Stone Age) 7500–5000 BC
Mesolithic (Middle Stone Age/Natufian) 10,000–7500 BC

The Ancient Near East

The great Egyptian and Mesopotamian rivers support an agriculture otherwise impossible in the dry, hot climate. Throughout the region cereals are a staple crop. Sheep and goats – tended by nomads or farmed – are the main livestock.

Scientists believe that in ancient times the climate of the Near and Middle East was wetter than now. In the central Sahara Desert plants were growing that are characteristic of the Mediterranean region now, and the area is still cut by dry water courses, which must once have carried water. There were fluctuations in climate with a general move towards arid conditions, but with wetter periods, during which it would have been possible for certain areas to be occupied that could not support a population of any number today.

Although the hottest part of the earth's surface should in theory be the Equator, it is in fact the area from the Sahara through central Arabia to the Punjab, a little to the south of the Near and Middle East. This is due to the large land masses and their effects on heat radiation. Heat transfer is by air currents, particularly the jet streams. These are winds high in the atmosphere blowing at extremely fast speeds. Major jet streams from the Mediterranean are responsible for bringing very warm air from the Sahara to the cold mountain ranges of western Asia. This warm air, combined with the melting snow in the Taurus Mountains of Turkey and the Zagros Mountains of Persia, creates the conditions for the annual flooding of the Tigris and Euphrates rivers. The agricultural cycle in Mesopotamia was dependant upon this.

Similarly, the unique pattern of air currents over the north-east Indian Ocean creates the conditions for the annual flooding of the River Nile. During the summer, an easterly airflow at high altitude creates turbulence at lower levels and carries moist air from the Indian Ocean to the mountains of Ethiopia and the Sudan in eastern Africa. The heavy rainfall of the monsoon flows into the Blue Nile, eventually depositing silt in the enormously long, level stretch below the First Cataract, where the Nile flows through Upper and Lower Egypt to the Mediterranean. By contrast, westerly jet streams prevail from November to March, together with an air current that peters out by the time it reaches the coasts of southern Arabia, which are among the world's most arid.

Whatever minor changes in climate may have happened, these broad patterns have always controlled the weather of the Near and Middle East. If anything, the area was rather more moist within the historical past, and able to support the size of population needed for the initial draining of the river marshes and the rise of civilizations in the two main river valleys.

Most of the Near and Middle East experiences a dry, hot climate, with large temperature variations between day and night. As the great river systems of Egypt and Mesopotamia draw their waters from mountain ranges well beyond their main valleys, they can support agricultural economies that would otherwise be impossible. However, even in much of the desert there are marginal areas that can support sheep and goats on sparse areas of pasture.

There are therefore two distinct types of livestock production – wandering herds led by nomadic herdsmen and shepherds, and the settled livestock farming with which the modern, developed world is more familiar. The

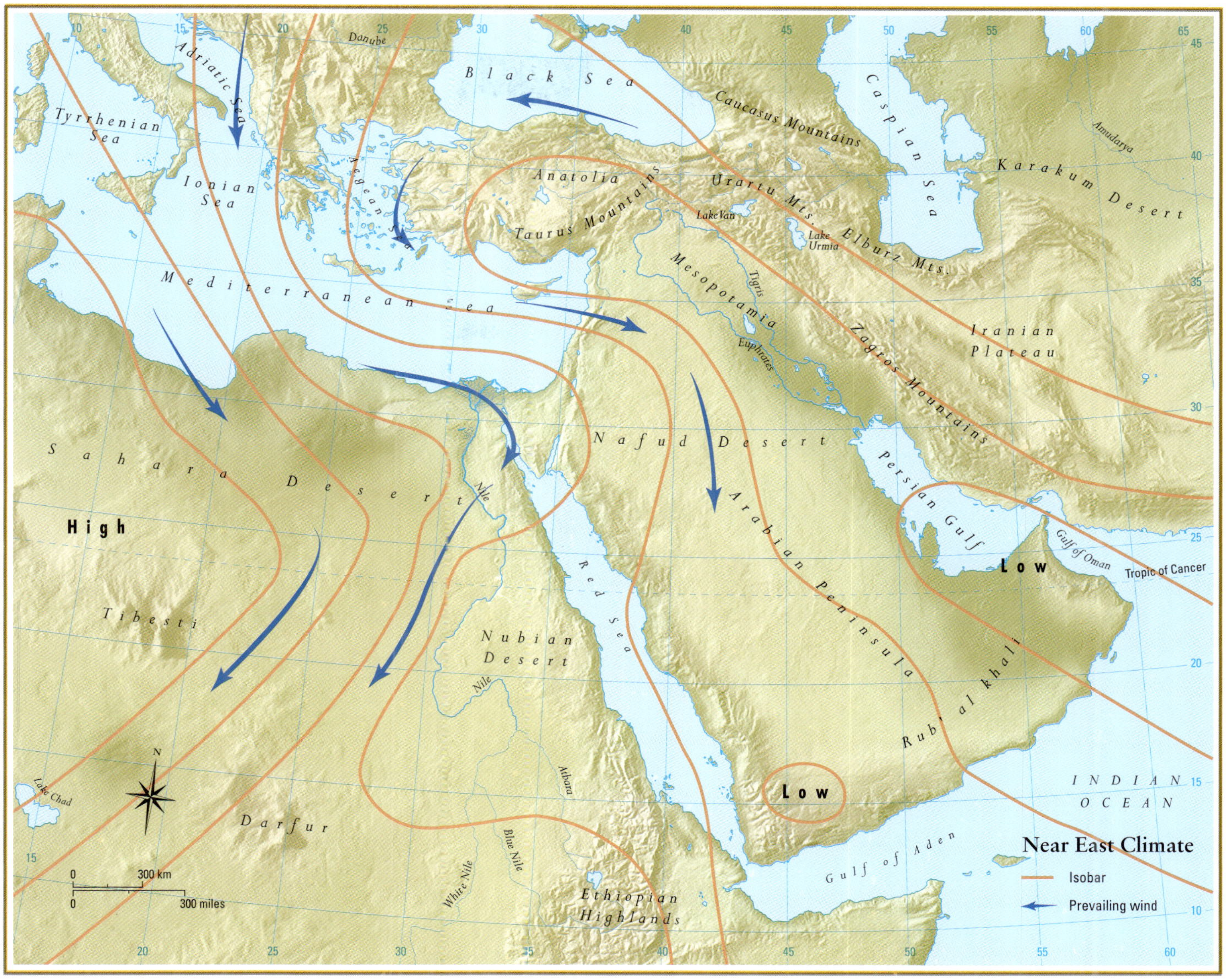

WEATHER PATTERNS

Prevailing weather patterns over the Middle East and north-east Africa create conditions where the annual flooding of the three main rivers – the Nile, Euphrates and Tigris – produce an environment where consistent agriculture thrives, supporting a large population.

two systems can co-exist happily, for the shepherds are not competing with the farmers for land. A further factor in ancient times lay in the different social structures of nomadic tribes and farming communities. The latter often lived in fortified settlements from which they farmed the surrounding agricultural lands, while the nomads travelled through the marginal lands and semi-desert areas without any close association with fixed settlements.

This accounts for tribal groups such as the Hebrews of patriarchal times (Genesis 12 onwards) that travelled large distances and across 'national' frontiers without much apparent hindrance from the settled peoples. The nomadic shepherds had to ensure that they were not competing with each other for routes to pasture lands, for it would have been fatal for one group to enter a marginal area where the ground had recently been grazed bare by another group. This explains why, in Genesis 13, Abraham and Lot agreed to take different parts of Palestine – they were nomads, rather than occupiers.

Cereals were the main agricultural crops, as wheat and barley are indigenous to the region. Barley was a currency in Mesopotamia as early as 2000 BC. Modern bread wheat is a hybrid crop, but the ancient native emmer wheat is still grown widely, as it is much hardier.

When the flooded rivers of Mesopotamia and Egypt returned to their beds each year, they left a rich deposit of silt that formed the basis of the agricultural economy. As the ground dried, it was ploughed and irrigated by cutting water channels through the riverbanks. This technique tended, though, to divide the land into small squares, which encouraged salt formation when the water evaporated. As the salt content of the land increased, harvest yields diminished. Records from the 2nd Millennium BC show that this was a serious problem in Mesopotamia. As well as cereals and dates, other indigenous crops of the Near and Middle East included olives, grapes, apricots, figs, pomegranates, cherries and peaches.

The Hebrew feast of Tabernacles, or Booths, which fell in the autumn, in September or October, was once a great feast of thanksgiving, marking the end of one year and the beginning of a new one. It no longer marks the new year in Palestine, but its old significance remains. A keen watch is kept for rain during the eight days of its harvest festivities. The long, dry summer of Palestine should be ending and the first rains falling to show that the agricultural year can start all over again.

The Mediterranean is a small body of water compared with the Indian or Atlantic Oceans, so the weather in Palestine is influenced more by the great land masses of Asia and Africa than by the sea. Most of the rain that falls on Palestine comes from the Atlantic, carried on the predominantly westerly airflow, with support from the Mediterranean. Much of the moisture has been lost by the time the stream of Atlantic depressions reach the eastern end of the Mediterranean. Seasonal weather patterns determine whether the moist winds will reach Palestine at all, and if they will release their moisture.

In winter, the Mediterranean has its own distinctive weather system. Atlantic depressions cross north-west Africa, Spain and Europe into the Mediterranean basin and on as far as Pakistan. As they travel, they become more constricted in area and more intense. Rainfall results from warm, moisture-laden air hitting cooler air streams, producing water vapour. Very little of the moisture trapped in the Atlantic depressions is released in Egypt as there is no high ground to force the air up to cooler levels. But the mountains of northern Palestine, and the ridge stretching from Mount Carmel down to Judaea, do so. Consequently there is a marked contrast in annual rainfall between the dry desert area south of Beersheba, which receives little rain, and the mountainous area of Upper Galilee where 140 centimetres (55 in) falls, mainly between November and April.

A different pattern prevails in summer. An area of high pressure, the 'Azores High', extends across north-west Africa to as far as Libya and Egypt. There, its edges meet a characteristic area of low pressure over

Cyprus and southern Turkey. This blocks the Atlantic depressions or forces them further north, and the area of low pressure draws dry air from central Asia, which reaches Palestine as hot, dry south-westerly winds. These winds seem to come from much the same direction as the wet, winter winds, but the air carries little moisture and no rain falls. In the wet months, the

rain usually takes the form of heavy cloudbursts, which produce deep gullies in the steep sides of the Jordan Valley. Flash floods occur because the sun-baked ground is unable to absorb the deluge of water that falls in a short period. As a result, the roads are flooded over long distances. Under such conditions, it is essential to dam gullies and direct the water into irrigation channels.

CLIMATE AND PLANT LIFE
The vegetation types of the Bible lands are predominantly influenced by the weather patterns created by the land masses of Asia and Africa.

The importance of water for Palestinian agriculture is shown clearly by the effects of irrigation – crops grow to a sharp line where the irrigation ceases, to be replaced by brown, parched earth. Almost everywhere that water can be taken proves to be fertile. An exception is the area around the Dead Sea, called the Salt Sea in ancient times. It lies only 80 kilometres (50 miles) from the Mediterranean, but is 400 metres (1,300 ft) below sea level and has no exit for the incoming waters of the River Jordan. Instead, the water evaporates quickly, causing high salt levels.

Yet even here, the abundant freshwater springs of Jericho, only 15 kilometres (9 miles) north in the same rift valley, provide luxuriant oasis conditions for one of the oldest of all settlements. Springs made occupation possible down the western shores of the Dead Sea in biblical times, supplemented by dams in the deep gullies from the Judaean hills. Such centres of population ranged from the great fortress of Masada, with its deep water cisterns on the top of the crag, to the Essene community at Qumran, where ritual bathing was an important part of life.

Only the northern highlands of Palestine and the coastal area, as far as about 60 kilometres (35 miles) inland, receive any appreciable and dependable amounts of rainfall. South of Gaza and Beersheba, rainfall is negligible, but evidence of ancient settlements in the Negev, the area south of Beersheba, suggest that it was either wetter in biblical times or very efficiently irrigated.

In the Bible, the area is described as '... a land of wheat, and barley, and vines, and fig trees, and pomegranates; a land of oil olive, and honey ... a land whose stones are iron, and out of whose hills thou mayest dig brass ... thy herds and thy flocks multiply' (Deuteronomy 8:8–13). The farming Canaanites tended the fertile areas by day, returning at night to fortified centres that could withstand long sieges. Thus, when the Hebrews began their occupation in the 13th Century BC, Canaan formed a patchwork of city states combined in various alliances. The nomadic Hebrews soon adopted the Canaanite way of life, but this placed considerable strain on their religious traditions as they adapted them to agricultural needs.

Nomadic shepherds continued to graze sheep and goats through the marginal areas, as part of their long routes from Egypt to Mesopotamia. The area supported a larger population than might be expected because of the great trading routes that passed through it. The region exported grain, oil, wine and honey, and was famous for the healing properties of the 'balm of Gilead' (Genesis 37:25; Jeremiah 8:22). Luxuries and raw materials such as metals and wood were exported to Egypt. Trading began to increase during the biblical period. However, the Philistines hindered Hebrew participation in this business by occupying the southern coastal area until the Hebrew King David gained control in about 1000 BC.

Palestine, which was settled by the Sea Peoples, was part of the so-called 'Fertile Crescent' linking the vast, rich valleys inhabited by two ancient civilizations – Ancient Egypt and Mesopotamia. The Hebrews were one of the nomadic groups grazing their flocks on the sparse pastures between desert and fertile land.

In the Fertile Crescent, the two great civilizations of the Near and Middle East in ancient times grew up in two vast river valleys. The Nile supported the ancient Egyptians, while the Mesopotamians lived on the banks of the Tigris and Euphrates. Between the two lay desert, the Dead Sea and Palestine. This tiny corridor of land provided the only fertile strip from the Persian Gulf to the Nile Valley. Its position was vital, as it linked the two valleys, forming a long stretch of fertile land from one end of the region to the other.

> *'... a land of wheat, and barley, and vines, and fig trees, and pomegranates; a land of oil olive, and honey ...'*
>
> *Deuteronomy 8:8*

Rising in the complex of great African lakes that straddle the Equator, the River Nile winds down through the Sudan and the eastern end of the Sahara Desert until it sprawls out into the fan-shaped swamp of river mouths and marshes that make up its delta. For most of its journey, it flows through desert, with minimal rainfall and no tributaries to feed it. The people who drained the marshes around the delta and learned to make use of the great river formed one of the oldest civilizations of the ancient world. The pyramids they built had been standing for more than 2,500 years when Jesus Christ was born.

The River Nile was the unifying factor for the peoples who lived along it. Its waters and the mud it left behind after the annual floods from the mountains of Ethiopia turned the desert into rich agricultural land and made Egypt the most dependable source of food in the eastern Mediterranean. Power shifted between the delta cities – Memphis in Lower Egypt and Thebes, the capital of Upper Egypt, which ended where the First Cataract interrupted navigation from the coast. Beyond the First Cataract lay Nubia and, eventually, tropical Africa.

RAINFALL IN PALESTINE

Water is the key to agriculture in Palestine. Areas of higher rainfall along the coastal strip and the hill country of Judah and further north, support most kinds of agriculture – vines, wheat, olives and dense woodland – especially in the north.

The Ancient Near East in the 3rd Millennium BC

Beyond the desert to the east of Palestine was Mesopotamia – drained by both the Tigris and Euphrates, which in ancient time entered the Persian Gulf separately, 200 km (125 miles) north-west of the present coastline. Between mountains to the east and desert to the west, Mesopotamia was peopled, like Egypt, by civilizations that had learned to control the rivers and use them for agriculture. Power was located at several centres – Sumer and Babylonia near the Persian Gulf, straddling the Euphrates, and Assyria about 700 km (435 miles) to the north on the Tigris. Beyond Assyria was Mitanni. For all its apparent strength, Mesopotamia was often threatened by incursions from mountain tribes, and no single power managed to dominate all of Mesopotamia for long.

Beyond Syria to the north, the Hittites inhabited the area that is now Turkey. The Hittites briefly extended their power into the Fertile Crescent, but their land had nothing comparable to the great rivers to give continuity, and they were overrun by migrants from the west.

The name Palestine is derived from the Greek for Philistine. The Philistines were among the waves of Sea Peoples who arrived from the west at the end of the

CIVILIZATIONS FROM 3000–2000 BC

By the 3rd millennium BC, powerful civilizations had become well established in the Fertile Crescent. Egypt traded with Akkad and Sumer in the east along busy trade routes leading through Palestine.

2nd Millennium BC. They briefly dominated the southern part of the land bridge from the Jordan Valley to the Mediterranean. Before the Philistines, it was occupied mainly by the Canaanites and is referred to as Canaan by the Hebrews. Its long desert frontier to the east exposed it to penetration from the nomadic desert people, including the Hebrews, while its strategic position between Egypt to the south and the Mesopotamian and Hittite peoples of the east and north made it politically sensitive. It seldom enjoyed peace, but its peoples profited from the trade routes that passed through it. From the south, the route from Egypt passed into the coastal area. Here, shifting sands forced travellers inland for 20 km (12 miles), through the town of Aphek and northwards to the ridge of Mount Carmel. The Philistines settled in this coastal plain, at Gaza, Ashkelon and Ashdod near the coast, and at Gath and Ekron further inland. From this coastal plain, minor roads led eastwards up through the lowland hills of the Shephelah to the hill country of Judah and the deep rift valley of the Dead Sea.

Beyond the Dead Sea lie mountain ridges, with steep gullies running down into the rift valley, and beyond these mountains the desert begins. The Judaean hills run northwards, parallel with the Jordan Valley, until they turn north-west to meet the Great Sea, as the Mediterranean was called in biblical times, at Mount Carmel and form the northern limits of the coastal plain.

The major coastal route crosses the Carmel ridge to enter the Plain of Jezreel at the ancient fortress of Megiddo, where it then splits in to two routes. A western branch hugs the coast, and an eastern branch carries on to Hazor and Damascus. Jezreel means 'God sows' in Hebrew, reflecting the fertility of this valley running from the Great Sea to the Jordan Valley, still more than 180 m (600 ft) below sea level where the River Jordan leaves the Sea of Galilee. This lake is called the Sea of Chinnereth in the Old Testament, and variously the Sea of Galilee, Lake of Gennesaret and Sea of Tiberias in the New Testament.

Northwards again, between the upper Jordan Valley and the sea, the land rises steeply into Upper Galilee. At the eastern side of the top of the Jordan Valley is Mount Hermon, which marked the northern limits of Palestine or Canaan. The road to Damascus and Mesopotamia passes south of Hermon. The King's Highway, a route used mainly by nomads, ran from Damascus southwards to Elath, situated on the Red Sea.

The towns of Beersheba in the south and Dan in the north marked the traditional limits of the ancient land of Israel. That area contains extreme geographical contrasts, including mountain ridges and the lowest point on earth, extremely fertile land, and desert-like terrain. Such conditions led to many kinds of peoples with vastly different ways of life settling there.

Archaeology of the Bible

Two branches within the science of archaeology focus on the Bible: biblical archaeology, in which the Bible lands and surrounding areas are selected for study, and the archaeology of Bible texts, where the research is centred on actual manuscripts.

Biblical archaeology is primarily a source of historical information. In conjunction with the Bible itself and other evidence, it helps us to ascertain and understand the sequence of biblical events, and to build up a picture of what life was like in Bible lands.

Many of the problems of biblical archaeology are those that are common to all branches of the science: the randomness of which items survive, and the fact that organic materials such as leather, wood and textiles generally fail to survive. The sheer vastness of potential sites for investigation, combined with limited resources, also present problems. Further difficulties are raised by the inaccessibility of many sites because they are inhabited, or because they are sacred to Christians, Jews or Muslims – or all three. Political tensions in the area persist, and cause misery on every level. Despite these difficulties, impressive finds have been made and, as the science of archaeology has become more exact, these have contributed greatly to Bible scholarship.

MESOPOTAMIA

The Fertile Crescent stretches from Sumer at the top of the Persian Gulf, up the Euphrates and the Tigris rivers through Babylonia and Assyria, westwards along the southern edge of the Armenian Mountains, southwards through Syria and Lebanon to the Jordan Valley and down to the Dead Sea. This is the route that Abraham took, and it could be said that the civilizations of the Middle East followed the same path. The archaeological sites in Mesopotamia are rich sources of evidence, given their long history of occupation by technically and culturally advanced peoples with a well-developed social organization.

The ancient civilizations of Assyria and Babylonia dominated this area for centuries. Although both were occupied from prehistoric times, the most interesting archaeological work has concentrated on the period when the city states of these empires were flourishing. Excavation on the site of the city of Nineveh began in the mid-19th Century, and it was not long before reliefs and inscriptions were found, which clearly came from the palaces of Sennacherib and Ashurbanipal. Huge numbers of inscribed tablets were found, providing invaluable information about Assyrian literature and civilization.

The site at Calah, south of Nineveh, has revealed the ruins of ziggurats, and enough of the remains of the temple of Nabu and the palace of Ashurnasirpal II (879 BC) to enable scholars to construct accurate plans of the original buildings. Scriptures, ivories and weapons were found in the outer town, and are thought to be booty captured by the Assyrian army.

GRAND ENTRANCE TO BABYLON

The magnificent Ishtar Gate, flanked by images of bulls, lions and dragons, was built around 575 BC by King Nebuchadnezzar to act as the main entrance to the city of Babylon. The gate, dedicated to the goddess Ishtar, was more than 12 metres (38 ft) high.

Babylon was always a centre of interest to explorers hoping to discover the remains of the legendary Tower of Babel, described in Genesis 11:1–9. This has never been found, although some have identified it with the ruins of a ziggurat found a few miles to the south-west. A tablet has also been found, dated 229 BC, which describes a tower restored by Nebuchadnezzar, parts of which were discovered in 1899. Excavations on the site of Babylon, from the mid-19th Century to the present, have uncovered much of the city of Nebuchadnezzar's reign. It was surrounded by a massive double wall, and entrance to the inner city was through various large gateways. The most magnificent was the Ishtar Gate, the bricks of which were glazed and decorated with pictures of animals. Remains have also been found of temples dedicated to Ishtar and Marduk, and part of the palace throne room.

The site of the ancient city of Ur has revealed far older artefacts than any other site of the region. In the 1920s, the English archaeologist Sir Leonard Woolley discovered a royal cemetery dating back to 2500 BC, which contained the remains of gold and silver beakers, jewellery, weapons and musical instruments.

The city of Mari is not mentioned in the Bible, but it was one of the most important of the Mesopotamian city states. Excavations have revealed a huge palace there, dating from around 1775 BC, containing various treasures, including over 20,000 cuneiform texts.

EGYPT

The other main route for the advance of ideas and technology into Palestine was from Egypt. The trade routes from the Nile delta to the east followed the

TREASURES OF THE AFTERLIFE
The Egyptian pharaoh Tutankhamun's internal organs were preserved and sealed inside an elaborate, gold-covered chest protected for their journey into the next world by the goddess Selket. Her emblem, the scorpion, rests on her head.

Mediterranean coast, turning north through Canaan, and there is considerable archaeological evidence of Egyptian influence on Bible lands. The sites in Egypt are even more impressive than those of Mesopotamia, because what survived is not arbitrary and accidental. The Egyptians wanted their rulers to have luxury in the next world, so they stocked their tombs with the costliest artefacts possible, and with the intention of preservation.

Archaeology in Egypt began when Napoleon invaded the country in 1798. It was, however, an Englishman, Howard Carter, who discovered Tutankhamun's tomb in 1922. Tutankhamun died within a hundred years of Moses' lifetime, and from the extraordinary treasures of his tomb we can discover what it was like for Moses to grow up in an Egyptian palace. It also throws light on the construction of the tabernacle and the Ark of the Covenant, for elaborate tent-shrines and wooden chests were found in the tomb.

Another discovery relating to Old Testament accounts was that of the ruins of temples and palaces at Tanis, now San el-Hagar, in the Nile delta. The buildings date from the 9th Century BC, but many of the blocks are inscribed with the name of Rameses II, who lived 400 years earlier. These blocks are thought to have been transported from Qantir, 29 km (18 miles) to the south, where the remains of a city were discovered. The city is believed to be Pi-Ramesse, or the Raamses that the Israelites were forced to build by their Egyptian taskmasters (Exodus 1:11).

CANAAN

Compared with the powerful empires to the east and south-west, the Israelites were a rough peasant people, with a less developed culture in the form of literature, art, or military or administrative skills. There are particular difficulties with some of the areas that conceal potentially valuable information. Damascus has been continuously occupied for thousands of years, and Jerusalem also dates back to ancient times. Because both are now huge, modern cities, major excavations are not usually possible.

Jericho is another ancient city, but it is uninhabited and so has been available for archaeological research.

Work began in 1868, but it was not until the 1950s that significant research was carried out by the archaeologist Kathleen Kenyon. She found that the remains of walls previously discovered and thought to be those destroyed by Joshua were, in fact, the ruins of buildings destroyed by an earthquake before 1500 BC. Pottery, weapons and furniture of this period have also been found. Nothing has been found of the city that Joshua conquered, but ruins have been found nearby of the winter palace of Herod the Great, built in Jericho about 100 BC.

Such excavations as have been possible in Jerusalem have also yielded evidence of magnificent buildings erected by Herod the Great, particularly the temple, which was ruined in AD 70. However, probably the most interesting Herodian remains have been found in Masada, west of the Dead Sea. On this isolated rock, Herod built a huge fortress and two palaces. Israeli archaeologists made extraordinary discoveries at Masada in the 1960s. Reservoirs had been cut into the rock, with channels and aqueducts to supply water to the fortress. A strong double wall enclosed barracks, storerooms and the two palaces, one built for administrative and official purposes, the other as a pleasure palace. Some of the best finds were from a later period, when Masada was occupied by Jewish zealots who were using the fortress as a stronghold against the Romans in AD 66–73. The remains of a synagogue and ritual baths were found, as well as fragments of leather scrolls, some bearing biblical texts.

THE DEAD SEA SCROLLS

In order to survive for long periods of time, texts and documents need to be written on stone or clay. These are slow to produce and extremely difficult to transport, so are characteristic of settled civilizations. The Hebrew people did not dwell securely enough or for long enough anywhere to leave much writing in a durable form. Most biblical texts have come down to us as a result of repeated copying in a perishable medium such as

THE QUMRAN CAVES

The Dead Sea Scrolls were discovered in several different sites here between 1947 and 1956.

WRITERS OF THE SCROLLS
The Essenes were located at the northern end of the Dead Sea. The monastic community was destroyed by the Romans because of its support for the revolt against Roman rule.

leather or papyrus. This can give rise to doubts about the historical authenticity of the texts. The most important archaeological breakthrough in this field of research has been the discovery of the Dead Sea Scrolls.

Qumran is the name of a wadi and a nearby ruin (Khirbet Qumran) located just north-west of the Dead Sea. Early in 1947, a shepherd chanced upon a cave in the cliff face and discovered some jars containing bundles of old cloth and rolls of leather with writing on them. He returned a little later with friends and found more of the same. The rolls went through many hands before finally making their way to the American School of Oriental Research in Jerusalem, where an American scholar, John Trever, identified them as scrolls of Hebrew texts and realized that one of them was a copy of the Book of Isaiah, which appeared to be older than any known Hebrew manuscript.

The results of Trever's research were made public in April 1948, and in the following years archaeologists explored all the caves in the area. More scrolls were found, although these were mainly fragments, not as well preserved as they had not been kept in jars. Between 1951 and 1956, the archaeologists turned their attention to the Khirbet Qumran site and excavated a building there that appeared to have belonged to a community of people. The evidence suggested that they had occupied the site for two centuries up to AD 68, with a 30-year break between about AD 4 and 34.

The community at Qumran seemed likely to have been a branch of the Jewish Essene sect, and it was clear that this had been their property. Pottery found in the caves and the ruins was identical, and jars found in the ruins were similar to those that had contained the scrolls. Roman troops, marching through Palestine to suppress the Jewish revolt, would have reached the Dead Sea region in about AD 68. The Essene community at Qumran probably hid their scrolls at that point, and were either killed or fled.

The manuscript that Trever identified as the Book of Isaiah was a roll of leather 61 centimetres (24 in) long and 25 centimetres (10 in) high. It was made of 17 sheets sewn together end to end and covered with 54 columns of Hebrew text. This scroll is around 1,000 years older than any existing Hebrew manuscript.

Much can be derived about the Essenes' theology from the biblical commentaries. They thought of themselves as the righteous remnant of Israel and rejected the Hasmonean dynasty. They spoke of someone whom they called 'The Teacher of Righteousness', but he appears to have been a leader and teacher of the sect rather than a Messiah figure. Members of the sect spent many hours in study of the law, and their interpretation of it was stricter than that of the Pharisees. Their interpretation of scripture was apocalyptic and they lived in expectation of the 'end-time'. They were expecting the last days to signal the end of the 'epoch of wickedness' and awaited the coming of a Messiah of David's line who would be a warrior prince, leading the faithful of Israel to victory over the 'sons of darkness'. They also awaited a judgement and a general resurrection at the end-time.

Eventually, fragments of every canonical book of the Hebrew Old Testament, except for the Book of Esther and some of the apocryphal books, were found in the caves. The manuscripts date from the period before AD 100. Most are in Hebrew, but some are in Aramaic. They include texts that the Masoretic scholars would have used and the text underlying the Septuagint. There are also texts similar to the Hebrew Pentatuech used by the Samaritans. The pieces are now in the Israel Museum in Jerusalem, and are still being studied and evaluated.

As well as Bible texts, the library in the Qumran caves included large numbers of texts that related to the life and beliefs of the community who lived there. Together with the remains of buildings and artefacts found in the ruins of Khirbet Qumran, they have enabled us to build up a picture of the 'people of the scrolls' who lived there.

WRITERS OF THE SCROLLS

The Essenes were located at the northern end of the Dead Sea. The monastic community was destroyed by the Romans because of its support for the revolt against Roman rule.

The non-biblical texts included Bible commentaries, rules for community life, and regulations for worship. This evidence is close enough to what has been learned about the Essene sect from contemporary writers such as Pliny and Philo for most scholars to be convinced that the Qumran community were Essenes. This sect flourished from about 100 BC to AD 100 and is of particular interest because of some similarities between its beliefs and practices and those of the early Christian Church.

Like other Essene communities, the people at Qumran lived a simple, rigorously disciplined, and austere life. The Essenes believed in the practice of hospitality and communal ownership of property. There was a novitiate of two years before anyone could join the community; admission was preceded by a ritual ablution or purification in water, and solemn fellowship meals were held in secret. Although there are some parallels with Christian rituals of baptism and communion here, there are also significant differences, and the Essene rituals did not have the sacramental significance of Christian ones.

PLACES OF THE BIBLE

The Old Testament and New Testament are full of place-names that chart the story of Israel and the Hebrew people. Some, like Jerusalem and Gaza, are still familiar, others have long since disappeared.

New Testament Sites
Tyre
PHOENICIA
UPPER GALILEE
LOWER GALILEE
NAPHTALI
ITUREA
Caesarea Phillippi
SYRIA
Ptolemais
Chorazin
Bethsaida
Capernaum
Kanah
Gennesaret
Gergesa(?)
Sea of Chinnereth
(Sea of Galilee)
Tiberias
ZEBULUN
Nazareth
GADARA
Yarmuk
DECAPOLIS
Great Sea
Western Sea
SAMARIA
Nain
Harod
Mt. Gilboa
Caesarea
Plain of Sharon
Aenon
Salim
Jebel Um ed Daraj
Jordan
Sychar
Zarqa
Antipatris
Joppa
Arimathaea
Ephraim
JUDAEA
Jericho
Emmaus
Mount of Olives
Jerusalem
Bethphage
Bethany
Bethlehem
Ashdod
Gaza
IDUMAEA
Salt Sea
(Dead Sea)
Transjordan
Negev
N
Hasa
Wadi el Jeib
0
20 km
20 miles
35°
36°
33°
32°
31°

HISTORY OF THE BIBLE

We are used to speaking of the Bible as a book, starting with the Old Testament. In fact, it is a collection of books, of different authorship and written at different times, which has been selected from a wider range of writings to make up the Bible as we know it.

The books of the Old Testament were written over centuries and some of them were added to or changed their form over many years. None of the original manuscripts have survived.

We use the word canon, meaning 'a rule', to denote the list of books considered to be the authoritative collection. The Pentateuch, or Five Books of Moses (Genesis, Exodus, Leviticus, Numbers and Deuteronomy), were already considered to be canonical by the time of Ezra and Nehemiah in the 5th Century BC. Recognition of the other books came at various times, but by the 2nd Century BC they were organized into the 24 books that make up the Hebrew Bible. The first Christians would have recognized these books as authoritative, although the manuscripts still existed only as separate scrolls.

The earliest translation of the Hebrew scriptures was the Septuagint, a translation into Greek of all the Old Testament canonical books and some that are regarded by many as apocryphal. The Jewish translators (traditionally, 72 of them) started work on the Pentateuch in Alexandria in the first half of the 3rd Century BC. The other canonical books appear to have been translated by the end of the 2nd Century BC, and non-canonical books at various times down to the 1st Century AD. The Greek of the Septuagint was much influenced by the Hebrew original, and the accuracy is sometimes questionable, but the Septuagint was the basis for several subsequent translations. In 382, St Jerome made a Latin translation, called the Vulgate, which is still used by the Roman Catholic Church.

For subsequent translations of the Old Testament taken from the Hebrew, the source had generally been what is known as the Masoretic text. The Masoretes probably started their work in about AD 500 and did not finish it until the 10th Century AD.

THE NEW TESTAMENT

The books of the New Testament were written in Greek during the 1st Century AD, with the earliest manuscripts dating from the 3rd and 4th Centuries AD. There are about 175 manuscripts dating from this period, written on papyrus or parchment, most of them well preserved. By the middle of the 3rd Century AD, parts of the New Testament had been translated into Latin, Syriac and Coptic.

In the 1st Century AD, and well into the 2nd, there was no conception of the New Testament canon. The Apostolic Fathers of the early Church often quoted sayings of Jesus in a form unrelated to any of the four canonical Gospels. Not all of the four Gospels were known to all the Fathers, and there was also various apocryphal material in use. The writings of Paul seem to have been well known and highly valued.

The idea of a canon of New Testament scripture started through various heretical movements of the 2nd Century AD. A teacher called Marcion broke away from the Church in Rome in about AD 150. He totally rejected the Old Testament and thus felt the need for an authoritative Christian scripture. He derived a canon that consisted of one Gospel (a form of Luke) and ten letters of Paul.

By the second half of the 2nd Century AD, the four Gospels were established as authoritative, and by the end of the century the Acts of the Apostles, Paul's Letters, and Revelation were also considered canonical. In the 3rd Century, a distinction was made by the ecclesiastical historian Eusebius, Bishop of Caesarea, between acknowledged books (the Gospels, Acts, Paul's Letters, I Peter, I John), disputed books (James, Jude, 2 Peter and 2 and 3 John), and spurious books (Hebrews and various apocryphal works). There is disagreement over whether Revelation was counted as acknowledged or spurious.

The canon was finally settled for the eastern Church by the 39th Paschal Letter of Athanasius in AD 367, and the West followed after Pope Damasus held a synod in Rome in 382.

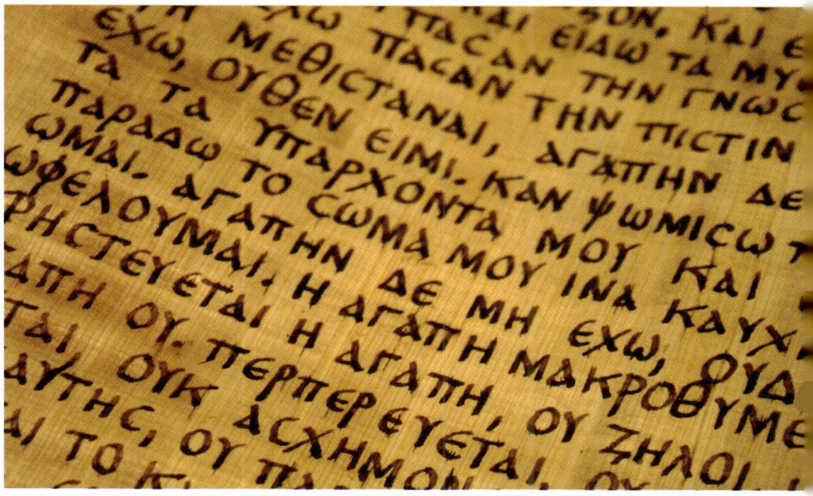

ANCIENT MANUSCRIPT
Like all books of the New Testament, Paul's Letters – like this section from I Corinthians – were written in Greek on papyrus.

THE APOCRYPHAL BOOKS

The word 'apocrypha' comes from a Greek word for 'hidden'. It is applied to all the books of scripture that are not included in the Protestant Bible, but particularly to the Old Testament books found in Roman Catholic versions. There are many other apocryphal books of both Old and New Testaments that have been rejected as spurious or of doubtful authenticity, and these are now usually referred to as 'pseudepigrapha'. The works below are those included in the Roman Catholic Old Testament canon, although not all Roman Catholic bibles contain all of them, and the names of the books sometimes vary.

1 Esdras

This book gives a parallel account of history recorded in the books of Chronicles, Ezra, and Nehemiah. There is also an addition, known as the 'Debate of the Three Youths', which is an adaptation from a Persian story. It features Zerubbabel, Governor under Darius. He takes part in a debate about the nature of power and uses it to remind Darius of his obligation to allow the rebuilding of the temple.

2 Esdras

This book is also known as 'The Apocalypse of Ezra'. It derives from a Hebrew source but has been expanded with Christian additions. The book describes seven visions. In the first three visions Ezra asks why God's chosen people have to suffer and be oppressed by other nations. An angel tells him that these things are incomprehensible to human beings, but salvation is close and the Jews will inherit the earth. The fourth vision is of a glorious Jerusalem, the next a symbolic vision of Rome, and the sixth is similar to the vision in Daniel 7. The last vision concerns the sacred books that Ezra is to restore.

Tobit

This story dates from the Babylonian exile. It tells of Tobit, a Jew in captivity in Nineveh. He is persecuted for burying the Hebrew dead, and becomes impoverished and blind. Tobit sends his son Tobias, guided by the archangel Raphael in disguise, to collect a debt. He falls in love with his cousin Sara, whose previous seven bridegrooms had been killed by the demon Asmodeus. Helped by Raphael, Tobias defeats Asmodeus and restores Tobit's sight by means of a fish he has caught in the River Tigris.

Judith

The story dates from a 2nd-Century BC Hebrew source. It tells of Judith, a beautiful Jewish widow of Bethulia. Her city is besieged by Nebuchadnezzar's forces, led by General Holofernes. Judith goes to Holofernes' tent on the pretext of telling him military secrets. He is taken with her beauty and asks her to dine with him. Judith encourages him to drink freely, and when he is in a drunken sleep she cuts off his head. When she returns to the city and shows the people Holofernes' head, they pursue the enemy who flees from them.

Additions to Esther

Although most scholars regard these passages as additions to the original Hebrew, some maintain that the Hebrew canonical work is an abbreviated version.

The additions include accounts of Mordecai's dream and an interpretation of it; the orders of King Xerxes (King Ahasuerus in the Bible) for the massacre of Jews and his subsequent edict permitting the Jews to defend themselves; prayers of Mordecai and Esther; and Esther's audience with the King.

Wisdom of Solomon

This work, of unknown authorship, has its roots in traditional Jewish Wisdom writing but was probably composed in Greek. It includes Greek philosophical thought and Platonic terminology. The book praises wisdom and exhorts followers to seek wisdom. In the book's second half, Jewish history is discussed in the context of the ways in which wisdom has helped the Jews.

Ecclesiasticus

This book consists of the wisdom of Joshua ben Sira, who lived in Jerusalem around 180 BC. The translation was made by the author's grandson. The book was well known and highly respected by both Jews and early Christians. It recommends observance of the law and a pious fear of God, and gives practical advice for daily living. The final chapters are devoted to the praise of the patriarchs and heroes of the Old Testament, and of Simon the High Priest, who lived about 200 BC.

Baruch

This book is supposedly the work of Baruch, who was the scribe or secretary of the Prophet Jeremiah. It is, however, thought to be of composite authorship. It begins with an address by Baruch to the exiles in Babylon, with a prayer of confession, and prayers asking for forgiveness and salvation. The next section speaks in praise of wisdom, and the last chapters are a lament of Jerusalem for the captives, with a final assurance that they will be restored to their home.

Additions to Daniel

The additions to the Book of Daniel are derived from the Septuagint. The first addition comes in chapter three and consists of the prayer of Azariah (Abednego) in the fiery furnace, in which he praises God's mercy and asks for deliverance. This is followed by the *Song of the Three Holy Children*, a hymn of praise uttered as they walk unharmed in the fire, with the refrain 'praise and exalt Him above all for ever'. The story of Susanna follows from the end of the prophecies of Daniel. It tells of a beautiful and pious woman married to a Babylonian. Two elders of the people see her bathing and, when she rejects their advances, have her falsely accused of adultery. She is condemned to death, but Daniel proves that the elders are lying. The people accept Susanna's innocence and put the elders to death. The last addition, the story of Bel and the Dragon, is written to mock idolatrous worship. In it Daniel proves to King Cyrus of Persia that neither the idol Bel nor a dragon are living gods.

Topography of the Near East

THE COMMUNICATIONS AND TOPOGRAPHY OF THE NEAR EAST

Along these ancient ways travelled ideas, spiritual and practical, as well as the commodities of everyday trade.

Prayer of Manasses

In 2 Chronicles 13, the reign of Manasseh, son of Hezekiah, is described. He was a worshipper of Baal and other idols, and heavily involved in occult practices. He was captured by the Assyrians and in his affliction prayed to the God of his fathers for release. God heard him and Manasseh was released, subsequently restoring the worship of God to

Judah. This book purports to be the prayer of Manasseh when in captivity. It is thought to be Jewish in origin, but was not known before the 3rd Century AD.

1 and 2 Maccabees

These books are concerned with Jewish history between 175 BC and 134 BC and the heroic family of the Maccabees. It describes their struggles against the Syrian king, Antiochus Epiphanes, the Hasmonean Wars and the line of priest-kings that they established. The first book was translated from a Hebrew work, in about 100 BC. The second book is said to be extracted from a work by Jason of Cyrene, of whom nothing else is known. It covers similar ground to the first book, but with various discrepancies.

MANUSCRIPT BIBLES

The first attempts at translating parts of the Bible into English began in the 7th Century AD. These were not so much translations as poetical works of paraphrase, and no manuscripts have been found. The Venerable Bede is said to have translated the Gospel of John, but again we have no concrete evidence of the work.

One surviving work is that of the Lindisfarne Gospels, a beautifully ornamented manuscript, which was written in Latin in about AD 700, but with an English gloss or interlinear translation added in about AD 950. Around 50 years after this, the West Saxon Gospels were produced. During the later Middle English period, various parts of the Bible were translated, but the most significant work was that associated with John Wycliffe (c. 1320–84), a reformer whose aim was to make the scriptures accessible to the people. There were two versions undertaken in Wycliffe's name, parts of which were written by Wycliffe himself. Both were translations from the Latin Vulgate, but the English of the later version, made by John Purvey, one of Wycliffe's followers, is more idiomatic and less archaic.

The Printed Bible

Although Bibles were being printed in Europe from the middle of the 15th Century, it was not until 1525 that the first Bible to be printed in English appeared. This was the Tyndale Bible, produced by William Tyndale, a scholar who, like Wycliffe, was determined to make the Bible more available to ordinary lay people. The first section of his Bible, the New Testament, was printed in Germany, partly in Cologne and partly in Worms. It was significant, not just as the first printed English Bible, but as the first to be translated from the Greek, rather than Latin. By 1534, Tyndale had produced a complete Pentateuch, the Book of Jonah, and other selections from the Old Testament, translated from the Hebrew texts. In 1535, Tyndale was arrested for heresy and executed in 1536. His translation had been enormously influential, and much of his work is preserved in the English of the King James Version.

ROYAL BIBLE CHAMPION

Dissatisfaction with earlier English translations of the Bible led King James I of England and Scotland to commission the King James Version.

At the same time as Tyndale was working on his translation, a complete English Bible was being prepared by Miles Coverdale, whose work was published in 1535. Coverdale was ignorant of both Greek and Hebrew and his version was taken in parts from the Vulgate, from the German versions, and from Tyndale. His was the first Bible in which non-canonical books were published under the separate heading of 'Apocrypha'.

In 1537, the English version known as Matthew's Bible appeared. It claimed to be 'truly and purely' translated into English by Thomas Matthew, but was the work of John Rogers, a friend and follower of Tyndale, and the Bible was not a new translation but a compilation of Tyndale's and Coverdale's work. In 1539, the Taverner Bible appeared, but this was only a revision of Matthew's Bible.

Another influential work, the Great Bible, so called because of its large size, appeared in 1539. It was prepared by Miles Coverdale, commissioned by Thomas Cromwell and based on Matthew's Bible, drawing also from Coverdale and Tyndale. This Bible was authorized by Archbishop Cranmer for distribution in all churches.

Under Mary Tudor, Protestants were persecuted, and many fled. A group of them who went to Geneva began to produce a Bible there. This Geneva Bible was mainly the work of William Whittingham, who based it on the Great Bible, but with attention paid to Hebrew scholarship. This was the first Bible where the chapters were divided into verses. When Elizabeth I took over the throne in 1558, England became safe for Protestants again, but the work continued to be centred in Geneva. It appeared in 1560, with a dedication to Elizabeth, but did not receive official endorsement. Instead, Matthew Parker, the Archbishop of Canterbury, ordered a revision of the work, the Bishops' Bible, which appeared in 1568, with a revised version in 1572. This formed the basis for the King James Version.

Just as Protestants had fled to Europe in Mary's reign, Catholics fled in Elizabeth's reign. A group that had settled in France published a New Testament in Rheims in 1582 and an Old Testament in Douay in 1610. The Douay Version is mainly a translation from the Vulgate.

James I commissioned the Authorized or King James Version in 1604, and it was printed in 1611. The basis for the translation was the Bishops' Bible, but the translators consulted the Greek and Hebrew texts, and followed Tyndale, Matthew's, Coverdale or the Geneva versions when it seemed to them that these translations were more accurate. The first edition was marred by typographical errors; subsequent editions have corrected these and modernized spelling and punctuation. The King James Bible became the standard version for Protestants all over the English-speaking world.

In 1870, work on a Revised Version of the King James was started, organized by the Church of England, but involving other denominations and American Bible scholars. The complete work was published in 1885 in England, with the American Standard Version published six years later.

Some 20th-Century versions that deserve mention include the Revised Standard Version of 1952, the Roman Catholic Jerusalem Bible of 1966, the Good News Bible of 1976, and the New International Bible of 1973.

SPECIALLY NAMED EDITIONS

Some Bibles have been given special names because of a typographical error or peculiarity of vocabulary. Some of these are listed below:

Breeches Bible: Another name for the Geneva Bible. Genesis 3:7 says that Adam and Eve 'sowed figgetree leaves together and made themselves breeches'.

Bug Bible: Another name for the Coverdale Bible in which Psalm 91:5 reads, 'Thou shalt not need to be afrayd for eny bugges by night'.

Ears to Ear Bible: An edition of 1810, where Matthew 13:43 reads, 'Who hath ears to ear, let him hear'.

Idle Shepherd: An 1809 edition in which the 'idol shepherd' of Zechariah 11:17 becomes 'the idle shepherd'.

Murderers' Bible: An 1801 edition where Jude 16 reads, 'These are murderers…' instead of 'murmurers'.

Placemakers' Bible: The 1562 second edition of the Geneva Bible, where Matthew 5:9 reads, 'Blessed are the placemakers'.

Printers' Bible: An early 18th-Century edition where Psalm 119:161 says, 'printers have persecuted me without a cause', instead of 'princes'.

Rebekah's Camels Bible: An 1823 edition that gives Genesis 24:61 as 'Rebekah arose, and her camels', instead of 'her damsels'.

Standing Fishes Bible: An edition of 1806 where Ezekiel 47:10 has, 'And it shall come to pass that the fishes shall stand on it', instead of 'fishers'.

To Remain Bible: A Bible printed in Cambridge in 1805. A proofreader queried a comma; the editor pencilled in 'to remain'. As a result, Galatians 4:29 read, 'He that was born after the flesh persecuted him that was born after the spirit to remain, even so it is now.'

Treacle Bible: A name for the Bishops' Bible because of its use of 'tryacle', for 'balm', as in Jeremiah 8:22, 'Is there no tryacle in Gilead?'

Unrighteous Bible: A Cambridge edition of 1653. In I Corinthians 6:9 the word 'not' was omitted, leaving 'the unrighteous shall inherit the kingdom of God;' and Romans 6:13 read, 'Neither yield ye your members as instruments of righteousness unto sin', instead of 'unrighteousness'.

Vinegar Bible: An Oxford edition printed in 1717 where the heading in Luke 20 reads, 'Parable of the Vinegar', instead of 'Vineyard'.

Patriarchs and Their World

God gave a series of covenants to a nomad named Abraham, his son Isaac and grandson Jacob. These agreements established Hebrew rights to the territory they later occupied. Meanwhile, the Hebrews migrated to Egypt. They travelled under the protection of Joseph, one of Jacob's sons, who held high office there.

About 3000 BC, the Middle East witnessed the rise of a new culture based upon bronze. Soft and malleable copper no longer met the requirements of populations that were becoming increasingly urban. Harder metals were needed. The Bronze Age lasted until c. 1200 BC, and it is divided into three eras. The first period (3000–2100 BC) witnessed the civilizations of the Old Kingdom in Egypt, the Kingdom of Sargon of Akkad and the Sumerian Empire in Mesopotamia. Following a blurred interim period, the Middle Bronze Age (2000–1600 BC) was integral to the flourishing of two great civilizations – the Middle Kingdom of Egypt (c. 2030–1640 BC) and a Mesopotamian culture under the rule of Hammurabi (c. 19th and 18th Centuries BC). The Late Bronze Age (1600–1200 BC) saw large-scale international contact being developed between Egypt, Canaan, Assyria, the Hittites and Babylonia.

The key to the growth of urban settlements lay in the cultivation of cereal production made possible by extensive irrigation systems, allowing wheat and barley to be grown extensively in the Tigris and Euphrates valleys in Mesopotamia. Permanent communities developed, employing stone or mud brick as building materials. The oldest and most developed of these cities was Jericho (Tell es-Sultan) in the Jordan Valley. Although largely agricultural in its origins, Jericho evolved into a major regional centre. Settlements spread with cultivation of once arid, semi-desert areas. As a result, many more settlements appeared on the edge of the Mesopotamian riverine plain.

The importance of irrigation systems and of river systems was paramount, since the control of these meant richer agricultural yields, and growth and domination over rival communities. For example, one of the major economic and strategic issues arising in Mesopotamia in the 2nd Millennium BC was the control of the Tigris and Euphrates and the struggle for water rights that ensued, which led to conflict between neighbouring city states. Some methods included damming the water above rival cities, to deprive them of water for irrigation, followed by the sudden release of the dam to create widespread flooding, as happened at Larsa (c. 1750 BC) under the Babylonian King, Hammurabi.

Once communities had moved beyond pure subsistence farming by the 4th Millennium BC, more people could engage in metalwork and building, along with other crafts, such as pottery, ceramics and jewellery. Stimulated by a parallel growth in commerce and transit trade between the communities of Greece, Mesopotamia and Asia Minor came the rise of civilizations built upon the development of city states.

As Middle Eastern cities developed into state societies by the 3rd Millennium BC, they became administrative and manufacturing centres of urban civilization, administered by rulers and literate elites. Earlier cities such as Jericho had been merely an agglomeration of populations; the new city states differed greatly and demanded administration and a high degree of social and economic organization. Such movements required the development of written languages, which allowed for greater sophistication in communication and a degree of centralized control in the hands of a ruling elite. These in turn managed the bureaucracies for the administrative functioning of societies and armies for external security.

Increased literacy was crucial to the early civilizations for the development of law codes, tax records and accounts, and such crucial evidence has provided historians with invaluable details of these ancient societies. Hittite royal archives in the 2nd Millennium BC contained a wealth of historical information concerning government, religion and mythology in Hittite society, and even a reference to a city known to us as Troy. In Mesopotamia and adjacent regions, cuneiform script was first utilized by the Sumerians, then by the Akkadians, Babylonians, Assyrians and Hittites. Sumerian influence was so great that it lasted long after the disappearance of the Sumerian city-states.

Archaeological excavations in Ur, Kish, Eridu and other cities have unearthed clay tablets with cuneiform inscriptions that recorded commercial transactions and in a later period bore religious, literary and scientific works. Historians have been provided with a wealth of material on Babylonian and Sumerian societies. The tale of a fruitless search for immortality by the Great King of Uruk, the *Epic of Gilgamesh*, recounts belief systems of Sumerian society and emphasizes mankind's dependence on the forces of nature. Similarly, the discovery of Hammurabi's law code, inscribed on a stele in the cuneiform script of Akkadian, the successor to Sumerian, tells us about the regulation of society.

In Mesopotamia in the 4th and 3rd Millennia BC, organized religions played a significant role in society, both in spreading belief systems and in the carrying out of administration from temples. Such activities probably included food distribution in times of poor harvests. The ziggurats in the temple of Uruk symbolized a transcendental link between heaven and earth in a society believing that kings came from heaven and that laws were granted by the gods, who in their anthropomorphic forms generated security for the people, and the fertility of their crops and livestock. The deities provided for different needs: Anu, the god of heaven; Enki, the god of water; and Enlil, the god of the earth.

MEMORIAL TO SUMERIAN CIVILIZATION
The exquisite Standard of Ur, which dates from around the middle of the 3rd Millennium BC, depicts a Sumerian king and his army, including donkey-led chariots.

By the 2nd Millennium BC, the major cities were recording the arrival of non-local products such as gold, silver, precious stones and wine, together with raw materials essential for industrial and technological production (copper, tin and oil), as well as luxury items (textiles, precious objects and furnishings). The interchange of luxury items carried by court officials, diplomats and professionals, such as physicians, was a part of international relations and the exchange of ideas. The major route followed, in and near Palestine, was named the Way of the Sea, and was the Philistine road from Egypt. Other routes were seaborne to the Philistine coastal cities and to the northern ports, such as Joppa, Byblos, Tyre and Ugarit. Sea trade from Africa and southern Arabia was augmented by caravans bringing gold and spices from Sheba through Tema to Dumah, for Babylonia, or westwards to join the King's Highway through Midian, Edom and Moab into Palestine, or northwards to Rabbath-ammon and outwards to Damascus. Lebanon contributed valuable wood, floated down the coast or dragged to streams for transit to eastern cities as tribute. In the north, tin from sources east of Mesopotamia was exchanged for copper, some tin reaching Canaan via Hazor from Mari.

Mesopotamia was one of the cradles of civilization, with an agricultural economy reliant on irrigation and rich river alluvial soil, but subject to terribly destructive floods from the Tigris and Eurphrates. About 3500 BC, from the north-east came the Sumerians, a non-Semitic people who pushed into south-west Mesopotamia, establishing a number of wealthy city-states, such as Babylon, Kish, Isin, Shurrupak and Uruk. Around 2300 BC, a powerful wave of Semitic nomads surged into the region from the Syro-Arabian desert, the Zagros Mountains and Persia, pounding the civilized areas and laying the foundations of the Akkadian kingdom. The Akkadians were united by Sargon (c. 2334–2279 BC) who developed trade routes to the north-east and to Asia Minor in the west, even reaching the Indus Valley. The empire established by Sargon and his sons stretched to the Persian Gulf and conquered Elam, Upper Mesopotamia and Syria, ruling from sea to sea. The Akkadians fell to the Gutians, invaders from the Zagros Mountains, but the Sumerians regained their power and their civilization enjoyed a renaissance, begun by Utukhegal of Uruk who drove out the Guti. This Sumerian renewal witnessed a golden age of literature, and Babylonian mathematics, with evidence of squares and square roots, of cubes and cube roots and the sums of squares and cubes required for the numerical evaluation of cubic equations and exponential functions.

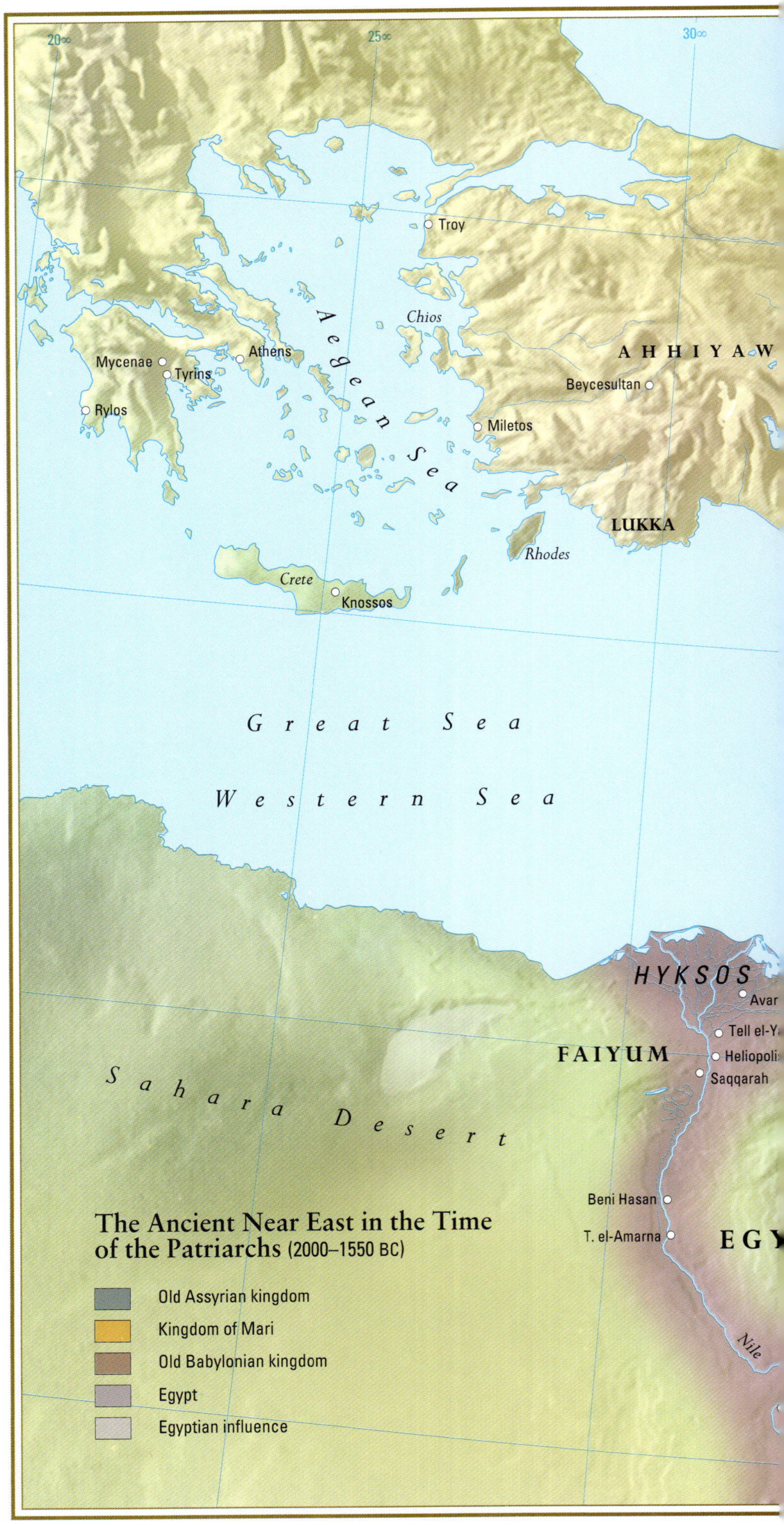

The Ancient Near East in the Time of the Patriarchs (2000–1550 BC)

Towards 2000 BC, Amorites and Semites from the Syro-Arabian desert settled in Mesopotamia, leading to the dynasty of the Amorite, Sumuabum of Babylon. Under King Hammurabi's leadership, Babylon defeated

Mari, and established an empire of letters, including 20,000 inscribed clay tablets from Mari alone. However, Babylonian power declined in the face of invasions from the Kassite, the Hurrians and the biblical Horites, drifting in from the Caucasus. Around 1500 BC, the Hurrians established the northern Mesopotamian Kingdom of the

CRADLE OF CIVILIZATIONS

The Nile Valley, along the east Mediterranean coast, then following the Euphrates and Tigris rivers to the Persian Gulf, proved to be the birthplace of early civilizations that were thriving by the time of the Patriarchs.

Mitanni, conquered by the Assyrians about 1300 BC. In turn, the Assyrians were pressed by the Arameans, but an Assyrian world empire emerged, its highest level of ascendancy being under Tiglath-pileser I.

Mesopotamian literature has left behind many texts. These are invaluable because they often reflect the conditions of the people and their belief systems. The Sumerians refer to their freshwater god, Enki, who fertilizes the goddess Ninhursag, the earth-mother. In his seed are found the origins of trees, and this 'Paradise Myth' demonstrates the importance the Sumerians accorded to water for irrigation and for life. Another tale witnesses the conflict between pastoralism and an agricultural lifestyle. Instead of the violence between Cain and Abel in Genesis 4, the Sumerian myth is located in the realm of the gods. The conflict, between Dumuzi, god of shepherds, and Enkimdu, the farmer's god, ends with a happy reconciliation. Equally interesting is the survival of a flood story. The chief character, Ziusudra, like Noah, receives a heavenly message that the gods are planning to inundate the earth. In order to survive, he is advised to build a boat. The myth ends thus:

'After, for seven days (and) seven nights,
The flood had swept over the land,
(And) the huge boat had been tossed about by the windstorms on the great waters,
Utu [the sun god] came forth, who sheds light on heaven (and) earth,
Ziusudra opened a window of the huge boat,
The hero Utu brought his rays into the giant boat,
Ziusudra, the king,
Prostrated himself before Utu,
The king kills an ox, slaughters a sheep.'

King Sargon was the subject of a myth reminiscent of Moses in the bulrushes, as written in Exodus 2:1–10:

'Sargon, the mighty king, King of Agade, am I.
My mother was a changeling, my father I knew not.
The brother(s) of my father loved the hills.
My city is Azupiranu, which is situated on the banks of the Euphrates.
My changeling mother conceived me, in secret she bore me.
She set me in a basket of rushes, with bitumen she sealed my lid.
She cast me into the river which rose not (over) me.'

A story in the *Epic of Gilgamesh* echoes Ziusudra and predates biblical Noah. Gilgamesh, on his journey searching for everlasting life, meets his ancestor Utnapishtim, who relates the event of a ruinous flood once sweeping the earth. The wise god Ea counsels him to build a ship to escape the danger. The ancient man stated:

'When the seventh day arrived,
I sent forth and set free a dove.
The dove went forth, but came back;
Since no resting-place for it was visible, she turned round.
Then I sent forth and set free a swallow.
The swallow went forth, but came back;
Since no resting-place for it was visible, she turned round.
Then I sent forth and set free a raven.
The raven went forth and, seeing that the waters had diminished,
He eats, circles, caws and turns not round.
Then I let out all to the four winds and offered a sacrifice.
I poured out a libation on the top of the mountain.'

In later texts, such themes may have been borrowed directly by the Bible. Alternatively, the tales were perhaps a common tradition among Middle Eastern peoples, dominated, nurtured and occasionally killed by the elemental forces of fierce floods or other disasters.

Another important and powerful people mentioned in the Bible are the Hittites. The Bible shows the existence of Hittite inhabitants of Canaan, with biblical writers believing that the Hittites belonged in north Canaan rather than Anatolia. Esau married some Hittite girls (Genesis 26:34; 36:2). Uriah, one of David's soldiers, was a Hittite (2 Samuel 11:3). The wives of Solomon included Hittite princesses (I Kings 11:1), and he traded with Hittite kings ((2 Chronicles 1:17). Finally, when the Arameans were besieging the city of Samaria, they fled, believing rumours that Hittite forces were coming to help Israel (2 Kings 7:6). Where, then, did the Hittites fit into the ancient world?

The Hittites were an Indo-European people, probably originating beyond the Black Sea, and invading Anatolia in the 2nd Millennium BC. After defeating the indigenous population, the Hittites, under Labarna, conquered nearly all central Anatolia, founding the capital of the kingdom (known as Hatti) at Hattusas (present-day Boĝazkale in Turkey). King Hattusilis (1650–1620 BC) extended Hittite

HIGHWAYS THROUGH THE PROMISED LAND

Major routes connecting Egypt, in the west, to the major states of Mesopotamia, ran through the bottleneck of Palestine. The Promised Land of the Hebrews proved to be of great interest to the superpowers of the Biblical period. Egyptians, Assyrians, Persians and others all passed through this small but strategic area.

power over northern Syria, his grandson defeating Aleppo and conquering Babylon (c. 1590 BC). The most powerful Hittite ruler was Suppiluliumas I (1380–1346 BC), who razed the capital city of the Mitanni and projected his power to Carchemish, which became a dependency, along with Ugarit and Aleppo. The Assyrian vassals of the Mitanni shrugged off their overlords and built their own state with a capital at Ashur, but a Mitanni rump state survived as a buffer between rival empires. Hittite power infiltrated the Aegean and trickled into Lebanon, where conflict with Egypt broke out with a drawn battle at Kadesh. Further disputes were prevented by a treaty between Pharaoh Rameses II and Mutuwallis of Hatti in 1275 BC, detailing a mutual defence agreement and a dynastic marriage. Soon after 1200 BC, the Hittite state collapsed under attack from migrating Sea Peoples, with Anatolia being overrun by Phrygians. However, many city states retained their Hittite identity.

'In the same day the Lord made a covenant with Abram, saying, Unto thy seed have I given this land, from the river of Egypt unto the great river, the river Euphrates ...'

Genesis 15:18

At the other end of the Fertile Crescent was Egypt, dependent for its agricultural survival on the annual floods of the Nile. Egypt's contacts with the outside world were dictated by its natural boundaries. To the west and east, deserts protected the Nile Valley. Southwards, rocky, desert upland secured the border, and in its upper reaches rapids made the Nile difficult to navigate. The northern frontier was defined by the Mediterranean, leaving the people to live safely along the fertile riverbanks and delta. At first there were two kingdoms, Lower and Upper Egypt, but these were unified around 3000 BC. Pharaoh Senusret III (1878–1843 BC) invaded Palestine along the Way of Horus to Gaza and beyond as far as Shechem. Egyptian artefacts from this period have been found at Bethsam, Megiddo, Gezer, Jericho, Lachish and Sharuhen. Trade also flourished, with Egyptian artefacts discovered at Byblos, Qatna and Ugarit, with known trade routes extending to Anatolia, Cyprus and Crete. Despite later internal divisions and Lower Egypt falling under the domination of the Hyksos ('rulers of foreign lands'), these Semitic-Asiatics were expelled about 1580 BC.

The Egyptians utilized the chariot, a weapon adopted from the Hyksos, to expand their power into Canaan and beyond. Pharaoh Thutmose III (1479–1426 BC) decided to reaffirm the Egyptian power in Palestine that began under his grandfather, Thutmose I. He attacked the Mitanni, claiming the banks of the Euphrates as his northern border, and invaded Palestine 17 times. He first marched via Gaza to Joppa, engaged and defeated an alliance of city states at Aruna and laid siege to Megiddo, taking it after seven months. He eventually reached the Euphrates, and erected another stele next to that of his grandfather. Kadesh, the last remaining Hyksos city, was also defeated. After 1400 BC, during the Amarna period, Egyptian foreign policy became more peaceful. Letters found at Amarna, addressed to the two pharaohs Amenhotep III and IV, mention a large number of virtual city-states, including Ashkelon, Hebron, Jerusalem, Gezer, Shechem, Megiddo, Acco, Damascus, Tyre and Byblos.

The strip of land joining Egypt to the seats of power on the Fertile Crescent was Canaan or Palestine, traversed by two major highways. The Way of the Philistines and Way of the Sea advanced along the coastal plain, joining Raphia and Gaza to Tyre before dividing, with roads going north and to Damascus. The second route, the King's Highway, passed south from Damascus through the highlands east of Lake Galilee and the Dead Sea. The road split into two: one road led west along the Way of Arabah and the Way to Shur through Beth-lahel-roi to Egypt; the other continued south through Punon, Petra and the Gulf of Eilat (Aqaba). The early history of the Israelites places the Patriarchs in this Canaanite locale and international backdrop. Canaanite city-states peppered the Negev and Judaean mountains as far north as Gishala, Bethsaida and Ashtaroth. Canaan itself was divided into roughly three parts: the narrow strip along the Mediterranean, known as Phoenicia; Aram, the area of the Aramean city-states, stretching from the Huran, south of Damascus, to the last Hittite states near the Euphrates; and Mount Lebanon to the west. The land fought over by the Israelites included the lowlands of the Shephelah and the hill lands, now known as the West Bank, but previously known as the old kingdoms of Israel and Judah. Into this territory came the Israelites after their flight from Egypt under Moses, probably in the reign of Rameses II.

GLORY OF EGYPT

Egypt created a cosmopolitan and thriving civilization, developing sophisticated architectural and highly stylized artistic styles. There was a strong emphasis on life after death in Egyptian culture, and this manifested itself in symbolism and mammoth building projects.

The Journeys of Abraham

'Neither shall thy name any more be called Abram, but thy name shall be Abraham; for a father of many nations have I made thee. And I will make thee exceeding fruitful, and I will make nations of thee, and kings shall come out of thee.'

Genesis 17:5–6

The Hebrews were latecomers to history. Across the Bible lands, civilizations and cultures had arisen and fallen for hundreds and thousands of years before Abraham was born. The ancestors of Israel's peoples were a mixture of many groups, although predominantly northern Semitic, who entered Palestine in the 2nd Millennium BC. These peoples sometimes found their way to Egypt during a time of low rainfall while pursuing a semi-nomadic lifestyle; they may have lived as virtual state slaves before rebelling and fleeing under Moses. Whatever the historical interpretation, many vicissitudes must have followed wandering clans and tribes. The biblical account of events and Abraham's life is rooted in traditions based on oral transmission rather than on historical records, so no true biography as we understand it can be written. The biblical story of Abraham encapsulates the tragedies, drama and dreams of a wandering people seeking somewhere as a stable home but promised Canaan by their God.

Terah, a descendant of Shem, lived in the city of Ur of the Chaldees, where his sons were born – Abram, Nachor and Aran. Terah, under divine inspiration, took Abram and his wife, Sarai (his half-sister) and Lot, son of the deceased Aran, travelling to Haran, where he died. Then, at the call of God, Abram, Sarai and Lot, and a party of people they had gathered in Haran, journeyed into Canaan to Sichem and Beth-el where Abram built an altar. When a severe famine hit Canaan, Abram moved into Egypt. Fearing Sarai was so beautiful that he might be killed for her, he claimed she was his sister. Reports of her attractions reached the Pharaoh who took her into his harem, but finding out the truth of her relationship with Abram, returned her untouched. He berated Abram for his lie and dismissed him from Egypt. Returning to Beth-el in Canaan and realizing that their combined herds and flocks were too great for the land to sustain, which would lead to strife between their respective herdsmen, Abram and Lot agreed to part company. Lot chose to enter the plain of Jordan, while Abram stayed in Canaan. There, God told Abram that all the land around would be his, and his progeny would be numberless. Abram then moved his tents to Mamre in Hebron.

A PATRIARCH'S GREAT JOURNEY
A painting by the Hungarian artist József Molnár (1821–99) depicts Abraham on his journey from the Mesopotamian city of Ur to the 'promised land' of Canaan.

ABRAHAM'S JOURNEY

According to Jewish tradition, Abraham, the first Patriarch, left his home in Ur to migrate westwards through the Fertile Crescent, eventually reaching Canaan. Though there is no scientific evidence to support the existence of Abraham as a person, archaeology confirms that Semitic shepherds lived a nomadic life at this time – probably seeking a suitable homeland in which to establish permanent settlements. Some settled in Canaan; others travelled east to Egypt or west to Mesopotamia.

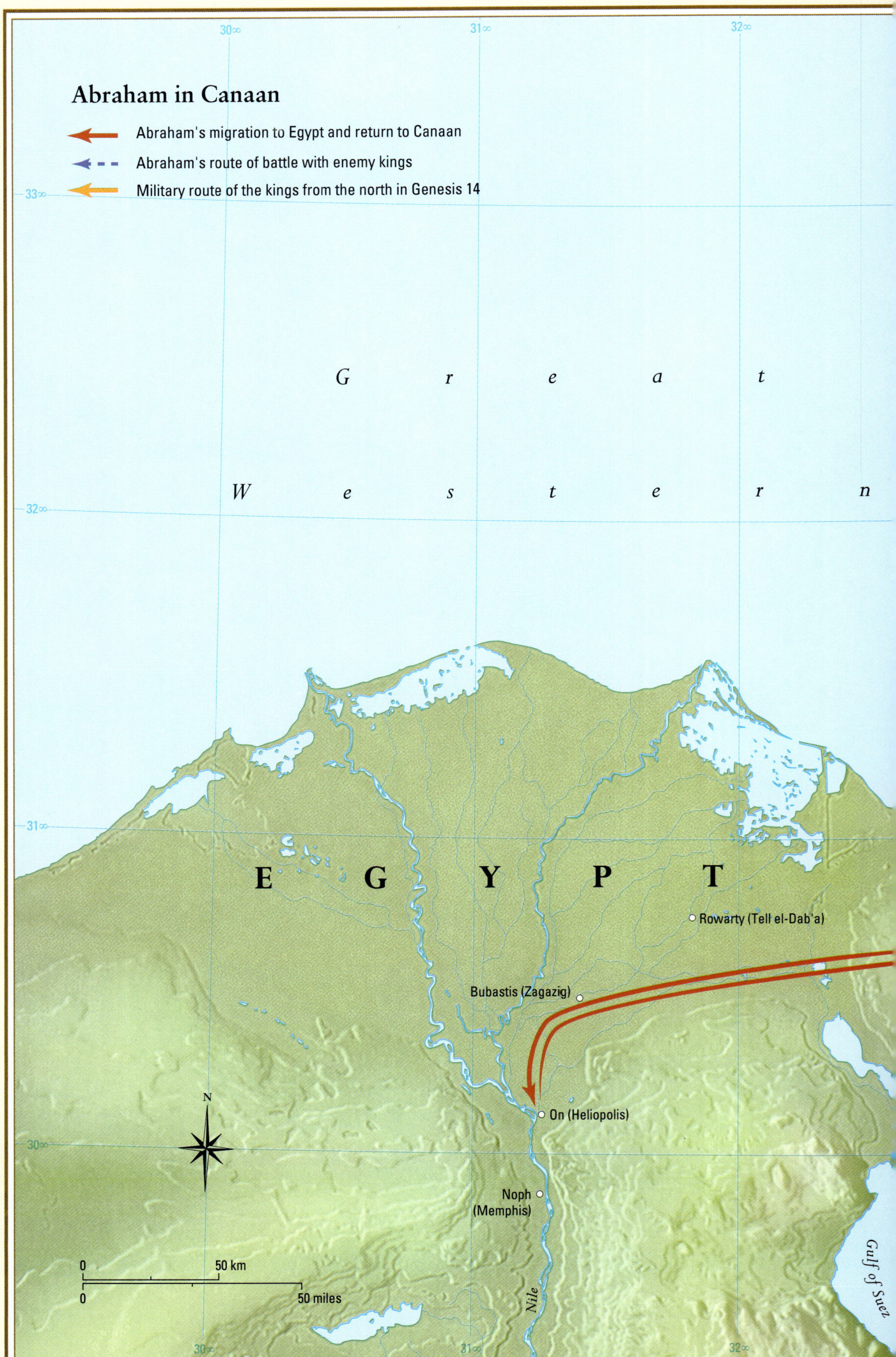

Dan
Hazor
Acco
REPHAIM
Sea of Chinnereth (Sea of Galilee)
Ashtaroth
Yarmuk
Dor
Megiddo
Beth-shan
Sea
Sea
Abraham leaves Canaan for Egypt
ZUZIM
Jordan
Samaria
Shechem
Aphek
Abraham receives the blessing of Melchizedek
Conflict arises between Abraham and Lot
Bethel
Ai
Jericho
Ashdod
Ekron
Salem
Abraham's attempt to sacrifice Issac at Mt. Moriah
God promises a son to Abraham and Sarah
Kiriathaim
Mamre
Hebron (Kiriath-arba)
Gaza
Salt Sea (Dead Sea)
Dibon
EMIM
Gera
Cave of Machpelah
Bab edh-Dhra
CANAAN
Beersheba
Possible location of Sodom, Gomorrah, Admah, Zebotim
Negev
AMORITES
Zoar (Bela)
Tamar
Beer-lahal-rol
AMALEKITES
Arabah
HORITES
Syro-Arabian Desert
Punon
Kadesh-barnea (En-Mishpat)
Wilderness of Shur
Wilderness of Paran
El-paran
Gulf of Aqaba (Ellat)

ESCAPE FROM THE WRATH OF GOD

In an engraving by the French artist Gustave Doré (1832–1883), Lot and his two daughters flee the burning cities of Sodom and Gomorrah, while his wife looks back and is turned into stone.

SACRED TOMB
A Jewish girl prays at the Cave of the Patriarchs, in Hebron on the West Bank, said to be the burial place of Abraham.

The political environment erupted when the kings of nearby Sodom and Gomorrah rebelled against their overlord, Chedorlaomer, King of Elam. The ensuing conflict saw the Elamite king victorious. Lot's community and flocks were seized while returning home. Hearing about his nephew's capture, Abram led an attack on Elam. While journeying home with his victor's booty, Abram was met by Melchizedek, King of Salem, who blessed him. Abram then gave him tithes of his spoils.

Meanwhile, Sarai, who was childless, told Abram to take her handmaid, Hagar, as a concubine, resulting in the birth of Ishmael. Thirteen years later God appeared to Abram and promised him a son by Sarai saying his legacy would be a great nation. Symbolically, he changed Abram's name to Abraham and Sarai's to Sarah in a covenant, which also established the rite of circumcision.

While sitting in his tent at Mamre, Abraham was approached by God and two angels in human form and offered them hospitality. The promise of a son, Isaac, was renewed, but when Sarah laughed at her child-bearing years being over, the Lord rebuked her. Abraham was informed about the impending destruction of Sodom and Gomorrah for the sin of wickedness. He pleaded with God to spare the cities. God agreed that he would do this if he could find ten righteous men there. The ten could not be found and God destroyed both cities. Seeing the smoke of destruction over the cities, Abraham moved south to Gerar. Again fearing for his life, he said that Sarah was his sister. She was taken by King Abimlech of Gerar, but her status was revealed to him in a dream and she was returned untouched. The king chastized Abraham for his deception. The two men were reconciled and God, in return, cured all the barrenness in the king's household.

Sarah gave birth to Isaac and he was circumcised on the eighth day. Jealous of Ishmael, Sarah had him and Hagar, the Egyptian, ejected into the wilderness. God saved them from dying of thirst, promising Hagar that her son would be the progenitor of a nation. Islamic tradition cites Ishmael as the father of the Arabs.

A dispute between Abraham and King Abimlech over a well ended with a treaty between them. Abraham dug a new well, naming it Beersheba. At Jehovah-jireh, Abraham next engaged in a trial of faith and God commanded him to sacrifice Isaac. Just as Abraham was going to strike his son, his hand was stayed by an angel and a ram was sacrificed instead. At Kirjath-arba, Sarah, aged 127, died and was buried in a cave in Machpelah, which Abraham had bought from Ephron the Hethite (Hittite).

Abraham's career continued when he found Rebekah, a wife for Isaac, from the city of Nachor where his brother, Nahor, lived. Thus, Isaac married into the clan left behind in Haran in Mesopotamia. Abraham married Keturah who bore him six sons. He died, aged 170, and was buried in the cave at Machpelah.

Isaac, Jacob and Joseph

'And it came to pass the same day, that Isaac's servants came, and told him concerning the well which they had digged, and said unto him, We have found water. And he called it Shebah: therefore the name of the city is Beersheba unto this day.'

Genesis 26:32–33

Isaac was a pastoral nomad, the son of Abraham and his wife, Sarah, and the heir of God's Covenant. As a youth, his father had offered him as a sacrifice. Certain that both Abraham and Isaac were totally obedient to His will, God accepted a ram as a substitute. Thus, the Hebrews rejected human sacrifice thereafter.

Isaac, or 'laughter' in Hebrew, was born to Sarah in the desert between Gerar and Beersheba. Spending most of his life constantly seeking water for his flocks and growing crops occasionally when suitable conditions prevailed, he replicated his father's lifestyle, seldom moving 80 kilometres (50 miles) from his birthplace in the northern Negev. When his mother died, Isaac lived at Beer-lahai-roi, an oasis on the caravan trail to Egypt and the place where an angel consoled the pregnant Hagar when she fled the cruelty of Sarah, her mistress. Isaac met his wife Rebekah at Beer-lahai-roi, and their twin sons, Esau and Jacob, were born there.

The Negev provides a hard living, especially when springs and wells run dry. Flocks and people can die. In early biblical times, Egypt was a fertile area that could provide shelter from climatic disasters. When famine hit Gerar, Isaac considered refuge in Egypt but obeyed God's will by not going there. The Gerar region has many wells and lies between real desert and areas of permanent settlement. The region is not barren, and irrigation systems can top up the 15–25 centimetres (6–10 in) of annual rainfall. Isaac reopened Abraham's old wells, sowed crops, and reaped a hundredfold in the same year. So wealthy and powerful did Isaac become that King Abimelech, feeling threatened, ordered him away. Isaac sought water in the Valley of Gerar, but disputed water rights with local herdsmen until he dug his own well, named Reheboth. Despite finding peace in that part of Gerar, Isaac obeyed God and went to the oasis of Beersheba.

Isaac's son, Jacob, was a quiet man unlike his older twin, Esau, who became a desert hunter. Esau hunted deer one day for Isaac, but when he returned exhausted and hungry, he sold his birthright to Jacob for some bread and a pot of lentils. At Beersheba, Rebekah helped Jacob, her favourite son, deceive her husband by placing the

'Thy name shall be called no more Jacob, but Israel: for as a prince hast thou power with God and with men, and hast prevailed ... And Jacob called the name of the place Peniel: for I have seen God face to face, and my life is preserved.'

Genesis 32:28, 30

THE JOURNEYS OF THREE GENERATIONS

Isaac lived his life in the Negev desert. His son, Jacob, travelled through lands that ranged from Haran, near the Euphrates, to the Nile delta. Jacob's youngest son, Joseph, travelled north from his home to seek his brothers. They sold him into slavery, and his enforced journey took him south into Egypt.

skins of goat kids upon his hands and neck, so that when the nearly blind Isaac touched him, he would mistake him for the hairier Esau. The fraud worked, and Isaac gave his second son, Jacob, God's blessing. Having lost his blessing and birthright, Esau planned to kill his twin. Jacob promptly travelled north to his mother's people, Aramaeans, in Paddan-aram near Haran, seeking safety and also a wife.

Jacob's likely route took him through the hill country via Hebron, Jerusalem, Shiloh and Shechem. A major event took place at Luz, called Bethel by Jacob. He dreamt he saw a ladder leading to God, who told him that his family and descendants would be numerous (Genesis 28: 10–22). The route from Bethel went through Damascus and then north via Hamath and east via Carchemish, or a southern road via Tadmor to Mari and Babylon. Paddan-aram is identified with Aram-Naharaim (Aram of the two rivers), the area between the River Khabur in the east and the great bend of the Euphrates to its west.

On Jacob's arrival at Haran, he met his cousin, Rachel, at a well where she was watering her father's flocks. She ran to her father, Laban, who welcomed Jacob. Laban offered Jacob work and pay, but Jacob requested Rachel in marriage and offered to serve Laban for seven years for the honour. At the wedding ceremony, Laban tricked Jacob into marrying Rachel's older sister, Leah. So Jacob worked for another seven years as a bride price for Rachel. He continued working for Laban, raised a family and became an extremely wealthy man. After residing with Laban for 20 years, Jacob decided to return to Isaac in Canaan, fleeing with his family and livestock as Laban was away tending his flocks. Laban pursued Jacob, overtaking his party in the hills of Gilead. Disputes over the ownership of the flocks and herds took place, but Jacob and Laban were reconciled, making a peace covenant.

Jacob moved to Mahanaim, below the limestone cliffs of the Jabbok Valley, sending peace messengers to Esau in Edom. Hearing that Esau was approaching with 400 men, Jacob divided his clan and goods into two and placed them in different locations, presuming that one company would survive if his brother wanted a fight. Jacob also sent gifts to his brother and prayed for a reconciliation. That night, Jacob wrestled with a man until morning. The man said, 'Thy name shall be called no more Jacob, but Israel: for as a prince hast thou power with God and with men, and hast prevailed … And Jacob called the name of the place Peniel: for I have seen God face to face and my life is preserved.' (Genesis 32:28, 30)

Jacob and Esau met, and the brothers made peace. Esau finally returned to Edom. Jacob reached Succoth

in the Jordan Valley, and built a house and shelters for his cattle. The heat was so intense and draining that he crossed the Jordan into Canaan up the Wadi Farah to the town of Shalem in Shechem, buying land nearby and erecting an altar called El-elohe-Israel. Disaster befell Jacob's daughter, Dinah, who was raped by Shechem, son of the Hivite Prince Hamor. Her brothers, Simeon and Levi, took revenge by killing the prince, his son and the men of Shechem, seizing all livestock and the Shechem women, and wrecking every house.

Jacob took his people to Bethel, where he built an altar. He retraced Abraham's route through the mountains. Rachel died giving birth to Benjamin near Bethlehem. Jacob was reunited with his father at Mamre near Hebron. When Isaac died, reputedly 180 years old, Esau and Jacob buried him in a cave. Esau returned to Edom, where he allegedly founded the Edomites, while Jacob personified the nation of Israel, his sons becoming the patriarchs of the 12 tribes of Israel: Reuben, Simeon, Levi, Judah, Issacher and Zebulon (from Leah); Joseph and Benjamin (from Rachel); Gad and Asher (from Zilpah, Leah's handmaid); and Dan and Naphtali (from Bilhah, Rachel's handmaid).

The story of Joseph, told in Genesis 37–50, probably took place some time between 1720 and 1500 BC, the

'Come, and let us sell him to the Ishmeelites, and let not our hand be upon him; for he is our brother and our flesh. And his brethren were content. Then there passed by Midianites merchantmen; and they drew and lifted up Joseph out of the pit, and sold Joseph to the Ishmeelites for twenty pieces of silver: and they brought Joseph into Egypt.'

Genesis 37:27–28

THE JUDAEAN DESERT

Esau, brother of Jacob, became a hunter, roaming the wilder parts of Judaea and Edom, where he sought out his prey. Elder son of Isaac and the first-born of twins, Esau was entitled to the family birthright but sold this to his brother, Jacob, in return for lentil stew. Jacob also tricked Esau out of his father's blessing. Esau hated his brother for this and wanted to kill him, but eventually the brothers were reconciled.

'And Joseph said unto his brethren, Come near to me, I pray you. And they came near. And he said, I am Joseph your brother, whom ye sold into Egypt. Now therefore be not grieved, nor angry with yourselves, that ye sold me hither: for God did send me before you to preserve life. For these two years hath the famine been in the land: and yet there are five years, in which there shall neither be earing [ploughing] nor harvest.'

Genesis 45:4–6

time when the Hyksos dynasty ruled in Egypt. The Hyksos were Semitic in origin, but had adapted completely to Egyptian culture. There is evidence that many Semites of various tribes were taken as slaves to Egypt at that time, with some reaching high office.

Joseph was the favourite son of his father Jacob. His father's favour and his own apparent arrogance earned him the enmity of his ten older half-brothers, who plotted to kill him. Finding him alone, they threw him into a well. Soon after, a group of merchants passed by on their way to Egypt, and they were happy to buy Joseph to sell as a slave there. The brothers covered up their crime by smearing goat's blood on Joseph's coat so that his father would believe he had been killed by wild animals.

Joseph was sold to Potiphar, one of the Pharaoh's officials. Joseph was so efficient that he was promoted rapidly and was soon running the whole household. All went well until the handsome young Hebrew caught the eye of Potiphar's wife, who set out to seduce him. Joseph constantly rebuffed her. Infuriated, she told her husband that his Hebrew servant had tried to rape her, and so Potiphar had Joseph imprisoned.

Joseph's abilities and intelligence again worked in his favour and he came to be entrusted with much of the prison's administration. When two of Pharaoh's officials, his chief butler and baker, were imprisoned, Joseph was assigned to look after them. Both had dreams that Joseph interpreted for them. He said that in three days' time the baker would be executed, but the butler would be pardoned. Joseph asked the butler to put in a good word for him with Pharaoh, but after his release the man forgot about Joseph.

Two years later Pharaoh himself had strange dreams that all his wise men were unable to interpret. At last the butler remembered the young man who had successfully interpreted his dream in prison. Joseph was sent for and was able to tell Pharaoh the meaning of his dreams. They signified that there would be seven years of good harvests, followed by seven years of famine. Joseph advised Pharaoh to store food during the years of plenty to draw on in the years of famine. Pharaoh was so impressed by Joseph that he made him a governor over Egypt, in charge of organizing the storage of grain.

There were such bountiful harvests in the first seven years that Joseph was able to provide grain during the famine, not only for the Egyptians but for people from other countries that were also short of food. One such country was Canaan, and when Jacob heard that grain was obtainable in Egypt he sent his ten older sons there to buy some.

When his brothers appeared, Joseph knew them immediately, but they failed to recognize him. He did not acknowledge them but accused them of being spies. He demanded that they prove their story that they were simply brothers from Canaan come to buy food, and that they should bring Benjamin, Jacob's youngest son and Joseph's only full brother, to Egypt. He forced them to leave one of their number, Simeon, as a hostage. Then Joseph loaded their packs with grain and money, and they returned to Canaan.

Jacob was reluctant to let his sons return to Egypt with Benjamin, but when the famine continued, he had to let them go. Again Joseph pretended not to recognize them, and tricked them by planting a silver cup in Benjamin's pack and then accusing him of the theft, insisting that he must remain in Egypt as a slave. Judah pleaded for his young brother, telling Joseph it would break their father's heart to lose his youngest son. At last Joseph relented and revealed who he was. He forgave his brothers and loaded them with gifts. Eventually Jacob and all his sons settled in Egypt.

LADDER TO HEAVEN
An engraving by the Dutch artist Gerard Hoet (1648–1733), from a 1728 book Figures de la Bible, *shows the sleeping Jacob at Bethel dreaming of angels ascending and descending a ladder up to God.*

The Exodus

Increasingly, the Egyptians regarded the Hebrews as aliens. At some point during the long reign of Rameses II, they escaped to Canaan. They were led by Moses, who had been given a sacred covenant naming the Hebrews as God's 'chosen people'. Hebrew law was an expression of the people's gratitude thereafter.

In about 1285 BC an Egyptian army led by King Rameses II (1290–1213 BC) ran into a trap at Kadesh in northern Palestine, just north of what is now Lebanon. The front section of the army, led by Rameses, was cut off by Hittite charioteers who attacked the second section, leaving the king and his section isolated. Only desperate fighting saved the situation.

Kadesh appears as a victory in Egyptian records, but the treaty that eventually followed left the Egyptian frontier in Palestine further south than it had ever been. Earlier in Rameses II's reign, the Egyptian capital had been moved to a site near the old Hyksos capital at Avaris, in the north-eastern part of the delta, as part of a vast, extensive building programme. Thus, the Nile delta was once more the most important part of Egypt and was vital to Egyptian security, with mounting pressure from Libya to the west and an uneasy peace with the Hittites.

These developments in Egyptian history have clear links with events described in the Bible. Therefore, it is assumed that it was during the reign of Rameses II that the Hebrews escaped from Egypt, as depicted in the Book of Exodus. When the Asiatic Hyksos rulers of Egypt were overthrown around 1550 BC, the descendants of the Hebrew nomadic shepherds who had settled near the delta found themselves under increasing suspicion as aliens. They would certainly have been chosen as one of many groups forced into labour gangs to build Rameses' new capital and frontier fortifications. This is described in Exodus 1:11: 'Therefore they did set over them [the Israelites] taskmasters to afflict them with their burdens. And they built for Pharaoh treasure cities, Pithom and Raamses.'

The Hebrew leader, Moses, is presented as the adopted child of an Egyptian princess. He therefore had access to the royal court. But of equal importance are his contacts with the Midianites of the Sinai Desert, who gave him shelter and a wife when he first had to flee Egypt. The Midianites, who were descendants of Midean, son of Abraham, worshipped the same God as the Hebrews, and Moses returned to Egypt with the conviction that God had chosen him to lead his people to freedom.

The famous plagues described in Exodus 7–12 can all be seen as natural phenomena, but for both the Hebrews and the Egyptians they were contests between the Hebrew God and the Egyptian gods – of whom Rameses II was one. The broad background to the account in the Book of Exodus is entirely consistent with the situation in Egypt at the time. Religion was territorial, and neither the Egyptians nor the Hebrews would want a Hebrew religious festival to be held on Egyptian soil, so the Hebrews asked permission to go into the desert to celebrate. This was the request that the Egyptian king at first refused and then granted after the series of devastating plagues.

THE POWER OF EGYPT

Egypt's empire and its area of influence reached from the region of Irem in the south to the frontiers of Syria and the Hittite Empire in the north.

'And the children of Israel were fruitful, and increased abundantly and multiplied and waxed exceeding mighty; and the land was filled with them. Now there arose up a new king over Egypt, which knew not Joseph.'

Exodus 1:7–8

The Hebrew escape from Egypt is described in the Book of Exodus 12–15. These chapters, and the subsequent ones that deal with the Covenant at Mount Sinai, must be the most heavily edited passages in the Old Testament, for the events they describe are as central to the Hebrew religion as the Crucifixion and Resurrection of Jesus are to Christianity. The account of the Exodus and Covenant reached its present form in the Book of Exodus about seven centuries after the events occurred, and some points are still disputed. But the final editors were able to refer to very old written sources, and firm traditions were kept alive through their regular use in Hebrew worship.

The description of the escape starts with the Passover regulations in Exodus 12. This celebration was, and still is, the key to Hebrew worship and the festival to which the other major feast is linked. It was originally a protection rite for nomadic shepherds as they moved along the routes in search of pasture. The blood of a sacrificed lamb, symbolizing and containing the life-giving power of God, gave them protection against any evil forces, and the meal then sealed the links between God and his people. The escape from Egypt gave this rite new meaning, as a commemoration of the Hebrew God's victory over the Egyptian gods and his covenant with his chosen people. All subsequent acts of deliverance throughout Hebrew history were then seen as consequences of his Exodus and God's deliverance and were celebrated therefore as extensions of the Passover. When the Hebrews became farmers after the occupation of Canaan, the Canaanite harvest festivals were celebrated as manifestations of the same power of God that had brought the people safely out of Egypt.

The actual crossing out of Egypt pursued by Egyptian soldiers, depicted in Exodus 14, occurred at what the Hebrews called Yam Suph. When this was translated into Greek, about 1,000 years later, a phrase meaning 'Red Sea' was used, implying that the Hebrews crossed the Gulf of Suez. However, the Hebrew should more properly be translated 'Sea of Reeds', which also agrees with the place-names given in the early part of the journey (Exodus 13:17–14:2). The 'way of the land of the Philistines' (Palestine) left the north-east edge of the Nile delta, where the ancient Egyptian capital of Memphis was then located, and followed the coast into Canaan. Succoth, where the Hebrews first camped on their journey, was probably west of Lake Timsah (today's Suez Canal), while Migdol was a border fortress near the coast at Tell el-Heir. Pi-hahiroth (Exodus 14:9) faced Baal-zephon, where there was a temple for sailors on a narrow peninsula.

This route takes the Hebrew escape well north of the Gulf of Suez, into the marshy area near the Mediterranean coast. This fits both the Hebrew 'Sea of Reeds' and the account of Egyptian chariot wheels being clogged, which comes from one of the earlier strands of the traditions woven together in Exodus 14. The crossing therefore probably occurred north of Lake Timsah. After this, the Hebrews turned south, both to avoid Egyptian officials on the main routes into Palestine and to reach the wilderness areas grazed by the nomadic shepherd tribes. One of these tribes was the Midianites, to whom Moses had fled before returning to Egypt as the leader of his people.

Despite a wealth of information in the Books of Exodus, Leviticus, Numbers and Deuteronomy, there can be no absolute certainty about the route the escaping Hebrews took from Egypt to the mountain of the Covenant and Canaan, nor how long the whole journey took. There are also some different views about the actual location of the mountain.

Some of the contradictory information becomes much clearer if it is accepted that the biblical accounts of the journey combine traditions about several waves of Hebrew penetration into Canaan, with at least two distinct journeys. One of these was opposed by kingdoms in the plains of Moab to the east of the Dead Sea, while an earlier journey was able to pass unhindered. In addition, there would have been Hebrews living in southern Canaan who had not gone to Egypt at the time of the entry of Joseph and his brothers.

Egyptian records lend support to such a view, for it appears that there were no organized kingdoms east of the Dead Sea in the 14th Century BC. But by the 13th Century BC, kingdoms had emerged in Edom and Moab, which would account for opposition to a Hebrew group during the latter part of the reign of Rameses II. In any event, there were fortified Canaanite cities across the south of Canaan that could prevent Hebrew groups of

THE HEBREWS LEAVE EGYPT

Most probably, the Hebrews crossed the marshy region to the east of the Nile delta where Moses' 'parting of the waters' would have occurred. They then journeyed to the sacred mountain, and their experiences in the Sinai Peninsula became the foundation of the nation's religion and identity.

MOSES AND THE TEN COMMANDMENTS

The mountain where the Covenant with God was revealed to Moses during the Exodus is believed to be either Mount Sinai, Mount Horeb or Mount Paran, all granite mountains in the southern Sinai Peninsula. In this painting by Rembrandt *(1606–69), Moses holds aloft the stone tablets inscribed with the Ten Commandments, revealed to him by God after forty days and forty nights on the mountain.*

'And Moses went up unto God, and the Lord called unto him out of the mountain, saying, thus shalt thou say to the house of Jacob, and tell the children of Israel; Ye have seen what I did unto the Egyptians, and how I bare you on eagles' wings, and brought you unto myself.'

Exodus 19:3–4

any size from penetrating past the region of Kadesh-barnea. Such groups would then have to cross eastwards to take the traditional nomadic route, the King's Highway. There is far less uncertainty about the location of the mountain itself. It is referred to variously as Mount Sinai, Mount Horeb and Mount Paran; and all three names point to the granite mountains in the southern Sinai Peninsula.

The most important incident of the whole tradition need not be doubted, and would account for the mingling of all the traditions into one: the Covenant at the sacred mountain from which the Hebrews derived their national identity and their sense of religious unity. All Hebrews would have the strongest motives for associating their ancestors with this tradition and for seeing the Covenant as their entitlement to the land of Palestine. The events at Mount Sinai are cast in a form similar to treaties between so-called saviour-kings and their subjects, whose relationships were based on a great victory or deed that placed the subjects under an obligation to their king. The relationship between them was then specified by laws accepted by the people, backed by the power of the gods and by sanctions. The Hebrew Covenant was therefore based on the escape from Egypt, the supreme manifestation of God's power and of His choice of the Hebrew people. Hebrew law then became the expression of the people's gratitude and their obligations to God and to each other as God's chosen ones. All Hebrew law, whether it already existed or developed subsequently, was an expression of the Covenant and so was incorporated into the narrative. As direct, absolute commands from God to the Hebrews, rather than laws presented in the form of cases and precedents, the Ten Commandments (Exodus 20:1–17 and Deuteronomy 5:1–21) have no known parallels in the ancient Near East.

'I am the Lord thy God which have brought thee out of the land of Egypt, out of the house of bondage. Thou shalt have no other gods before me.

Thou shalt not make unto thee any graven image, or any likeness of any thing that is in heaven above, or that is in the earth beneath, or that is in the water under the earth.

Thou shalt not bow down thyself to them, nor serve them: for I the Lord thy God am a jealous god, visiting the iniquity of the fathers upon the children unto the third and fourth generation of them that hate me; And showing mercy unto thousands of them that love me, and keep my commandments.

Thou shalt not take the name of the Lord thy God in vain; for the Lord will not hold him guiltless that taketh his name in vain.

Remember the sabbath day, to keep it holy. Six days shalt thou labour, and do all thy work. But the seventh day is the sabbath of the Lord thy God: in it thou shalt not do any work, thou, nor thy son, nor thy daughter, thy manservant, nor thy maidservant, nor thy cattle, nor thy stranger that is within thy gates. For in six days the Lord made heaven and earth, the sea and all that is in them is, and rested the seventh day: wherefore the Lord blessed the sabbath day, and hallowed it.

Honour thy father and thy mother: that thy days may be long upon the land that the Lord thy God giveth thee.

Thou shalt not kill.

Thou shalt not commit adultery.

Thou shalt not steal.

Thou shalt not bear false witness against thy neighbour.

Thou shalt not covet thy neighbour's house, thy shalt not covet thy neighbour's wife, nor his manservant, nor his maidservant, nor his ox, nor his ass, nor any thing that is thy neighbour's.'

Invasion and Conquest

The Near and Middle East was entering a long period of turmoil. The powers that had previously occupied Canaan collapsed or were wracked by civil wars. Local peoples and migrants, such as the Philistines and Hebrews, struggled for control of Canaan.

The most probable date for the Hebrew escape from Egypt, the Exodus, is the latter part of the reign of King Rameses II of Egypt (1290–1213 BC), which would mean that the Hebrews penetrated into Canaan from the east at the end of the 13th or beginning of the 12th Centuries BC. Canaan was soon to become known as the 'Land of the Philistines', and eventually, Palestine. This time marks the beginning of nearly three centuries of weakness and turmoil for the great powers, which normally considered Canaan an essential part of their defences and trading interests. It was certainly not a period of peace for the area, with the protagonists local to Canaan, or migrants such as the Hebrews.

The geography of the area forced the international routes from Egypt to Mesopotamia and Asia Minor through the narrow land of Canaan, between the desert and the sea. Throughout its recorded history, Canaan was at the mercy of the dominant powers of the Near and Middle East; it was nearly always occupied by one of these powers, and served as a battleground between them. During most of the 2nd Millennium BC, Canaan had been under the control of Egypt. The Canaanite city-states, always at war among themselves, had seen Egypt as a source of support against each other. But from the beginning of the 15th Century BC, the powers of Asia Minor and upper Mesopotamia had resisted Egyptian pressure and forced the Egyptians back from Carchemish in the north. The Battle of Kadesh (c. 1275 BC), between Egyptians and the Hittites of Asia Minor, left the northern limits of Egyptian control running from Damascus to the Phoenician coast. Egyptian-controlled territory would probably have been pushed back to the Nile delta itself if the Hittites had not themselves been overwhelmed by migrants known as the Sea Peoples, who had probably been driven out of the Balkans and Greece.

Egypt might have gained full control of Canaan, but in turn had to fight off the Sea Peoples who attacked the delta region of Lower Egypt during the reign of Rameses II's successor, Merneptah (1213–1203 BC). Egypt repulsed the migrants from the delta but could not prevent them gaining control of the coastal strip in southern Canaan, where they became known as the Philistines. They established themselves in five main cities – Gaza, Ashkelon, Ashdod, Gath and Ekron – where they were technically subject people of the Egyptians. The Philistines' presence points to Egyptian weakness. Egypt was entering a period of internal disorders and economic problems. The priests grew enormously powerful on wealth that they built up through the temples and kept secure from the state. Gradually Upper Egypt fell under the control of the priests of Thebes, while Lower Egypt

HEBREW SPIES *(right)*
Moses sent one man from each of the 12 tribes of Israel on a spying mission into the land of Canaan to seek out invasion routes and gather any useful information. They returned with tales of fortified cities and of the fierce people that lived in them. But the lure of the land was irresistible.

Wanderings of the Hebrew Spies
Route of the spies
Route of entry into Canaan according to Numbers 21
Route of entry into Canaan according to Numbers 33
to Damascus
Samaria
Shechem
Jordan
Aphek
Joppa
Plains of Moab
Rabbah-ammon
Bethel
Anathoth (Jeremiah)
Jericho
AMMON
Great Sea
Western Sea
Ashdod
Ekron
Jerusalem
Mt Nebo
Heshbon
Bamoth
Ashkelon
Gath
Almon-diblathaim
Nahaliel
Salt Sea (Dead Sea)
Hebron
Kiriathaim
Gaza
Dibon
Arnon
Mattanah
Gerar
PHILISTIA
CANAAN
MOAB
Beersheba
Hormah
Arad
Bab edh-Dhra
Wilderness of Moab
Zered
Zoar (Bela)
Iye-abarim (?)
Negev
Wilderness of Zin
Tamar
Zalmonah (?)
Beer-lahai-roi
Arabah
Mt Hor (?)
Punon
Kadesh-barnea (En-Mishpat)
EDOM
Wilderness of Edom
Wilderness of Paran
Edomite Fortress
N
Arabian Desert
Jotbathah
0 25 km
0 25 miles
Sinai

MIGRATION BY WATER

The movement of the Sea Peoples created a period of great instability. Against this background the Hebrews and the Philistines struggled to settle and control Canaan.

was ruled by the kings from Tanis in the delta. Libya increased its pressure on Egypt from the west and Nubia gained its independence. Egypt would not be fully united and powerful again for several centuries.

In this period of turmoil the Hebrews arrived in Canaan. Joshua sent spies to gather intelligence and find possible invasion routes. Camped on the plains of Moab at Abel-shittim were the Hebrews, making their preparations for the invasion. The invasion epic, found in the books of Joshua and the Book of Judges, was probably based on the combined experience of many invading groups, covering some decades, perhaps even centuries. There is no doubt, however, that the Hebrews had to fight to gain control of the land of Canaan – their 'Promised Land'.

At the moment Joshua launched the first invasion, the Hebrews crossed the Jordan over a dry riverbed. The river had providentially been blocked upstream, stemming the flow of water, at least while the army crossed. Joshua selected Gilgal as his base, then set about extending Hebrew authority over the immediate area. This would form a secure centre of operations from which to launch his campaign against the local settlements and on into the central highlands. The first major city to be attacked, and one of the best-known battles of the Bible, is Jericho. For six days the Hebrews marched around the city walls. On the seventh day, priests blowing rams' horns continued to circle the city, and the walls eventually fell. The Hebrews entered and massacred its inhabitants, taking the treasure they found there for 'the house of the Lord'.

However, extensive archaeological work on the site of Jericho reveals no walled city from the period of the Hebrew conquest. There was a walled city, but its violent end came some 300 years earlier, possibly the result of local wars or invaders. Perhaps the Jericho stories were handed down and woven into the biblical epic when the Hebrew conquest stories began to take shape.

The Canaanites, the people facing this Hebrew assault, were predominantly farmers living in heavily fortified settlements from which they could work the fertile land within safe reach. Agriculture and defence were the two keys to their way of life and religion, but the rivalry between the many fortified towns meant they did not achieve political unity and were thus unable to offer, at least initially, a united front to stem Hebrew advance. The shifting patterns of alliances and leagues are similar to those of Greece during the classical period about 1,000 years later. It is possible that the Hyksos rulers of Egypt, from the mid-17th to mid-16th Centuries BC, were originally Canaanites, and that this was a brief period of political unity and power in an area stretching from Lower Egypt to the borders of Asia Minor.

Ai, a typical Canaanite settlement of some 1,000 people, stood in the way of the Hebrew advance. Joshua launched a direct attack but was repulsed, with the loss of 36 men. He then formulated a plan that drew the defenders of Ai into the open to the north, while another force attacked from the west. Ai fell, the town was burned and the inhabitants slaughtered.

The case of Shechem presents an interesting insight into the Hebrew settlement of Canaan. The Shechemites were of mixed origin, and their city commanded an important area of the hill country. Some of its people may have been part of the movement that had earlier brought Abraham to Canaan. These people may have had affinities with the Hebrews, and this might explain the gathering at the pass between Mounts Gezarim and Ebal of 'sojourner as well as homeborn' for the blessing of Israel. The Hebrews moved into and through this area by treaty with these indigenous people.

The control of the lands around the vital area of Gibeon was also by treaty. The people in this area called themselves Hivites, not Canaanites. The treaty, though created to deceive the Hebrews, was still honoured. This agreement gave Joshua and his invading army access to the Shephelah, the low hills bordering Philistia.

The Canaanite city of Megiddo was on a fortified hill commanding the coastal road where it emerged into the Valley of Jezreel from a pass in the ridge of Mount Carmel, and branched into its northern and Mesopotamian routes. The city was repeatedly destroyed and rebuilt as each victor took advantage of its strategic position. Excavations at the site have revealed some 20 layers of occupation. It was to receive its most impressive additions during the reign of King Solomon (c. 970–931 BC), but it was also powerful and wealthy during the 13th Century BC. At that time, Megiddo already had a great fortified palace to the east of the main gate, and a fortified temple. A hoard of carved ivory, precious beads and jewellery, including gold earrings, point to the wealth in the city at the time. It was a feudal society, under the absolute authority of a king.

> ***'And the Lord said unto Joshua, See, I have given into thine hand Jericho, and the king thereof, and the mighty men of valour.'***
>
> *Joshua 6:2*

Most of the Canaanite cities were dependent on agriculture and water supplies within their fortifications. Therefore, they were almost all situated near the coastal plain, with a few scattered across to the edges of the Jordan Valley. The destruction of the coastal city of Ugarit by the Philistines about 1200 BC makes it possible to put a final date to the hundreds of written texts discovered on the site. They were in the form of clay tablets, which included religious and mythological material. From these, and from the excavations of Canaanite sanctuaries, it is possible to reconstruct something of the beliefs and practices of Canaanite religion without having to depend too closely on the hostile and critical descriptions contained in the Bible.

The next phase of the Hebrew assault on Canaan was towards the fertile hills and forests of Galilee to the north. The major city of the area was Hazor, which,

FIGHTING FOR THE PROMISED LAND

The invasion of Canaan began by the crossing of the Jordan. From a base at Gilgal, Joshua attacked and captured Jericho. He then moved into the central highlands, but the city of Ai blocked his route. After an unsuccessful first attack he eventually captured the city. His campaign continued through the highlands and towards Philistia.

with its moat and defensive walls, was the largest city in Canaan. Joshua gathered his forces in Upper and Lower Galilee in order to launch a surprise attack. He met the Canaanite army in the narrow defiles and forests at Merom, where the Canaanite cavalry and chariots were of little value – there was simply no room to manoeuvre. Using the terrain to its advantage, the Hebrew army won a major victory, putting the Canaanites into shambolic retreat. The Hebrews cut off the Canaanite escape route to Hazor, leaving the them no option but to withdraw northwards. Hazor was left undefended. The city suffered the same fate as cities to the south – its population was slaughtered, and the city was razed to the ground. Extensive archaeological research conducted between 1920 and 1960 confirmed the city's destruction in the 13th Century BC.

The Old Testament shows that some of the language and symbolism of the Canaanite religion was also used by the new Hebrew settlers, particularly the name of the chief god, El, and some of the aspects of the Canaanite creation myths. El is called 'El the Bull' in some of the Canaanite texts, while Baal has titles such as 'Rider of the Clouds', with control over the storms and rain that water the soil for crops. In the creation myths, Baal fights the death god and the god of the chaotic waters and at one stage is himself killed. His sister forces the death god, Mot to give Baal life for half of the year and the water god is banished to the sea. Wherever the Hebrews have drawn from such ideas, they have subordinated them to the unique saviour-God of the escape from Egypt and the Covenant. However, the influence of the Canaanites can be seen most in the Hebrew sacrifices and festivals.

The Canaanites offered animals, crops and incense as sacrifices, in which all or some of the offering was burnt, and as communion sacrifices with an associated sacred meal. The main Canaanite festivals were celebrations of the various stages of the harvest. They appear in Hebrew religious celebrations as the three major harvest festivals, known in English translations of the Bible as the festivals of Unleavened Bread, Pentecost (or Weeks) and Tabernacles. Whatever their origins, the Hebrews associated these festivals with the God of the Covenant and so detached them from their Canaanite origins.

Everyday life for the great majority of people in the ancient world was almost totally concerned with survival. The essentials of life were food, which had to come from their crops and livestock, and protection, which came from being part of a social unit that could defend its members. For the nomadic pastoral peoples, such as the Hebrews during the earlier part of their history, the clan, or tribe, provided protection. For all others, security depended on being a member of a territorial group, as small as a fortified town or as large as a country. Their security was only as sure as their ability to defend that territory. To be conquered by invaders meant slavery or death. Every detail of life – housing, family structures, religion and even the selection of children for survival – evolved as a result of these basic concerns.

In the nomadic tribes the social structure reflected the natural authority and the basis of the family. Blood ties were all important. The family was polygamous (men had more than one wife), but the basic rights of members of the extended family were recognized and protected. Even slaves related to the family by blood had limited rights; other slaves had no rights. The flocks and herds were the common property of the group.

The social systems of agricultural settlements dependent on a particular territory were far more rigidly structured. A strict hierarchy of authority and subordination existed, with rule by an absolute monarch. Egypt does not even appear to have had codified laws. Mesopotamia regulated its social structures with a written code from at least the start of the 2nd Millennium BC. Houses were built of mud brick with flat roofs, which could be used for drying crops. They usually consisted of one room, with a raised sleeping platform on which a mat would be spread. For defensive reasons, at least in Canaan, the houses were clustered in positions that could be fortified and surrounded by heavy defensive walls. The main gate was usually approached by a ramp, set at an angle so that attackers had to expose their right, unshielded, sides to the defenders. Access to water during a siege, either by storage or fortified spring, was important, as were safe storage facilities for harvested crops. The olive tree was much valued as a source of oil from the pressed fruits, for use in lamps, cooking, cosmetics and in medicine. It was such a universal symbol of health, prosperity and security that the Hebrews eventually used it to show that authority had been conferred on a person by anointing them with olive oil. From this practice comes the word 'messiah', literally meaning 'the anointed one'.

In monarchical systems, law was administered by the king or his delegates. For the patriarchal nomads, the father or grandfather acted as judges, considering cases in the presence of the whole family or tribal group. This practice continued after the Hebrews developed a monarchy, in the form of town elders sitting in judgement in the open area just inside the town gate. Just as there was no clear boundary between religion and the secular, so the law dealt with religious and secular offences in the same 'court'. Education was within the family group and related to the family's trade, unless the child was destined for one of the specialized administrative skills, such as scribe, priest or royal official, when technical training would be given. Such professions were not usually distinct from each other, especially in the earlier period.

There were no extensive roads, as we would know them, until the Romans developed their system of paved roads wide enough to take wheeled vehicles. The donkey was the usual means of transport, used as a pack animal, although towards the end of the 2nd Millennium BC the camel came into use for crossing deserts. It was a static world for most non-nomadic peoples, who, by modern standards, had a short life and harsh standards of living.

The Hazor temple, captured in Joshua's attack, has particular significance because its general architecture is similar to that of the Hebrew Temple in Jerusalem built by King Solomon in the 10th Century BC. In the court outside the temple building at Hazor were several smaller altars, and a drainage channel to carry away the blood from the sacrificed animals. At the Hebrew Temple, as at Hazor, the animal sacrifices took place outside the building, while incense was burned inside. Other Canaanite temples of this period, particularly at Shechem and Megiddo, had features similar to the Hazor temple.

For the Hebrews, as for other people of the time, sacred places were used for the worship of their own god even when they had associations with other gods. The Hebrews found no problems in using Canaanite sacred centres – but not for the worship of Canaanite gods.

The events of the conquest happened over a short or long period, with or without coalitions. The biblical narratives end with a list of conquered Canaanite cities, but they also mention areas still to be taken, perhaps indicating the complex nature of the settlement process. As the Hebrews took over the land and were exposed to new styles of life, they transformed from wandering nomads to become farmers living in fortified settlements. Farming and exposure to new religious practices were to some extent challenges to their old beliefs. They had arrived in the Promised Land.

THE RUINS OF GEZER

The Canaanite city of Gezer was one of the last to fall into the hands of the Hebrews.

PUTTING DOWN HEBREW ROOTS

The Hebrew settlement of Canaan probably took many years to complete. At first the Hebrews tended to occupy the marginal land that had not been brought under cultivation by the Canaanites and only later did they capture the cities. The Canaanites themselves were too disunited to offer any coherent resistance.

STRUGGLES OF THE JUDGES

Although various tribes fought many bitter wars against the Canaanites and other common enemies, there was little central Hebrew organization until Saul was chosen as king about 1030 BC. The Hebrews were challenging the rule of the Philistines, who had conquered much of Canaan and renamed it Palestine.

The Book of Judges is organized around the deeds of 12 'judges' who rallied groups of Hebrews to resist attack from Canaanites or from peoples beyond Canaan's borders. They had a charismatic gift for leadership in times of danger, rather than serving in the normal Hebrew authority structure, based on heads of families and tribes. Judges also tells the history of Israel from the death of the prophet and leader Joshua to the time just before the prophet Samuel. The book is of considerable historical value as the only biblical source for ascertaining the events and social conditions of that period. Most historians consider Judges to be a composite work written between the 7th and 6th Centuries BC,. Contained within the book are ancient fragments of Hebrew literature, such as the *Song of Deborah*.

The international historical setting of the Book of Judges is important to an understanding of how a loose tribal or clan confederacy formed and survived at this time. Had the Egyptian empire held firm, then Hebrew history could have taken a different direction. The Egyptian 20th Dynasty established itself in power under Set-nakht and his son Rameses III (c. 1187–1156 BC). This latter Pharaoh faced assaults by the Sea Peoples as well as by Libyan tribes. Rameses listed the Pelasata (the Philistines) among others who he could not eject from his territories, being forced to allow them to settle – possibly as mercenaries to man garrisons – and give their name to Palestine. The Egyptian Empire never recovered from the alien incursions.

The remnants of Egypt's Asian holdings were up for grabs. The Hittite Empire had vanished. Assyria had weakened with the assassination of Tukulti-ninurta I (c. 1207 BC), and even the resurgence under Tiglath-pileser I (c. 1115–1077 BC), who had defeated Babylon, Armenia, Anatolia and northern Phoenicia, did not last. The international political scene was in a state of flux, which gave a nascent Israel freedom to develop without immediate threat.

Canaan, weakened without the defence of an imperial power, faced the Israelites who occupied the highlands of Palestine, the Sea Peoples nibbling away at the coastal plains and Aramean pressure dominating the Syrian hinterland. Canaanite enclaves endured and the bulk of the population remained with their land. Elsewhere the Phoenicians recovered from attacks by the Sea Peoples and regenerated quickly, with Byblos and other cities becoming bustling trade centres.

The Book of Judges describes Israel's history as one of continuous if intermittent fighting, alongside periods of peace or deep crisis. The Hebrews' territories were not a well-knit whole. The mountain areas were mainly in their hands, but Israelites could not move onto the plain for fear of facing the chariots of the city-states along the coast. The coastal strip and the Plain of Jezreel (Esdaelon)

THE TRIBAL LAND OF THE JUDGES

God commanded Joshua to 'allot the land of Israel for an inheritance', though much of Canaan remained to be conquered. The question of the exact locations and borders of the Hebrew tribes is one of the most difficult to resolve.

THE GREAT RIFT VALLEY OF JORDAN

The geographical barrier of the Jordan valley, with its river, inland seas and rocky terrain, made it difficult for tribes based either side to act together.

were outside Israel's control. Any Israelites settling there intermarried with Canaanites or became subject to them.

Geographical features made an impact, too. The Galilean tribes were cut off from their kin by Canaanite lands in the Jezreel Valley. The Jordan Rift Valley separated eastern and western tribes and the highlands were so riven with valleys and broken terrain that communities tended to develop in some isolation, developing their own customs, interests and, often, their own patriarchal traditions. Localization militated against any common Hebrew unity. When danger threatened Israel, only those nearest to the issue reacted. Thus, the Book of Judges demonstrates the incredible disunity of the tribes, despite the spiritual power of the Covenant.

Compared to their neighbour, the Hebrews were a poor, socially homogenous group with no pretensions of developing an aristocracy. During the Judges period, though, camel caravans and links to seaborne trade allowed some tribes to develop some prosperity. The judges entered this situation by criticizing Israel for absorbing alien elements through its mass conversions. Although the Israelite league swore loyalty to Yahweh, pagan cults did not automatically die out. Some worshipped fertility cults as commensurate with an agricultural life and others accommodated their allegiance to Yahweh with worship of Baal.

The 12 judges emerging to deliver Israel are presumably mentioned in chronological order, but precise dates are impossible to determine. No common characteristics can be assigned to the individuals. Gideon was motivated by a divine vocation, whereas Jephthah was a bandit who found Yahweh. He sacrificed his virgin daughter to fulfil a vow, an event that is described tragically and piteously: 'And she said unto her father, Let this thing be done for me: let me alone two months, that I may go up and down upon the mountains, and bewail my virginity, I and my fellows. And he said, Go. And he sent her away for two months: and she went with her companions, and bewailed her virginity upon the mountains. And it came to pass at the end of two months, that she returned unto her father, who did with her according to his vow which he had vowed: and she knew no man.' (Judges 11:37–40).

All judges had one thing in common: they were capable of firing up the tribes to fight. Othniel, the first judge to be mentioned (Judges 3:9–11), repulsed the invasion of Cushan-rishathaim of Aram-naharaim. Interpretations have variously portrayed this incursion of originating from Edom or the district of Qusanaruma in northern Syria (Aram).

Ehud's victory over Moab (Judges 3:12–30) occurred in the 12th Century BC. Moabite territory north of the River Arnon had been grabbed by Sihon the Amorite, from whom Israel seized the land, subsequently being occupied by the tribe of Reuben. Moab had regained this land and encroached into Benjaminite territory. Although the Moabites were repulsed, it is unknown whether they

JUDGES AND INVASIONS

The Book of Judges begins with an account of the tribes' efforts to conquer their territories – some successful, some total failures. Canaanites remained in several areas especially in the north, and Israel also faced many invasions: from the Philistines in the west, and from the Moabites, Edomites and Amalekites in the south and east.

THE TRIBES IN THE TIME OF JOSHUA

Some tribes possessed land east of the Jordan, granted to them by Moses. To the west of the river, the land was allotted by Joshua, with some areas going to these same tribes. Not all tribes completed the conquest of their areas, but instead settled down alongside the Canaanite population.

THE DAUGHTER DOOMED BY A JUDGE
A painting by the French artist Édouard Debat-Ponsan (1847–1913) depicts the virgin daughter of Jephthah, sacrificed by the Hebrew judge to fulfil a vow made to God.

were ejected from Reubenite territory. Reuben was an early victim and was no longer an effective leader.

Shamgar (Judges 3:31) is an enigmatic figure. He was not even an Israelite, but existed before Deborah when the Sea Peoples were encroaching upon Hebrew territory. Reputedly, he was a city king of Beth-anath in Galilee who repulsed the Philistines killing 600, saving both himself and Israel.

Deborah and Barak of Naphtali (Judges 4–5) are best placed historically about 1125 BC or a little before. Israel was almost cut in half by the Valley of Jezreel and Canaanite leagues that dominated neighbouring Israelite clans. Deborah and Barak rallied six tribes from Benjamin to Galilee that were aided by a rainstorm churning up the land, bogging down Canaanite chariots and allowing Israelite infantry to slaughter their crews.

Gideon's career developed when Jezreel and the nearby highlands were attacked by camel-riding nomads from the desert – Midianites, Amalekites and Benê Qedem. Annual raids occurred at harvest time, generating an economic downturn and starvation. Gideon, a Manassite, rallied his tribe and his neighbours and drove the raiders from the land, his victories giving him immense authority. His people wanted him to assume a kingship, but he categorically refrained even though his son, Abimelech, established himself as king in Shechem for a short time before being killed. Such local kingship was not customary in Israel.

The tale of Jephthah depicts human sacrifice occurring in Israel despite its incompatibility, since the time of Isaac, with Yahwehism, and shows how easily civil war could happen. Samson's career (Judges 13–16), with its marital adventures, accurately reflects the situation on the Philistine borders before open war erupted. It is possible that Samsonite-style raiding provoked the Philistines into more militant action against the Hebrews.

Judges demonstrates that the tribal league survived as a loose governmental form for a long time, throughout a series of defensive wars. Possibly, the Israelites controlled less land by Samuel's time than at Joshua's death. The tribe of Reuben was virtually erased. Dan could not retain control of the central Shepheleh and moved north to seize land around Laish, north of the Sea of Galilee. All tribes were tormented by the Canaanite enclaves remaining in their midst.

Israel Defeated and the Ark Captured

'And the Philistines fought, and Israel was smitten, and they fled every man into his tent: and there was a very great slaughter; for there fell of Israel thirty thousand footmen. And the ark of God was taken; and the two sons of Eli, Hophni and Phinehas, were slain.' 1 Samuel 4:10–11

An understanding of what the Ark of the Covenant meant to the tribes of Israel is essential if the significance of its loss is analysed. The central shrine of the Israelite league of 12 tribes provided a cult, with its sacred rites and occasions, and above all it contained Covenant law. The moveable tent-shrine was a feature of desert origin, and is sometimes known as 'the tent of meeting', where Yahweh – God – met His chosen people and made known His will. Sometimes, the shrine was regarded as 'the Tabernacle', where God tented among His people. 'And let them make me a sanctuary; that I may dwell among them' (Exodus 25:8). This type of shrine was well known, with Ugaritic texts describing a portable shrine of El and the copper mines at Timna witnessing the uncovering of a Midianite tent-shrine.

Descriptions of the shrine can be found in Exodus 25–31 and 35–40. Here, the ornate, resplendent Ark and Tabernacle are depicted in great detail as if the writer is attempting to project backwards a later temple, legitimizing it with the past. Another, probably more realistic, description can be found in the tent-shrine set up by David. 'And they brought in the Ark of the Lord and set it in his place, in the midst of the tabernacle that David had pitched for it: and David offered burnt offerings and peace offerings before the Lord' (2 Samuel 6:17). This shrine was the successor to the league shrine captured by the Philistines. The portable tent-shrine is symbolic of the Israelites' origins in the desert and carries the heritage of a primitive desert belief system. Additionally, the shrine was the focal point for the tribal league and the core institution for the tribes. Accordingly, there had to be a central official shrine, which did not preclude worship at other places.

The Bible places the tribal centre, after the conquest of Canaan at Shiloh, in the holdings of the tribe of Ephraim. Maybe this site had no associations for the tribes who had no vested interests in it. The tribal centre might have been previously located elsewhere during the conquest. Gilgal was an important site (Joshua 4 and 5) both then and later. 'And all the people went to Gilgal: and there they made Saul king before the Lord in Gilgal; and there they sacrificed sacrifices of peace offerings before the Lord; and there Saul and all the men of Israel rejoiced greatly' (1 Samuel 11:15). Some historians believe that the central shrine was first erected at Shechem, then at Bethel, before the final resting place at Shiloh. It seems

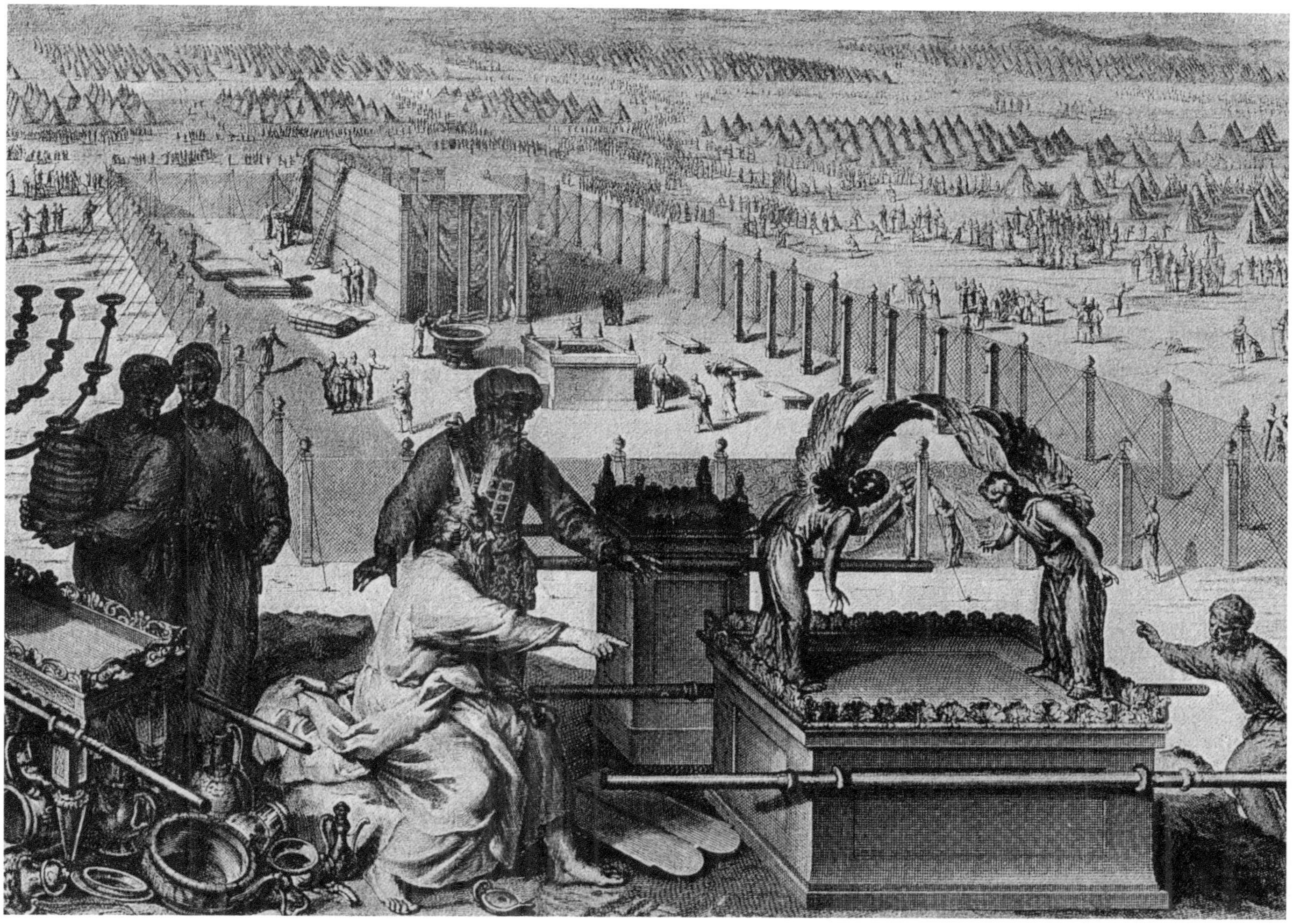

THE ARK AND THE TABERNACLE
A 1728 engraving shows a tabernacle being erected to hold the Ark of Covenant – the most sacred of all Hebrew symbols, said to hold the tablets of the Ten Commandments.

likely that a regular rite of Covenant renewal took place during certain feasts at the shrine.

During Pharaoh Rameses III's reign, Egypt was assaulted by Libyans and the Sea Peoples. These tribes had been attacking the eastern Mediterranean coastline for many years. Probably originating in the Balkans, these peoples destroyed the Hittite state in Anatolia and the Bronze Age states of Greece. Rameses III witnessed them moving southwards by land and sea with their possessions, women and children. No one knows what motivated this wave of people – were they marauders or dispossessed refugees? A naval attack was pushed back at the Nile delta and Egyptian records list some tribes: Shakarusha Tjikar, Danuna and the Pelesata (the Philistines). The Philistines and Tsikal were allowed to settle in Palestine, named after the Philistines, either as vassals or as mercenaries to man Egyptian garrison posts. Thus, the Philistines appeared in the region only a few years after the Israelite tribes. The Philistine migrants established themselves in the coastal area between the Shephelah and the sea, part of which is now the Gaza Strip. The Philistines captured five Canaanite cities: Gaza, Ashkelon, Ashdod, Gath and Ekron. The last two could control the main route of the coastal road from Egypt to the north and to Mesopotamia. The other three were on the route to Joppa, the only sheltered harbour south of Acco. Under the Philistines, each city had its own king, but it was a closely knit federation that appointed a single leader for warfare. They were technologically more advanced than the Canaanites or the Hebrews. With iron weapons, chariots and good discipline, the Philistines soon extended their control into the Negev, the central mountains and the Valley of Jezreel. Neither the Canaanites nor the Hebrews were able to withstand them, and they effectively ended Egyptian control of the area. Never particularly numerous, the Philistines were essentially a military aristocracy ruling a mainly Canaanite population. The Philistines also possessed the ability to act in concert,

THE ARK IN PHILISTINE HANDS

A painting from the 3rd Century AD Dura-Europas synagogue in Syria shows the Ark in the Philistine temple of Dagon.

something at which Canaanite cities failed, as did the Israelite tribes.

The Hebrews may have been perceived as a threat to Philistine security or to the trade routes leading inland from the coast. Hence, they attempted to win control of all western Palestine. No one knows when the Philistines began their aggression. One imagines they sought to dominate the remaining coastal Canaanite city states and other Sea Peoples settling in the region. The tribes of Judah and Dan felt pressurized, the latter moving from its lands. Doubtless, border incidents, skirmishes and guerrilla warfare were the norm, as evidenced by the Samson stories.

Around 1050 BC, the Philistines attacked under the leadership of the King of Gath from their base in Aphek, at the edge of the coastal plain. The Israelites were crushed at Ebenezer, with 4,000 killed. The Ark was brought from Shiloh, in the hope that God would bring victory. The Israelite army was destroyed, the Bible recording 30,000 dead. The Ark was captured and the priests in charge,

'And they laid the ark of the Lord upon the cart and the coffer with the mice of gold and the images of their emerods. And the kine took the straight way to the way of Bethshemesh, and went along the highway, lowing as they went, and turned not aside to the right hand or to the left; and the lords of the Philistines went after them unto the border of Bethshemesh. And they of Bethshemesh were reaping their wheat harvest in the valley: and they lifted up their eyes, and saw the ark, and rejoiced to see it.

I Samuel 6:11–13

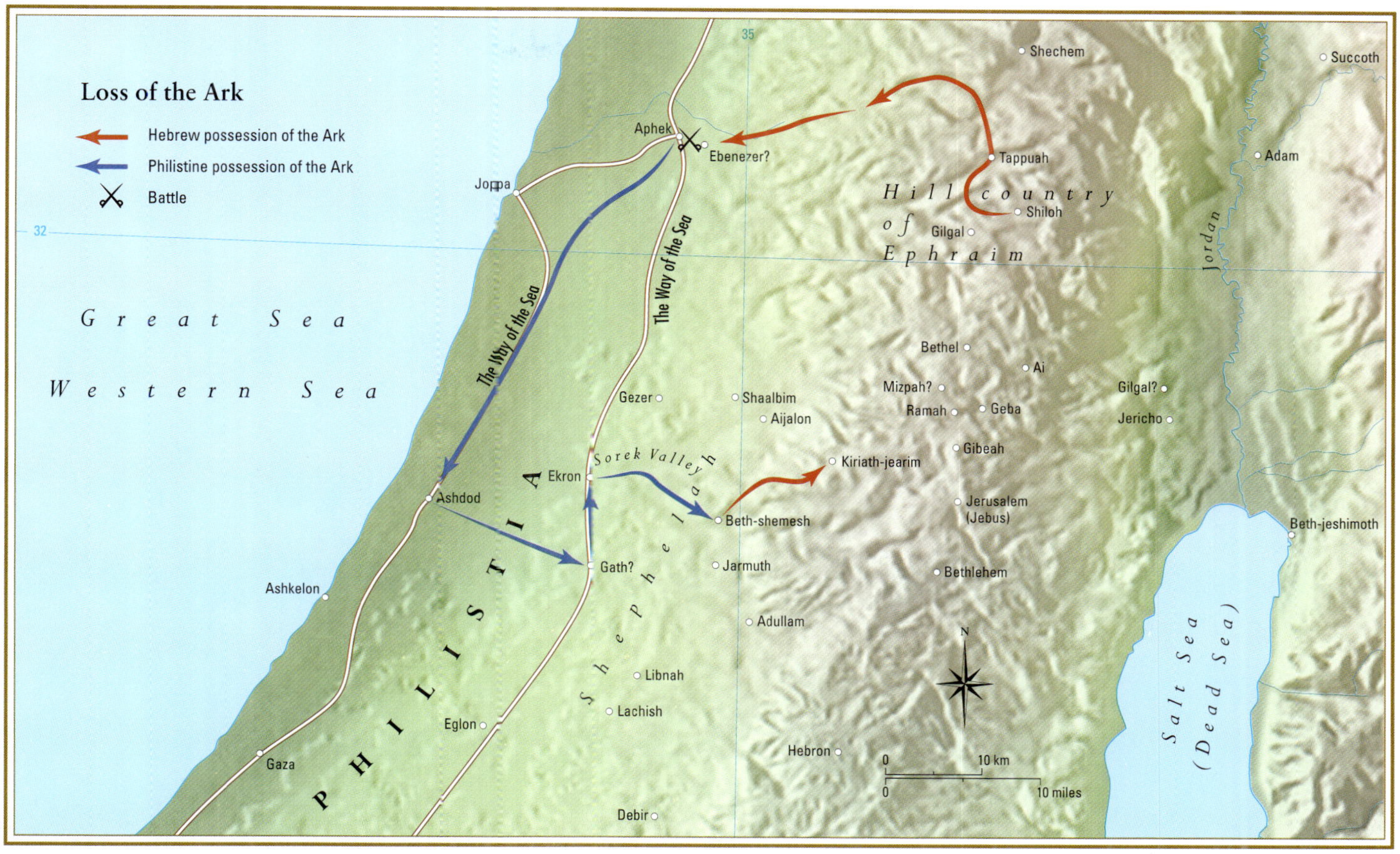

A HEBREW DISASTER

The Philistines attacked the Hebrews near Aphek and defeated them. The Hebrews withdrew to rally their forces and counterattack. This time they took the Ark of the Covenant into battle. They were defeated again and, worse still, the Ark was lost.

Phinehas and Hophni, were killed. The Philistines then occupied the land, took Shiloh, and destroyed the tent-shrine of the tribal league. Occupation garrisons were placed at key military points. The Philistines prevented the manufacture of weapons and, retaining a monopoly of iron, took away any metal industry from the Israelites, making them dependent on Philistine smiths. 'Now there was no smith found throughout all the land of Israel: for the Philistines said, Lest the Hebrews make them swords or spears. But all the Israelites went down to the Philistines, to sharpen every man his share, and his coulter, and his axe and his mattock. Yet they had a file for the mattocks, and for the coulters, and for the forks, and for the axes and to sharpen the goads. So it came to pass in the day of battle, that there was neither sword nor spear found in the hand of any of the people that were with Saul and Jonathan' (I Samuel 13:19–22). Iron remained uncommon in Israel until the reign of King David.

The Philistine occupation was incomplete, but Philistia held much of the Negev region, the central mountain range and the Valley of Jezreel. Philistine control was probably not exercised over all Galilee and not in Transjordan. Even the garrisoned central mountains were impossible to police, since the Israelites managed to arm themselves and develop resistance techniques. The Israelite league was without an army temporarily, its tent-shrine destroyed and much of the priesthood killed. The situation looked hopeless.

The Philistines took the Ark to Ashdod, placing it in the temple of their god, Dagon. Later, their idol was found fallen on its face. Upon replacing the statue, next day it was found with its head and hands cut off. Ashdod and its environs then suffered a plague of 'emerods', or hemorrhoids (I Samuel 5:6). After this, the Philistines moved the Ark to Gath and then to Ekron, but the plague struck each place in turn. After seven months, the Philistines decided to return the Ark, accompanied by expensive gifts. The Ark arrived at Beth-shemesh and was then transported to Kiriath-jearim, where it remained for 20 years, doubtless under watchful Philistine eyes. The old Hebrew tribal league, however, was smashed forever; a monarchy was about to be established.

SAMUEL, SAUL AND THE NEW JEWISH MONARCHY

Samuel appears in the Bible as both a judge and a prophet. Pressed by an irresistible public demand for a strong leader, he chose the war-like Saul as the first King of Israel.

In the Bible story, Samuel's mother, Hannah, who thought she was unable to bear children, prays to God for a son. As a result, Samuel is born, and Hannah, eternally grateful, dedicates him to the service of the chief religious sanctuary of the ancient city of Shiloh. After he is weaned, Samuel leaves his birthplace of Rameh and is placed in the care of Eli, the Shiloh priest.

Samuel grew up at a time when border strife with the Philistines intensified. United under the King of Gath, the Philistines crushed the Jews at Ebenezer, capturing the Ark of the Covenant. Eli's sons were killed in the battle and the Shiloh shrine was destroyed.

When his mentor Eli died, Samuel inherited the spiritual leadership of the Hebrews. Samuel was convinced that his people could only be free and secure if their faith was strong. Accordingly, he called the Hebrews to the city of Mizpah, where they confessed their sins, Samuel praying to the Lord on their behalf. The Philistines learned of the Hebrews congregating and attacked Mizpah: '… But the Lord thundered with a great thunder on that day upon the Philistines, and discomfited them; and they were smitten before Israel' (1 Samuel 7:10). Despite their rout, the Philistines were soon back in force at Geba, in a strong position dominating the main eastern approach through the Saddle of Benjamin into the Judaean hills. Eventually the Hebrews pushed them out.

Border warfare continued unabated with the hills and the Shephelah lowlands as a battleground. Nevertheless, the times were peaceful enough for Samuel to conduct an annual ministry circuit from his home at Ramah to Mizpah, Bethel, Naraan, Gilgal and Geba. Whilst visiting these communities, Samuel dispensed judgement and justice in disputes.

As Samuel aged, his sons were considered unworthy to succeed him. The future looked uncertain, with no respected spiritual leader available. The Hebrew elders thought that only a centralized government, with power held in the hands of a strong leader, could respond quickly and decisively against the Philistines. Their means of survival was a request to Samuel to anoint a king to govern them as monarchies did in places elsewhere. Samuel argued against the notion, claiming that royal power could be abused, but the elders ignored his pleas.

Ultimately, the Bible states that the Lord commanded Samuel to heed the Hebrews' wishes and find a king. Samuel's choice fell upon Saul of Gibeah, a known warrior fully capable of leading men. He possessed few supporters and, therefore, no power base for abuse, and would as a result be constrained in his actions. Saul of the tribe of Benjamin was anointed and installed as king.

SAUL IS CHOSEN *(right)*
In an engraving by the French artist Gustave Doré (1832–83), Samuel blesses Saul as the new King of Israel. Doré produced this and many other illustrations for an English edition of the Bible, published in 1866.

According to one folktale, Saul sought out a local seer as he searched for his father's donkeys in a neighbouring village. That man was the prophet Samuel, who promptly anointed him. Another version of events sees Samuel summoning the tribes of Israel at Mizpah to choose and publicly select a king by drawing lots.

Saul was the reluctant choice and he returned to Gibeah in Benjamin to his wealthy father, Kish. All Israel hoped he would unite the tribes – a loose confederation, the unity of which was dependent on its religious faith and Covenant with God. These bonds were renewed at intervals, in ceremonies at the central shrine of Shiloh. By this time, Saul had to fight better-armed and organized Philistines, who had iron weapons and chariots. However, his first test of resolve and leadership was not against this strong enemy, but against the Ammonites.

The Ammonite leader Nahash besieged the Israelite town of Jabesh-gilead, across the River Jordan in the north. Nahash demanded the right eye of every townsman as a condition for making peace. 'On this condition will I make a covenant with you, that I thrust out all your right eyes and lay it for a reproach upon all Israel' (I Samuel 11:2). The Jabeshites sent out messengers seeking help. At Gibeah, Saul responded by summoning the men of Israel to the town of Bezek, on the way from Shechem to Beth-shan. He led his forces at night across the Jordan through the Wadi Yabis to a valley below Jabesh-gilead. A three-pronged dawn attack caught the Ammonites unawares and they were hunted down and killed – it was a total victory. Saul's reputation as a military leader was made and he was re-acclaimed as King at Gilgal.

To the west, barely 24 kilometres (15 miles) away at Geba, Philistine forces sat astride the strategically important pass that lead into the Israelite hill territory. With the tribes united, probably for the first time, Saul caught the Philistines with their guard down. He took Gibeah, which controlled the southern end of a strategic crossing of a steep valley that separated the settlement from Michmash. Saul collected 3,000 men, taking 2,000 with him, leaving the remainder under his son Jonathan at Gibeah.

The headstrong Jonathan launched a surprise attack on Geba, defeating its garrison. Saul broadcast news of the victory in order to rally more Hebrews to his command. However, the Philistines collected together their garrisons and outposts into a large concentration of infantry and charioteers. 'And the Philistines gathered themselves together to fight with Israel, thirty thousand chariots and six thousand horsemen, and people as the sand which is on the sea shore in multitude: and they came up, and pitched in Michmash, eastwards from Beth-aven' (I Samuel 13:5).

Saul's terrified army disintegrated, and he retreated to Gilgal. Deserters hid in caves and other secret places throughout the region. An impatient Saul waited for Samuel to offer a burnt sacrifice to God, but the judge was delayed and Saul made the offering himself, breaking religious practice and protocol. Saul then had to face an angry Samuel, who claimed that Saul's kingdom would fail and that God would seek a man after his own heart as king. Samuel then abandoned Saul.

Despite this inauspicious start to the campaign, Saul took his remaining 600 men, moving to Gibeah and avoiding three large companies of raiders leaving Michmash. Jonathan and his armour-bearer carried out their own raid, destroying a Philistine outpost of 20 men on a rocky crag. The Philistines panicked and Saul threw his entire force at the enemy camp, causing confusion and slaughter. As the Philistines fled, Israelite deserters emerged from hiding and joined the hunt of the routed Philistines westwards to Beth-horon and past Aijalen to Philistia, stopping at the border. This victory ensured the security of the highlands, the core of Saul's kingdom.

Saul then waged war against all surrounding enemies: Moab, Ammon, Edom, Zobah and the Philistines. Samuel returned to Saul and said God demanded the destruction of the Amalekites, who had treated the Hebrews harshly when they first entered the Promised Land. Saul captured the Amalekite king, Agag, and killed his followers but, despite being ordered to destroy every living thing, he sent the best of the flocks and oxen to Gilgal. Samuel denounced Saul for not destroying all as the Lord required, saying again that God rejected him as king. The judge was adamant, ignoring Saul's repentance, and himself hacked Agag to death with a sword. Saul established a victory monument at Carmel, south-east of Hebron, possibly to demonstrate his claim to political power in the region.

Saul was victorious in many campaigns and remained a military figure. His sole royal official seems to have been Abner, Saul's cousin and a military commander. The court was austere, occupying a simple country fortress at Gibeah. It was here that David, a future king, came to Saul's notice – as a harpist with the ability to soothe the king's bouts of melancholy. 'And it came to pass, when the evil spirit from God was upon Saul, that David took an harp, and played with his hand: so Saul was refreshed, and was well, and the evil spirit departed from him' (I Samuel 16:23).

SAUL GOES TO WAR

The Philistine efforts to expand their lands and contain the Israelites created a situation they had hoped to avoid – the unification of their enemies under a single leader, Saul.

The Struggle for Power

David is a hero in Israel's history – his legend surrounded by myth as much as historical events. Anointed in secret by Samuel, he came to serve Saul, thanks to his warrior and musical skills, only for the king to turn against him, consumed by jealousy.

Minor skirmishes with the Philistines continued to occur regularly. It was in one such action that David distinguished himself as a brave warrior. The version of events in 1 Samuel 17:32–51 pits the young shepherd boy David against Goliath, the huge Philistine. Border warfare had been renewed, the Philistines again attempting to acquire the Shephelah foothills. They were concentrating their forces between Socoh and Azekah, intending to attack the Judaean highlands. Saul placed the Israelite army in a blocking position in the Valley of Elah. The positions of both contenders were strong, and military stalemate was reached.

An old tradition maintained that single combat between champions could resolve such situations. Goliath represented the Philistines, but he was knocked down by a sling stone cast by David who then seized Goliath's sword and beheaded him. The Philistines fell into disarray and fled to the cities of Gath and Ekron.

David was now a hero, and entered the king's service, immediately befriending Jonathan, Saul's son. David became a renowned military leader, killing 200 Philistines and winning Michal, Saul's daughter, in marriage. Saul became jealous of David's success. 'And the women answered one another as they played, and said, Saul hath slain his thousands and David his ten thousands. And Saul was very wroth, and the saying displeased him; and he said, They have ascribed unto David ten thousands, and to me they have ascribed but thousands: and what can he have more but the kingdom?' (1 Samuel 18:7–8).

Saul grew to hate David and even threw a spear at him – twice – while he was playing his harp. Michal warned her husband that Saul was plotting his murder, and he ran from Gibeah, leaving a mannequin in his bed. David travelled to Rameh to win the support of Samuel, the judge who had anointed him as Israel's future king. Saul's agents, sent to seize David, vanished; Saul himself went to Ramah, but became possessed by frenzied religious dancing and collapsed. David sought Jonathan's intercession but was again warned about Saul's hostility. Without an unarmed escort, he fled to Nob and persuaded Ahimelech, the shrine's chief priest, that he was Saul's agent, leaving with food and Goliath's sword, originally left there as tribute. Ahimelech and other priests were later slaughtered by Saul for helping David.

David then travelled to Philistia in search of sanctuary. He reached Gath, where he was quizzed by King Achish, who was suspicious about the motives of this notorious Philistine killer. To ensure survival, David feigned madness and was dismissed, walking 16 kilometres (10 miles) through the Shephelah to Adullam, in no-man's-land between Philistia and Saul. There, he encamped in inhospitable terrain, but with a water supply and a cave system for hiding places. At first, he was joined by his brothers and clan members, then by the discontented, the disaffected and the indebted, until he formed a renegade band of 400 men. David took his parents to the sanctuary of the Moabite king, while he moved from Adullam to the Forest of Hereth.

DAVID AND SAUL FIGHT IT OUT

David had served in Saul's court and had already acquired a powerful military reputation with a band of followers. However, because of Saul's jealousy he fled to Philistia serving the King of Gath as a mercenary.

Learning that Philistines were attacking Keilah, an independent town, David assaulted and dispersed the besiegers. The ungrateful population of Keilah, though, planned to betray David and his men to Saul. Consequently, David had to flee Saul's forces to Horesh and into the Wilderness of Ziph. The inhabitants of this barren plateau informed Saul, and, pursued by 3,000 men, David moved south to the Wilderness of Maon. Had the Philistines not raided the north – forcing Saul to give up his campaign against David – then the latter would probably have been captured. Instead, David reached the Dead Sea at En-gedi.

The Bible states that, having dealt with the Philistines, Saul again chased David. Saul even entered a cave where David was hiding, but David refrained from killing the king while he was asleep, instead surreptitiously cutting away a piece of Saul's clothing. Afterwards David shouted to Saul, showing him the portion of his robe, making Saul realize that he been at David's mercy. Immediately remorseful, Saul returned to Ramah, and David continued to his Adullam stronghold.

After Samuel died, David moved from the area of Rameh and returned to the Wilderness of Maon, and at nearby Carmel met his future wife Abigail. The Ziphites again betrayed David's presence to Saul. David and a companion crept into the king's camp at night, but David refused to let his comrade slay Saul. 'As the Lord liveth, the Lord shall smite him: or his day shall come to die; or he shall descend into battle and perish. The Lord forbid that I should stretch forth mine hand against the Lord's anointed: but I pray thee, take now the spear that is at his bolster, and the cruse of water, and let us go' (1 Samuel 26:10–11). Again, David demonstrated his actions, showing the spear and water bottle to the king as evidence. As before, Saul retreated.

David still felt insecure and marched with his company of 600 proven soldiers to seek sanctuary at Gath. Saul now left the chase, knowing he could not enter Philistia. Achish gave David the Philistine town of Ziklag, in the Negev, to rule as his vassal. He wanted David to assault the Israelites in the Judaean foothills, but, instead, David raided into the Negev against the Amalekites, the Geshurites and the Gezrites. These victims were all killed and their livestock seized. David persuaded Achish that he had attacked southern Judaea against the Jerahmeelites and Kenites. In reality, he was undermining Israel's southern enemies. Sixteen months were spent with the Philistines, but David eventually had to face the problem when his host mustered a large army at Aphek in preparation for a final battle against Israel. The issue was removed from David when Achish sent his company back to Ziklag because he felt that David might betray him in battle.

On his return to Ziklag, David found the town burnt and his men's families and possessions taken by vengeful Amalekites. David organized a quick pursuit of the camel-borne raiders beyond the Beser into the Negev. The raiders were found feasting. The men were killed, and the families, including David's two wives, were returned safely along with the loot of the Amalek raid into Philistia. David demanded that the booty should be shared equally amongst the elders of southern Judah – a shrewd move, winning the potential support for a future move on the kingship.

The Philistines moved from Aphek into the Jezreel Valley, making their camp at Shunem under Mount Moreh. Saul's forces were at Mount Gilboa in the south, maybe near the mountain's springs. Saul was terrified at the sheer size of the Philistine army, and he could not receive an answer to his prayers about the battle's outcome. Anxious, he journeyed to the witch of Endor, begging her to speak to Samuel's spirit. Samuel's ghost appeared and prophesied: 'Because thou obeyest not the voice of the Lord, nor executest his fierce wrath upon Amalek, therefore hath the Lord done this thing unto thee this day. Moreover, the Lord will also deliver Israel with thee into the hand of the Philistines: and tomorrow shalt thou and thy sons be with me: the Lord also shall deliver the host of Israel into the hand of the Philistines' (1 Samuel 28:18–19).

The Israelites were vastly outnumbered, and even if the terrain rendered Philistine chariots unusable, they were still severely disadvantaged. The Philistines stormed the Hebrew ranks and neither Saul's nor Jonathan's bravery could deny the overwhelming enemy victory. Saul's forces were utterly overrun, fleeing up the sides of Mount Gilboa, where they were hunted down in a savage pursuit. Here, three of Saul's sons fell: Jonathan, Abinadab and Malchishua. Saul was wounded by an arrow, and committed suicide by falling on his sword, rather than allow the Philistines to capture him.

DAVID SLAYING GOLIATH *(left)*
The painter Peter Paul Rubens (1577–1640) captured the moment when David cut off Goliath's head, using the giant Philistine's own sword.

DAVID TAKES CONTROL

As David, in the service of the Philistines, fights the Amalekites in the south, his employers march against Saul, meet him in battle at Mount Gilboa and destroy the Israelite army. The wounded Saul commits suicide rather than be captured. On hearing the news, David holds a wake for the dead king, then sets about taking the reins of power.

The captured Israelite royals were beheaded and their weapons placed as an offering in the temple of Ashtaroth at Beth-shan. Saul's head was given to the temple of Dagon. The royal Israelite corpses were hung from the city's walls.

News of their mutilation and the fate of the bodies spread far and wide. Men from Jabesh-gilead, remembering how Saul had saved them earlier, removed the bodies secretly and ritually burnt them, burying the bones under a tree at Jabesh.

The Israelites had now lost the area bordering the Jezreel valley, abandoning their cities as refugees. News of the defeat reached David three days later. He and his men held a wake for Saul, his sons and the Israelites who had fallen in battle. David's heightened emotional state produced the well-known biblical lament, right.

Saul was a tragic hero, deranged in his slaughter of 85 priests and their families at Nob for helping David, but with a military prowess that prevented the complete occupation of his kingdom by the Philistines. David was able to take the remnants and work as a new deliverer of Israel from the hands of its triumphant enemies.

'The beauty of Israel is slain upon thy high places: how are the mighty fallen! ... Saul and Jonathan were lovely and pleasant in their lives, and in their death they were not divided: they were swifter than eagles, they were stronger than lions ... How are the mighty fallen, and the weapons of war perished!'

2 Samuel 1:19, 23, and 27

BATTLE LANDS OF SAUL AND DAVID
Ancient stone megaliths stand sentinel on the Shephelah foothills of southern Judaea, looking across the coastal plains of Philistia towards the Mediterranean Sea. It was through this terrain that the Hebrews fought long and costly campaigns against the Philistines.

King David

Faced with a divisive political situation after Saul's death, David united rival Hebrew tribes, secured their loyalty by providing a neutral capital – Jerusalem – and subdued their various enemies.

The main sources of information about David and Solomon were heavily edited by historians of the southern Hebrew Kingdom of Judah. Jerusalem was Judah's chief city, captured by David and made the first effective capital of the united Hebrew people. The sources are therefore suspect and may underrate Saul and the northern Hebrews to emphasize the glories of David and Solomon. However, unattractive aspects, such as David's murder of his officer, Uriah (2 Samuel 11), are included to show that the accounts are not mere propaganda. Biased they may be, but 1 and 2 Samuel present a convincing picture of David as an outstanding leader.

After Saul was made king, he exercised loose control over the central highlands from Judah to the edge of Mount Carmel, the area east of the Jordan, the Valley of Jezreel and Galilee. The centres of his power lay in Benjamin country, just north of Jerusalem, and Bethlehem, just south of Jerusalem. The recognition by Samuel of the young David as future leader of the country (1 Samuel 16) is consistent with the role of Samuel as a seer, but the account was written with hindsight.

David was born in Bethlehem, the most northerly town in Judah. He joined Saul's court as other young Hebrews from various tribal areas did, and became a successful officer and favourite. There is also some doubt about David's slaying of Goliath at an engagement with Philistine forces between Socoh and Azekah (1 Samuel 17) as certain versions of the Bible attribute the killing (in 2 Samuel 21:19) to one of David's soldiers.

David's marriage to one of Saul's daughters is told within the context of Saul's mounting jealousy of David, whose popular reputation as a warrior had now surpassed Saul's own (1 Samuel 18). This would have been dangerous at any time in the turbulent history of Hebrew kings, including David's own reign, and so the marriage should be seen as a way of securing David's loyalty to Saul. Shortly afterwards, Saul tried to kill David because he was a threat to his authority. This is still a period when the leader's authority rested on his pre-eminence in battle, as it had for the judges, and Saul could not afford to have his own reputation surpassed by one of his court.

The subsequent actions of David, after his flight from King Saul, all show the political skill which he would eventually use to unite the various Hebrew groups and factions. He was helped by the members of the sacred city of Nob, near Jerusalem, where the priests of the central sanctuary had fled when Shiloh was captured and destroyed by the Philistines after the Battle of Aphek. David welcomed the survivor, Ahimelek, when Saul had Nob's priests executed. During this period David lived as an outlaw in the Judaean hills and in caves along the shores of the Dead Sea. He gathered around him the men who would become the nucleus of his own court. Eventually, he and his group became mercenaries in the service of the Philistines, following a long Hebrew tradition of service as mercenary soldiers. Even during this time, his sense of political realities kept him from antagonizing any Hebrews whose support he would need if he were to unite the people. Saul died at the Battle of Gilboa (c. 1000 BC). David and his men had been left behind because of their previous service under Saul. Thus, no Hebrew group could claim that David had fought against them.

DAVID TACKLES HIS ENEMIES

By defeating the Philistines, King David gave his people national security in Palestine. He established his rule from Damascus to the Egyptian border, and from the Great Sea (Mediterranean Sea) to the Syrian Desert. The Hebrews had won a small empire centred on Palestine.

DAVID THE EMPIRE BUILDER

By establishing an empire that extended many miles beyond his core territory, David was to test Palestine's ability to hold on to its varied and disparate possessions.

ENTRANCE TO DAVID'S CITADEL
In David's time, Jerusalem lay to the south of the present-day 'old city'. Traditionally, the gateway above is supposed to be the entrance to David's Citadel, although its authenticity is extremely doubtful. Despite this, it remains a popular tourist attraction in modern Jerusalem.

Saul's reign ended in disaster. He lost the support of Samuel and of the traditional Hebrew religion, and eventually was defeated by the Philistines he had successfully resisted during his time in power. Despite his reputation as a failed king, Saul did, for most of his reign, force the Philistines to relinquish control over the whole of the central highlands from Judah to the Valley of Jezreel. Saul's reign should be seen as an essential interlude of monarchical experiment between the ineffectiveness of the judges and the successful monarchy founded by David.

David heard the news of Saul's defeat and death while he was at Ziklag, deep in the southern part of Judah, and immediately set about securing his own succession and acceptance by all the Hebrew tribes. He faced a delicate political situation, and his first steps were to dissociate himself from any involvement with the death of King Saul at the hands of the Philistines. David composed a lament, which demonstrated to Saul's supporters that he mourned the king's death. He also executed the messenger who said that he had killed Saul, at the king's own request, when it was obvious that the Battle of Gilboa was lost. We know that Saul took his own life (I Samuel 3 :4). As he was about to become king himself, David had every reason to enforce respect for the person of the king.

It is clear that the Hebrew tribes constituted two distinct groups at this time – a southern group consisting mainly of Judah and Simeon, to which David belonged and the northern tribes of the central highlands, Galilee and the Jordan area. The land between them, which included Jerusalem, may not yet have been under Hebrew control. In any case the northern tribes had not looked for help from the southern tribes during the period of the judges. It is even probable that the southern Hebrews had not been among the Hebrews who escaped from Egypt.

The southern Hebrews anointed David king at the ancient southern sanctuary of Hebron, and at first there was open war between the southern and northern Hebrew tribes. Saul had been succeeded by his son

SON AGAINST FATHER

Towards the end of his reign, the ageing King David became increasingly remote from daily life. Taking advantage of this, David's third son, Absalom, raised a revolt. David, however, regained control and defeated Absalom, who was killed by Joab, the commander of David's army.

Ishbaal (Ishbosheth), but he offended his senior army commander, Abner, who then negotiated with David to transfer his loyalties and those of the northern tribes. Fortunately for David, Abner was murdered by David's own senior army officer, Joab. David could dissociate himself from the murder and give Abner a solemn funeral to show his disapproval of the act. Ishbaal was now the only remaining obstacle, and he was assassinated by two of his own officers who were then foolish enough to take Ishbaal's head to David. Once more David could demonstrate his disapproval of murdering kings by having the assassins executed. David's way was clear, and his reign over the united Hebrew tribes dates from his acceptance as king by the northern group of Hebrews, whose leaders went to Hebron to anoint him.

David secured his hold over the united Hebrew people by giving them a capital – Jerusalem – that had no political or religious associations for any of the Hebrew tribes. The small Canaanite city was on a narrow ridge that fell away steeply on each side and flattened out into a gentle hill at the northern end. The Gihon spring at the foot of the eastern slopes of the ridge provided a dependable water supply for the inhabitants and was protected by the city's defensive walls. Sitting as it was, caught between two Hebrew groups, Jerusalem had never been in Hebrew hands before David's soldiers captured it. Both groups could accept it without loss of face and David sealed its new significance for his people by fetching the sacred Ark of the Covenant from the borders of Philistine territory and installing it in its tent at the northern end of the city.

Once he had secured the loyalty of all the Hebrew tribes, David turned to their enemies – the remaining Canaanite cities, the Philistines, the small kingdoms east of the Jordan Valley and the nomadic groups who attempted to settle in what was now Hebrew territory. Although the Philistines retained their foothold in the southern coastal area with its five cities, David took control of the cities of the Shephelah and of the coastal plain north of the Philistines. The Philistines were only able to survive as subservient to the Hebrews. King David's successor, Solomon, inherited the areas traversed by the coastal

BRINGING THE ARK BACK HOME
The Ark of the Covenant is a chest described in the Book of Exodus as containing the stone tablets on which the Ten Commandments were inscribed. In this painting, attributed to the Flemish artist Pieter van Lint (1609–1690), King David, singing and dancing, leads the Ark into Jerusalem.

road as Hebrew territory, and David also imposed his rule over the areas through which the eastern route – the King's Highway – passed. He thus controlled both of the great international routes through Palestine, as well as the land area from Damascus to the Egyptian frontier, and from the Mediterranean to the Syrian Desert.

David's political success was confirmed and secured by a major act of religious symbolism. He planned to build a temple to house the Ark of the Covenant (2 Samuel 7), and his successor, Solomon, did so. The prophet Nathan had told David that his descendants were to be the 'house' of God's Covenant, together with the Hebrew people. The Hebrew monarchy itself was to be the sign of the Covenant and its guardian, so the Davidic succession became a form of divine right that should have provided the people with a secure and just administration. This idea of kingly responsibility held great importance for the Hebrew people. For instance, when David had one of his officers murdered, so that he could take the officer's wife without scandal, Nathan rebuked him. This would have been normal behaviour, perhaps, for a Canaanite king who owned his subjects in the name of the god Baal, but a Hebrew king must administer Hebrew Covenant law and be bound by it himself. The king was to be the guardian of the Covenant. David's reign (c. 1000–962 BC) included a major rebellion, led by one of his sons, Absalom. However, David regained control and nominated his son Solomon as his successor just before his death.

SOLOMON'S RULE AND EMPIRE

Solomon consolidated David's administrative system and extended his influence through trade links, reaching from Egypt in the west to Mesopotamia in the east and to Ophir and Sheba in the south.

The triumph of Solomon in the succession struggle marked the eclipse of the older, conservative religious traditions, and the ascendancy of the new way of life introduced by the conquest of Canaan. The Hebrews had become a predominantly settled, agricultural people, rather than nomadic shepherds. The priest of David's court, Abiathar, who had survived the slaughter of the old Hebrew priest-guardians of the Ark of the Covenant by King Saul, backed the losing side and was banished by Solomon to Anathoth. Zadok, a priest who first appeared after the capture of Jerusalem, became the most prominent religious figure in Solomon's court. It is reasonable to assume that Zadok was the priest of Jerusalem in its Canaanite days, before its capture by King David, and that his prominence under King Solomon marks a distinct movement towards the Canaanite expression of religious beliefs.

If religious symbolism does not alter with the changing needs of the people, it then fossilizes and becomes irrelevant. From the time of Solomon onwards, a tension can be detected among the Hebrews. Some of them remained loyal to the old religion of the nomadic shepherds, while others expressed the essentials of the Covenant religion in ways that reflected the needs of the Hebrews' in their new economic, social and political situation. The Hebrew Temple in Jerusalem, built by King Solomon, became the visible sign that the nomadic religion of the Hebrews who had fled from Egypt was now being expressed in new forms.

The new temple was more than a permanent home for the Ark of the Covenant. It asserted that the Hebrew people had taken over the Canaanite way of life, with its fortified settlements, agricultural economy and monarchical form of government. Not only was the Temple the shrine of the Ark, it was also the royal chapel, administered by priests appointed by the king. At this time a separate class of priests emerged to serve the Temple.

The plan of Solomon's Temple is similar to that of other temples in Canaanite areas, particularly the temple destroyed by the Hebrews at the city of Hazor. The temple itself was a comparatively small building – at most some 37–46 metres (120–150 ft) long by 14–18 m (45–60 ft) wide – which was not designed to accommodate worshippers. It stood in the great court, which also contained the royal palace, and had its own inner court to which there was direct access from the palace. The Temple was entered though a porch between two ceremonial pillars, erected as a symbol of God's greatness. It then opened out into the Hekal or main hall. This communicated with the Debir, the innermost shrine, which was raised higher than the rest of the building and housed the Ark of the Covenant.

The main hall contained an altar for burning incense, the table for the 'bread of the presence' – which originally

SOLOMON CEMENTS HIS POWER

Solomon, the second son of King David and Bathsheba, had been anointed before David's death. On his accession, Solomon ruthlessly removed any potential rivals, ensuring an unthreatened transfer of power.

may have been a food-offering to God – and ten lampstands. The main focus for worship was the bronze altar of whole burnt offerings, a great raised hearth about 9 metres (30 ft) square and 5 metres (15 ft) high, which stood before the Temple porch and on which the main sacrifices were offered. Near it was a bronze basin some 5 metres (15 ft) in diameter and 2.5 metres (8 ft) high, with ten wheeled basins for carrying water.

Solomon employed Phoenician architects and workmen for the Temple, sent by King Hiram of Tyre, who also supplied the cedarwood with which it was panelled. It is no longer possible to say precisely where the Temple was situated in relation to modern Jerusalem, for the Babylonians destroyed it in 587 BC, and its replacement, a temple built by King Herod the Great, was destroyed by the Romans in AD 70. It probably stood where the spectacular Muslim Dome of the Rock today protects a rocky outcrop with sacred associations.

The Temple and the royal palace were only a small part of the vast programme of building undertaken by Solomon, for which he used forced labour, a normal practice of the time. A number of Palestinian cities have remains of massive fortifications constructed during Solomon's reign. These included recessed stone gateways that were designed to provide several lines of defence, and walls of great thickness with hollow chambers built between the inner and outer surfaces that give access to the water supply. The latter, which have been found at Megiddo, are now thought to date from the period immediately after the reign of Solomon.

Solomon consolidated the centralized administrative system begun by King David, from which emerged the first reliable Hebrew written records. He took advantage, too, of Palestine's central position in order to develop existing trading connections both by land and by sea, with caravan routes into the Arabian Desert and a merchant fleet in the Red Sea. He also developed the Hebrew copper industry from ore deposits in the Jordan Valley and the area south of the Dead Sea. King Solomon's administrative ability is the foundation of his famed reputation for 'wisdom', which created a golden age for the Hebrew people. His achievements required large-scale organization of labour, and his success owes much to his understanding of divisive tendencies in Hebrew society, with its traditions of tribal loyalties. Solomon managed to maintain a form of national unity for the Hebrews, but it collapsed with his death in about 931 BC.

ANCIENT JERUSALEM

A view from the Mount of Olives shows the magnificent Dome of the Rock, which dominates the clustered buildings of the Old City of Jerusalem, including the Church of the Holy Sepulchre.

ON THE ROAD TO RICHES

Solomon's empire was effectively the nerve centre of a network of long-established trading routes and therefore ideally situated to take advantage of them.

David and Solomon's City

Jerusalem is the Holy City for Jews as the site of Solomon's temple, and for Christians it is held sacred as the scene of Jesus Christ's trial, crucifixion and Resurrection.

Inhabited for over 4,000 years, Jerusalem has been under the rule of many different nations and has often been attacked, destroyed and rebuilt. It is now a city full of contrast and variety, where modern buildings tower over the old Arab and Jewish quarters that evoke the city's rich biblical past.

The first written reference to Jerusalem is in a text dating back to 2500 BC. There is some evidence of prehistoric settlement, but little is known of the city's early history before the 14th Century BC, when Jerusalem was apparently under Egyptian rule. There is no mention of Jerusalem under that name in the first five books of the Bible. However, it is believed that Salem, which was ruled by King Melchizedek and is mentioned in Genesis 14:18, is identical to Jerusalem.

At the time when the Israelites entered the land of Canaan in about 1210 BC, Jerusalem was in the hands of a Semitic people called the Jebusites. Their settlement was south of what was to become the Temple platform and ran down to the Pool of Siloam. Although Joshua and his army defeated the Jebusites and their allies in battle, the city remained under Jebusite rule (Joshua 15:63), and it was left to David to capture Jerusalem in about 1000 BC (2 Samuel 5). Under the Jebusites, the city was already known as 'Zion' – a word whose meaning is obscure, but which has remained synonymous with Israel – and now it also acquired the title 'City of David'.

The city became the Israelite capital, where the holy Ark of the Covenant at last found a home. David had Jerusalem's fortifications improved and new buildings erected, but it was his son, Solomon, who built the first Temple in the city. He spared no expense, employing the finest materials and the most expert craftsmen to build and decorate a place fit to house the Ark of the Covenant, which was kept in the inner sanctuary, called the 'holy of holies' (1 Kings 5–8). Once the Temple was complete, the city became a religious centre where people gathered to celebrate festivals and holy days, and it soon began to acquire symbolic significance as a holy city. The Psalms are full of references to the city, with such memorable exhortations as 'Pray for the peace of Jerusalem' (Psalm 122:6) and 'If I forget thee, O Jerusalem, let my right hand forget her cunning' (Psalm 137:5).

After Solomon's death in around 930 BC, the kingdom was divided into two: the northern kingdom of Israel and the southern kingdom of Judah. As the capital of the smaller southern kingdom, Jerusalem declined in importance to some extent. The city was now frequently under attack – by the Egyptians in 922 BC, the Philistines in 850 BC, the northern kingdom in 786 BC and the Assyrians in 701 BC – and, more than once, the palaces and Temple were sacked and looted. In 586 BC, Jerusalem was besieged and captured by the Babylonians, under their king, Nebuchadnezzar II. The entire city and the

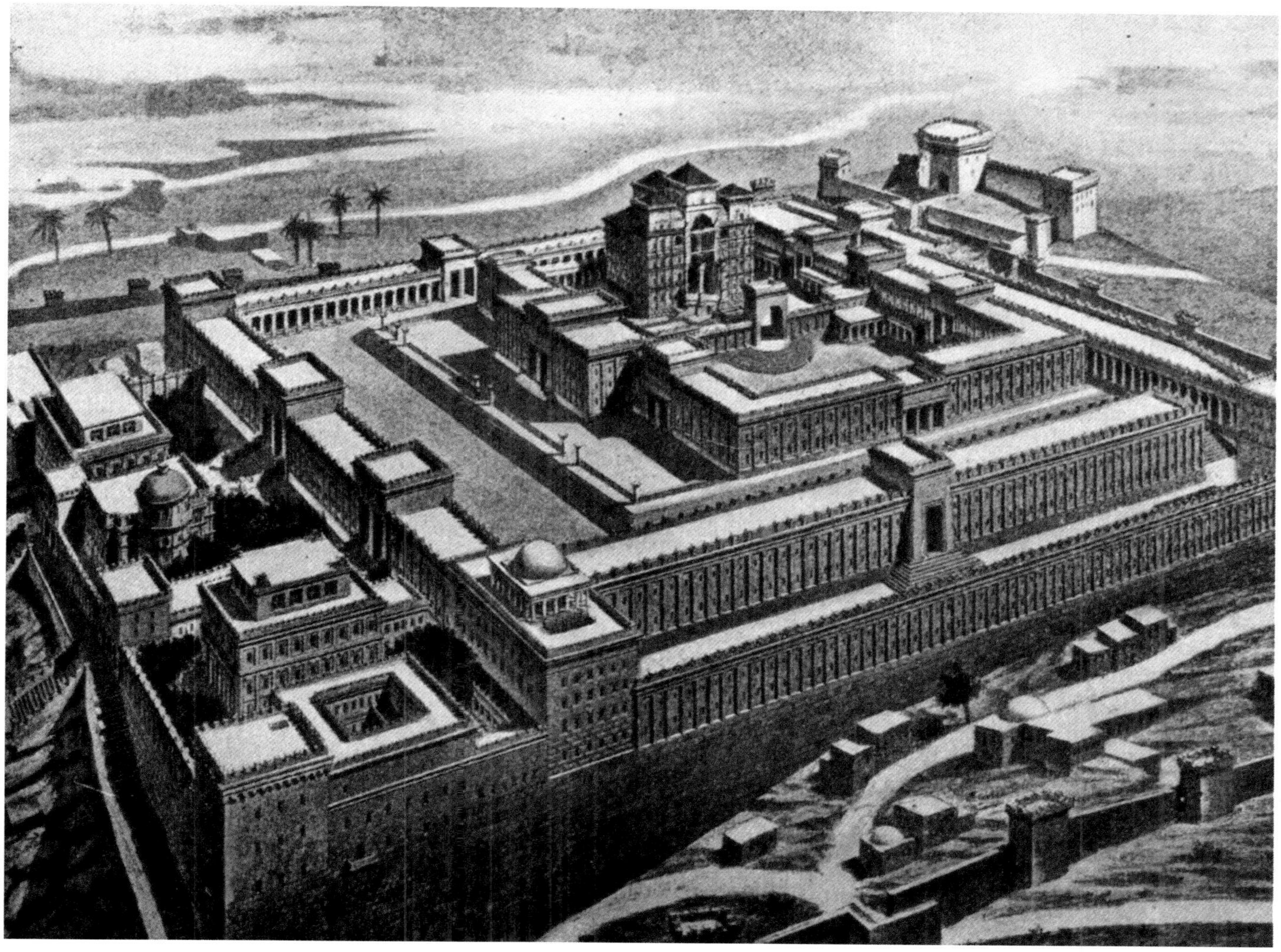

THE TEMPLE OF SOLOMON
This reconstruction of Solomon's Temple in Jerusalem appeared in a 19th-Century Swedish encyclopedia. It is based on details of the construction described in the Bible, in 1 Kings 6–7 and 2 Chronicles 3–4.

Temple were destroyed, and the people were taken into captivity in Babylon (2 Kings 25).

In 538 BC, Cyrus II of Persia overcame Babylon and allowed the Hebrew exiles to return to Jerusalem. The Temple was rebuilt (Ezra 1–5), and later, under Nehemiah, the city walls were restored (Nehemiah 3–6). Two centuries later, the city came under the rule of Alexander the Great, and subsequently Ptolemy, and then it fell to the Syrians in 198 BC. The Temple was desecrated again, but after a Jewish revolt under Judas Maccabeus it was re-dedicated in 165 BC.

Jerusalem remained under Jewish rule until it was taken by the Roman military leader Pompey in 63 BC. However, Roman influence was countered by the power of the Herodian dynasty. Herod the Great repaired the ravages of the various plundering armies and began the work of rebuilding the Temple on a grand scale, one among many of his ambitious building projects. Under Herod, Jerusalem became great again, but his successors were less competent and the city became part of a minor Roman province under the rule of a procurator. So it was when Jesus was exercising his ministry, and it was the procurator, Pontius Pilate, who sentenced him to death (Matthew 27). The city was the scene of Jesus' trial, crucifixion and Resurrection. Jerusalem became the first centre for the early Church (Acts 1–7) until Christians there began to be persecuted; most of them then scattered into other regions to spread the Gospel (Acts 8:1). The city was now a symbol of God's glory for Christians as well as Jews, and in the last book of the Bible, John describes his vision of Heaven as 'the Holy City, new Jerusalem' (Revelation 21:2).

In AD 66, the Jews rebelled against their Roman rulers, and four years later Roman forces under Titus besieged and destroyed the city. There was never to be another temple in Jerusalem, but the Emperor Hadrian built a new city, Aelia Capitolina, on the site in AD 130. After Constantine became Emperor of the Roman Empire in AD 324 and made Christianity legal, churches and shrines were built and Jerusalem began its 'golden age' as a Christian city. The layout of this city, on a typical Roman grid plan but smaller than before, is the basis for the modern city centre.

In AD 638, Jerusalem came under Muslim rule and the great mosque, the Dome of the Rock, was built on the Temple Mount in AD 691. For some centuries the Muslim rulers were tolerant of the Jews and Christians who lived and worshipped in the city, as well as the many pilgrims who visited it from all parts of Europe. However, in 1071, the Muslims destroyed the Christian shrines and cut off the pilgrim routes. The European powers, with whom the Muslim rule of the Holy City had long been a sore point, decided to invade. In 1099 the Christian army of the First Crusade captured Jerusalem and established a state there; new churches were built and mosques were converted into churches. But forces led by Saladin, the Egyptian ruler, regained Jerusalem in 1187, and it was re-established as a Muslim city.

Egyptian rule ended in 1517, when Jerusalem was taken by the Turks. For 400 years after that, the city was part of the Ottoman Empire, slowly declining in importance. It was primarily a Muslim city, but Jews and Christians lived there and practised their religions; Christian pilgrimages continued and Jewish immigration increased, particularly during the 19th Century. In 1917, following the defeat of the Turks in World War I, Jerusalem came under the British mandate.

British rule in Jerusalem lasted from its capture in 1917 until 1948, by which time the Zionists and Arabs were fighting each other and both fighting the British.

City of David

Present wall of Old City

Site of the City of David

DAVID'S CAPITAL

David conquered Jerusalem, taking it from the Jebusites. He made it his new capital, established on the border between Judah and Benjamin, probably in the hope of ending inter-tribal rivalry.

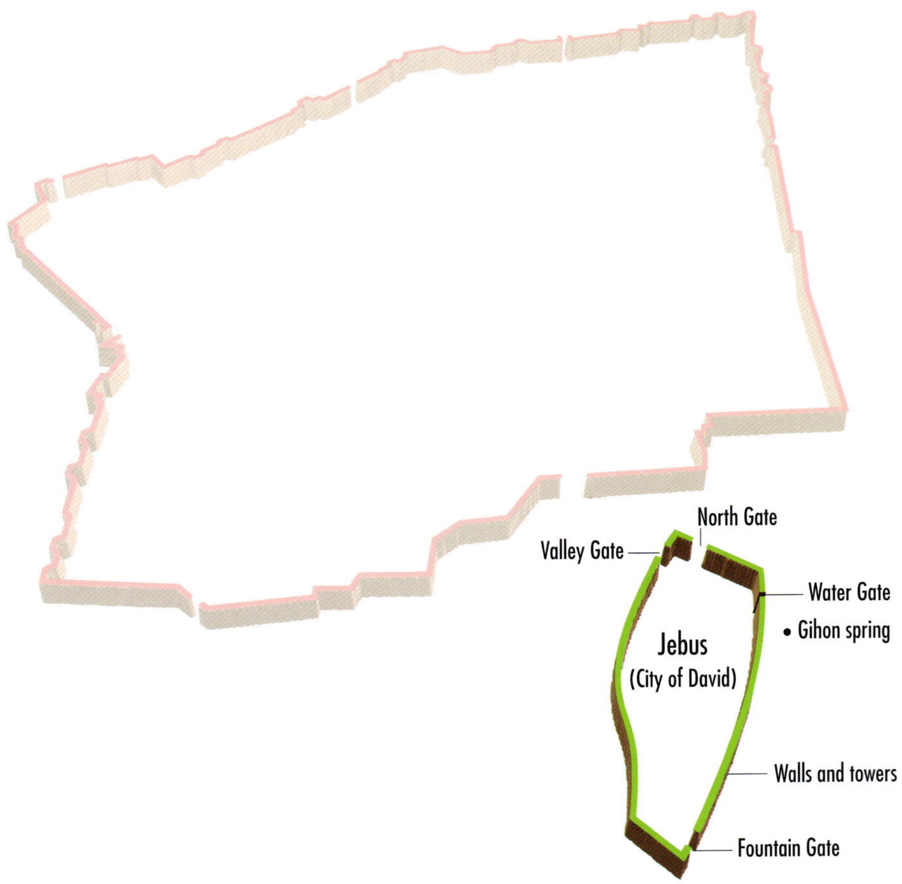

N

0 250 metres

0 250 yards

Eventually, the city was split between Israel and Jordan. After the Six Day War in 1967, Israel troops won control of the whole city, but it remains an area of disputed claims. Although the state of Israel regards it as her capital city, it is not internationally recognized as such, and many international organizations and foreign embassies are sited in Tel Aviv rather than Jerusalem. The Israelis have expanded the city and erected many modern buildings, including government offices, cultural institutions and extensive housing projects.

The Old City has been preserved intact. Although it is now only a small district of Jerusalem, the area is by far the most fascinating part of the city for both tourists and pilgrims. Divided roughly into Jewish, Muslim, Christian and Armenian quarters, the Old City is essentially Oriental in character with narrow streets and bustling bazaars and markets. Dominated by the Dome of the Rock and the adjacent al-Aqsa mosque, it is also crowded with churches, ancient synagogues and Jewish study houses. The focus of Jewish pilgrimage is the Western Wall (or Wailing Wall), which is all that remains of Herod's Temple. Here, Jews pray and lament the destruction of Solomon's Temple. Christian holy places include the Church of the Holy Sepulchre, believed to be the site of Christ's crucifixion and burial – especially since modern research has established that the church is situated outside the perimeters of the original city walls.

The fact that Jerusalem has been continuously inhabited since the 2nd Century BC makes archaeological work extremely difficult. Excavations began there in the 19th Century and have continued to the present day, particularly since 1967, with most of the work concentrated on the Temple Mount area. Extensive research into ancient documents has helped to reveal many clues to the structure and history of the Holy City over the vicissitudes of the past 4,000 years.

Jerusalem from Solomon to Hezekiah

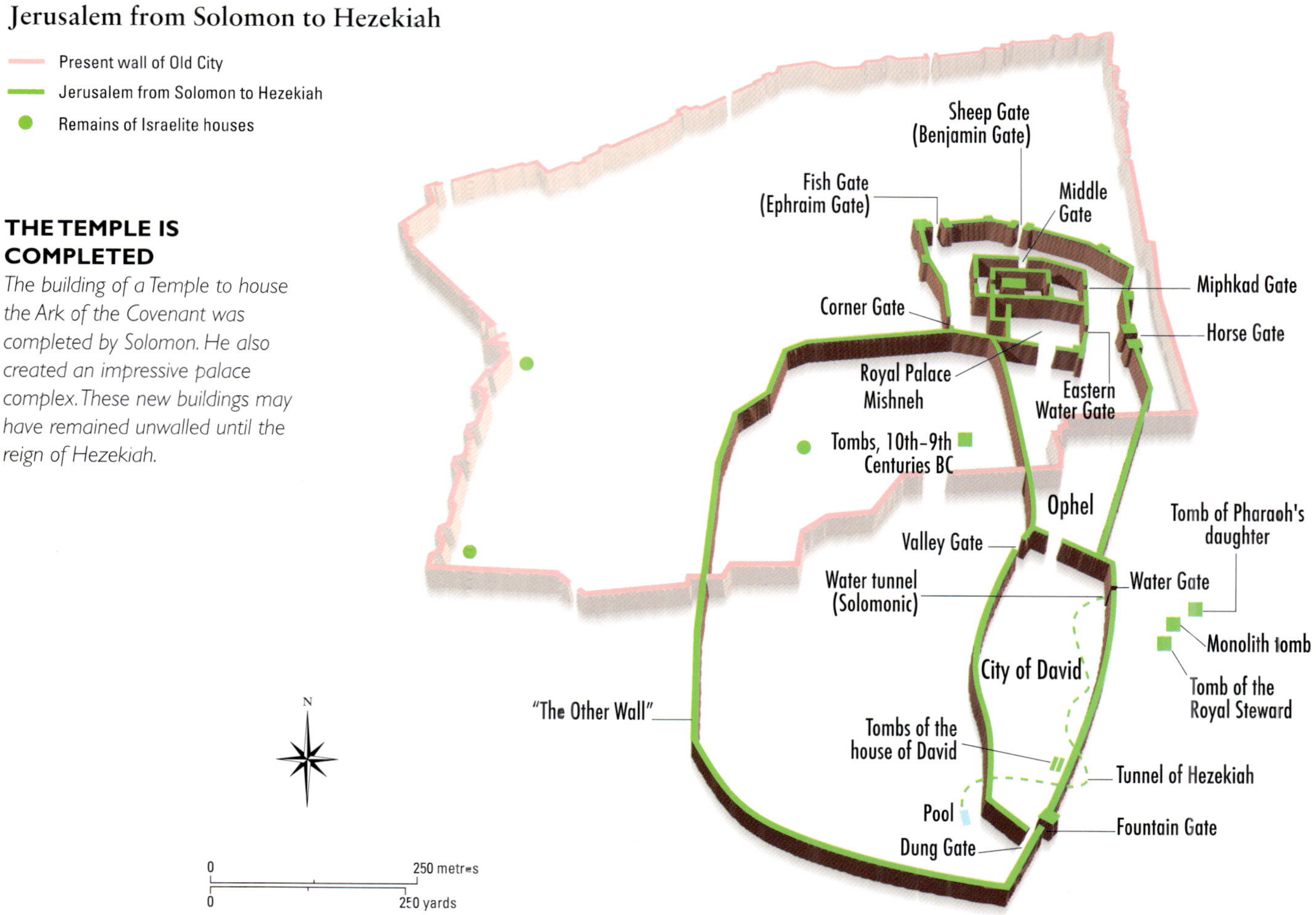

THE TEMPLE IS COMPLETED

The building of a Temple to house the Ark of the Covenant was completed by Solomon. He also created an impressive palace complex. These new buildings may have remained unwalled until the reign of Hezekiah.

JERUSALEM – OLD AND NEW

Biblical Jerusalem – the Old City – still exists among the expanding, though divided, modern city. This is a place sacred to Jews, Christians and Muslims alike.

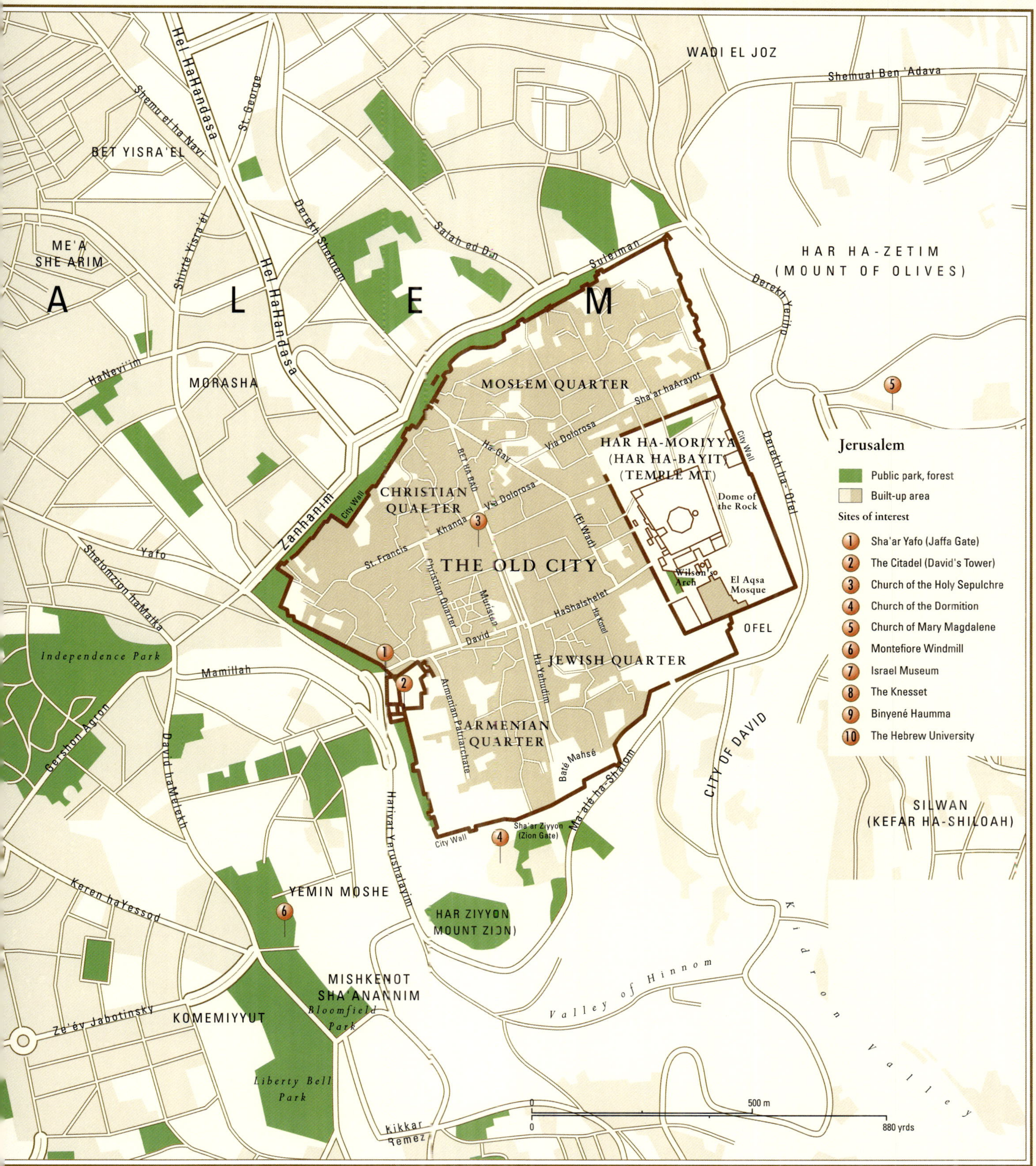
Jerusalem
Public park, forest
Built-up area
Sites of interest
1 Sha'ar Yafo (Jaffa Gate)
2 The Citadel (David's Tower)
3 Church of the Holy Sepulchre
4 Church of the Dormition
5 Church of Mary Magdalene
6 Montefiore Windmill
7 Israel Museum
8 The Knesset
9 Binyené Haumma
10 The Hebrew University
WADI EL JOZ
Shemual Ben 'Adava
BET YISRA'EL
ME'A SHE ARIM
A L E M
HAR HA-ZETIM (MOUNT OF OLIVES)
MORASHA
MOSLEM QUARTER
HAR HA-MORIYYA (HAR HA-BAYIT) (TEMPLE MT)
CHRISTIAN QUARTER
THE OLD CITY
Dome of the Rock
Wilson's Arch
El Aqsa Mosque
OFEL
JEWISH QUARTER
ARMENIAN QUARTER
CITY OF DAVID
SILWAN (KEFAR HA-SHILOAH)
Independence Park
YEMIN MOSHE
HAR ZIYYON MOUNT ZION
MISHKENOT SHA'ANANNIM
Bloomfield Park
KOMEMIYYUT
Liberty Bell Park
Valley of Hinnom
Kidron Valley
Sha'ar Ziyyon (Zion Gate)
City Wall
Hel HaHandasa
St. George
Shivte Yisra'el
Derekh Shekhem
Salah ed Din
Suleiman
Derekh Yeriho
Derekh ha-'Ofel
Sha'ar haArayot
Via Dolorosa
Ha-Gay
Bet HaBad
Khanqa
St. Francis
Christian Quarter
Muristan
David
HaShalshelet
Ha Kotel
(El Wad)
Ha Yehudim
Armenian Patriarchate
Baté Mahsé
Ma'ale ha-Shalom
Hativat Yerushalayim
HaNevi'im
Zahanim
Yafo
Shelomzion haMalka
Mamillah
Gershon Agron
David haMelekh
Keren haYessod
Ze'ev Jabotinsky
Kikkar Remez
500 m
880 yrds

THE NATION DIVIDED

Shortly after Solomon's death, differences between the northern tribes – who were angry at being economically exploited and uneasy about religious changes – and the southerners culminated in the kingdom's collapse. The Old Testament was written during the centuries of civil strife, invasion and exile that followed.

Kings David and Solomon proved to be the only kings to reign over a union of the various Hebrew tribal groups – traditionally 12 in number – that settled in Palestine. At the death of Solomon in about 931 BC, the united kingdom split into two factions, consisting of the northern and southern groups of tribes, along the old demarcation line through the centre of Palestine. The split led to two separate Hebrew kingdoms. The southern one, Judah, with Jerusalem as its capital, was ruled by descendants of David, until it was destroyed by the Babylonians in 587 BC. The northern group formed the kingdom of Israel, ruled by a series of dynasties with, eventually, Samaria as its capital. It survived until 721 BC, when it was destroyed by the Assyrians.

The precarious unity of the Hebrew peoples had lasted little more than 70 years, from the choice of David as king by the two main groups of Hebrews to the death of Solomon. Unity was only maintained by the outstanding abilities of the two kings. Shortly after the death of Solomon, Egypt reasserted control over Palestine, but the Egyptians did not cause the split. The main causes were economic and religious, which amplified all the tensions that already existed between the two Hebrew groups.

The economic problems can be understood from the scale of King Solomon's building activities and the splendour of his court. Archaeology has confirmed the extensive building programme, while, even allowing for possible exaggeration in the biblical accounts, it can be assumed that his court was resplendent. Both the taxation and the forced labour required for this building were sources of anger, and there is evidence in the Bible that at least part of the taxation fell more heavily on the northern group of Hebrews. A list of Solomon's administrators, given in the First Book of Kings (4:7–19), shows that the territory north of Jerusalem, from the coast to the eastern side of the Jordan Valley and the Dead Sea, was divided into 12 districts. Eight of the districts consisted of Hebrew tribal areas, while the four districts along the western coast, from the Philistine border to Mount Carmel, consisted of former Canaanite cities occupied by the Hebrews late in the settlement period. Between them, these 12 northern districts were made responsible for the expenses of Solomon's court, each district covering the cost of one month of the year. There is no mention of the southern Hebrew areas, occupied by David's tribe of Judah and by Simeon. Undoubtedly the northern Hebrews were far more prosperous and numerous than the southern ones, but this evidence of inequality of taxation provides at least one good reason for their subsequent split.

To economic differences must be added differences in religious traditions. When David made his capital, Jerusalem, the religious centre for the Hebrew people and Solomon built the Temple for the Ark of the Covenant, they made it possible for the old Hebrew religion to

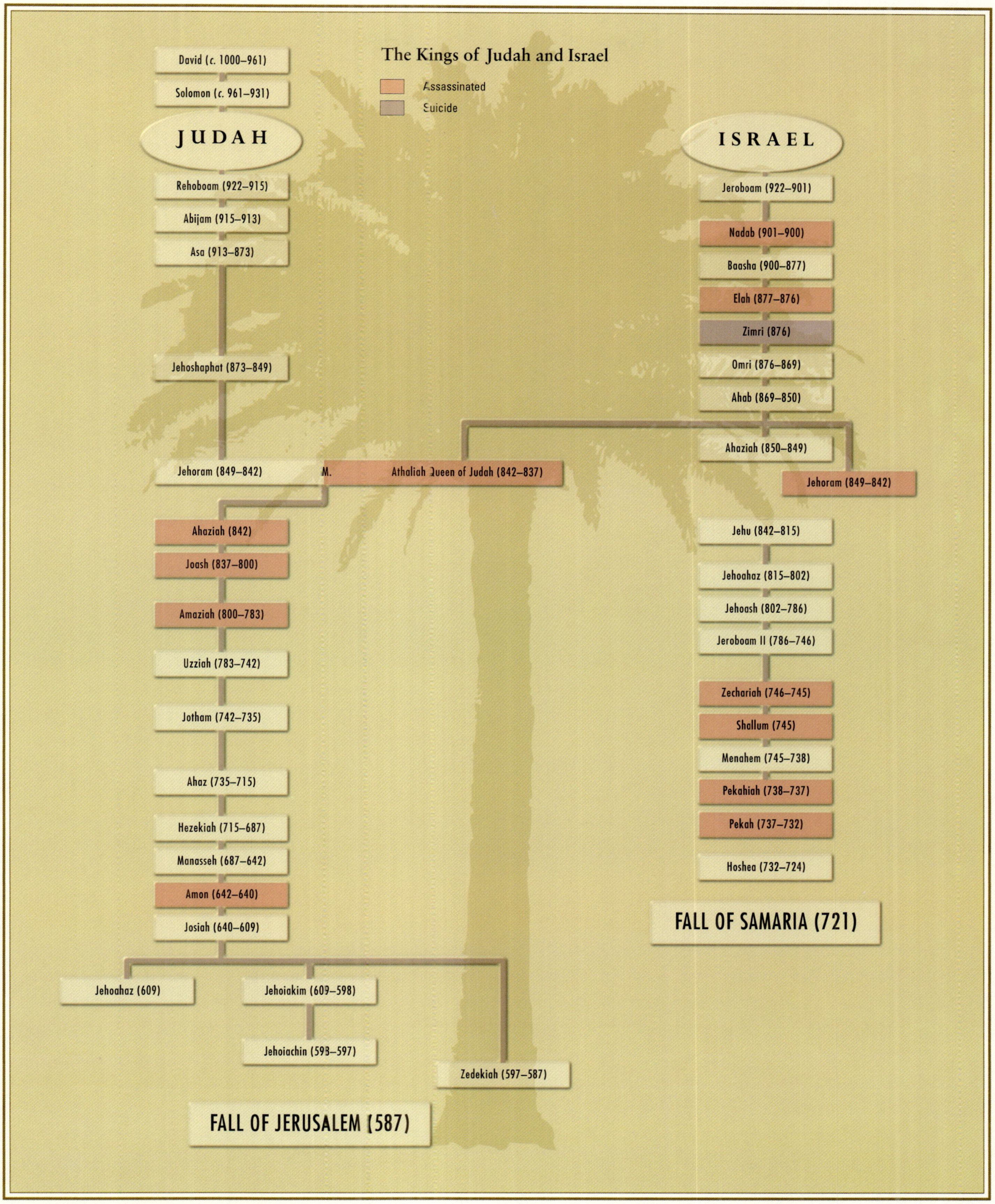

A PEOPLE IN TWO HOUSES

After the stable administrations of King David and his son, King Solomon, the nation divided into two kingdoms – Judah and Israel – ruled by a succession of ineffectual rulers, many of whom were assassinated.

serve the new needs of the Hebrew people as they changed from nomadic shepherds to settled farmers. But many Hebrews remained loyal to the old nomadic symbolism of the Hebrew religion, associated with such ancient sanctuaries at Bethel, Shiloh and Shechem. The new Temple in Jerusalem could easily be seen as a departure from tradition, especially as the traditional priestly organization of the old tribal confederation had been eclipsed by the new line of priests. The rebellion of the northern group, late in the 10th Century BC, was led, eventually, by one of Solomon's own senior officials, Jeroboam, who was in charge of the forced labour levies drawn from the northern Hebrew areas.

The biblical accounts of the Hebrew monarchy were edited into their present form after the destruction of the northern Hebrew kingdom, Israel, by the Assyrians in 721 BC. It is therefore reasonable to beware of a bias in favour of the southern kingdom and so of the Davidic dynasty, reigning from Jerusalem, and the religion of the Temple. This is borne out by the historical books, which select incidents to be included for their religious significance and their effects on the survival of the kingdom of Judah. The reader is told that the information that applies to the northern kingdom, Israel, is available in other records, long since lost (2 Kings 8:23; 10:34).

The leader of the split between the two Hebrew groups, Jeroboam, was an important official in Solomon's administration. He had rebelled during the king's lifetime and fled to Egypt. When Solomon's successor, Rehoboam, refused concessions to a delegation of northern Hebrews and threatened to increase their burden, they made Jeroboam king of the northern tribes and fortified Shechem and Penuel. King Rehoboam of Judah assembled an army to put down the rebellion, but prophetic advice dissuaded him from attacking the northerners. It is possible that the prophets, as distinct from the royal priests, sympathized with the northern desire to curb the power of the Jerusalem kings and the Temple priests. In any case, the northern group was by far the stronger of the two, and in the many years of brutal civil warfare between the two Hebrew kingdoms, the northern kingdom became dominant.

The split was sealed by the northern emphasis on the importance of two sanctuaries, Bethel, near the southern frontier with Judah and Dan in the far north of Israel (1 Kings 12:26–33). The one at Bethel, in particular, would provide a centre for northern Hebrews inclined to look to Jerusalem. Each of them contained a religious image in the form of a golden bull, a traditional symbol for the Hebrew god, Yahweh, but one that could easily be seen as a representation of the Canaanite god, Baal. The traditional Canaanite fertility religion was to be the main danger for the Hebrew people, both northerners and southerners, for the rest of the period of the monarchy. It is only natural that the biblical histories roundly condemn these two sanctuaries of the northern Hebrew kingdom.

'And the king answered the people roughly and forsook the old men's council that they gave him; And spake to them after the counsel of the young men, saying, My father made your yoke heavy, and I will add to your yoke: my father also chastised you with whips, but I will chastise you with scorpions. Wherefore the king harkened not unto the people; for the cause was from the Lord, that he might perform his saying, which the lord spake by Ahijah the Shilonite unto Jeroboam the son of Nebat.'

1 Kings 12:13–15

The internal struggles between the two Hebrew kingdoms was not, though, the only factor that led them to lose control of Palestine. A few years after Solomon died, Shishak (Shoshenq I), the first King of the 22nd Dynasty, re-established Egyptian control of Palestine by a m litary campaign, which took him as far as the Phoenician cities and revived Egypt's trading relationships with Byblos, north of Damascus. Egypt thus once more had command of the coastal road to the north and to Mesopotamia. Shishak took Jerusalem and stripped the royal palace and the Temple of its treasures. Egyptian supremacy was comparatively short lived, for the 22nd Dynasty collapsed in civil war late in the 8th Century BC. By then the Hebrew kingdoms were too weakened by their mutual enmity to take advantage. Moreover, the Assyrians had begun their great expansion and would soon be the dominant power of both the Near and Middle East.

THE DIVIDED KINGDOMS

After Solomon was buried in Jerusalem, the Hebrew nation split in two. Jeroboam became King of Israel while Solomon's son, Rehoboam, became King of Judah.

Egypt Invades

Shishak became Pharaoh during Solomon's reign. Relations were amicable, but Solomon's Empire had emerged as an economic force, controlling trade routes and curtailing Egyptian influence and territorial ambitions. Now was Egypt's chance to intervene.

The dissolution of Solomon's united monarchy into Israel and Judah and the subsequent war between Rehoboam and Jereboam presented the Egyptian ruler Shishak with a superb opportunity to exploit this weakness. An Egyptian invasion is mentioned in the Bible (1 Kings 14 and 2 Chronicles 12), where the Pharaoh, Shishak, captured 15 Judaean fortresses and appropriated the gold from Solomon's Temple in return for sparing Jerusalem. The Bible claims that the Egyptian host comprised 1,200 chariots and 60,000 cavalry, suggesting that the invasion was no mere large-scale raid but a serious attempt to destroy the two Jewish successor states. Shishak had an account of his campaign inscribed in the Temple of Amon at Karnak. The carvings list over 150 places captured, demonstrating that communities were attacked in Judah, Israel, Transjordan and in the Negev.

Archaeological evidence is rich and supports the Egyptian account of the invasion. Fire marks can still be seen on gates and walls, and destroyed shops and houses show the results of Egyptian attacks. The path of destruction blazed across Judah and Israel 3,000 years ago provides the story for historians. The temple carvings also show the god Amon holding ropes attached to captured kings while other captives kneel before him.

Advancing through the plains of Philistia, the Egyptians marched to Gaza and there split their forces. One detachment attacked Sharuhen in the Negev. The inventory of captured places at Karnak lists 70 in the Negev region, including Beersheba, Arad-jerachmeel, Ramat Matred and Ezion-geber. Evidence of destruction at Beersheba and Ezion-geber could readily be attributed to Shishak. The Egyptians intended to weaken Judah's hold in the Negev and its influence over the region of Edom and also open up the trade routes to Arabia.

The Egyptians' northern force marched to Ashdod and Ekron, where a two-pronged attack was launched into Judah. One element of Shishak's army went north, turning eastwards along the Way of Beth-horon, through upper Beth-horon, while a second element tore into the central hill country eight miles south along the Way of Beth-shenesh through Kiriath-jearim. The two forces met at Gibeon, six miles from Jerusalem. According to the Bible, this is where Rehoboam came to ransom Jerusalem with the Temple's gold.

The Egyptian army travelled the central ridge route to enter the Kingdom of Israel. No large, fortified cities existed to form a defensive chain. In fact, there was no defensive perimeter for Israel. Judah had not been considered a severe danger, Jereboam having been a political exile in Egypt, and it was thought that such an Egyptian invasion would be unlikely because Shishak was wrongly regarded as an ally. The powerful invasion force was unstoppable, and Davidic and Solomonic fortifications offered little resistance to Egyptian military technology. Solomon's military engineers had favoured casement walls, where a double wall was connected by cross walls, thereby hampering battering rams. These and three-chambered gates as uncovered by archaeologists

A PHARAOH'S ADVENTURE

Around 925 BC, five years into Rehoboam's reign over _udah, the Pharaoh Shishak invaded the Hebrew kingdoms, blazing a path of destruction across the region.

at Gezer, Hazor, and Megiddo were inadequate. Passing and probably destroying Shechem, the Egyptians attacked and damaged the new capital of Israel at Tirzah. The Wadi Farah river provided a route to the fords at Adam on the Jordan. The river was crossed. The Egyptians marched north to Succoth and through the Jabbok Valley to Mahanaim and Penuel, the latter being a royal city of Israel. Possibly, Shishak wanted to destroy Israelite power across the Jordan.

Shishak then retraced his route down the Jabbok Valley and moved north, destroying Zaphon before recrossing the Jordan and following the Jezreel Valley at Beth-shan. The cities of Rehob, Beth-shan, and Shunem were captured. The southern edge of the Great Plain saw Taanach destroyed and torched. Five miles away, Solomon's great city of Megiddo was attacked and burnt, and then rebuilt as an Egyptian outpost guarding the Way of the Sea trail as it passed the Mount Carmel ridge. A fragment of a stele commemorating Shishak's victory there provides evidence of Egyptian occupation.

The main campaign over, Shishak turned toward Egypt and followed the Way of the Sea, capturing towns along the route. Among those captured, as listed at Karnak, were Aruna, Borim, Gath, Yaham, and Socoh. In this fashion the Pharaoh controlled trade routes not just in the northern valleys but also in the Plain of Sharon and along the coast, all the way back to Philistia. Shiskak's return itinerary is incomplete because the Karnak inscription breaks off at this point.

Shishak had now devastated Judah and Israel, but was forced to quell insurrections at home. Even though Shishak had not managed to rebuild Egypt's old Asian empire of Pharoah Thutmose III, he ensured that there was no longer a strong power potentially threatening his northern border.

EGYPT SPREADS ITS INFLUENCE

Egypt's empire continued to seek to control Palestine, creating defense in depth for its eastern border and control over valuable trade routes.

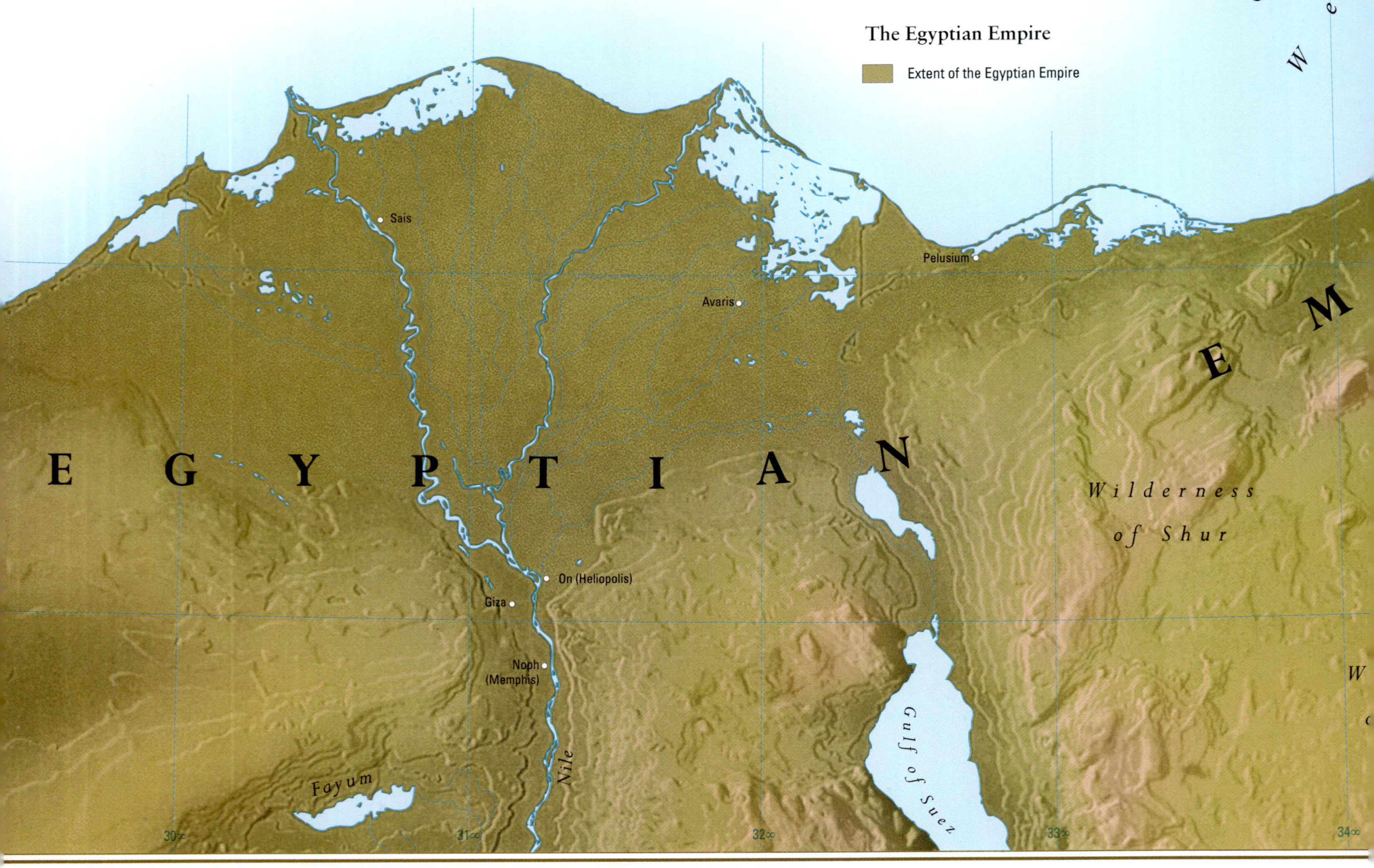

EGYPTIAN TEMPLE GODS

The complex of temples at Karnak, near Luxor in Egypt, contains the temples of many gods erected by a succession of pharaohs. Carvings at the Temple of Amon include a list of Pharaoh Shishak's conquests in Palestine.

'And it came to pass in the fifth year of King Re-ho-bo-am, that Shi-shak king of Egypt came up against Jerusalem: And he took away the treasures of the house of the Lord, and the treasures of the king's house; he even took away all: and he took away all the shields of gold which Solomon had made. And king Re-ho-bo-am made in their stead brasen shields, and committed them unto the hands of the chief of the guard, which kept the door of the king's house.'

1 Kings 14:25–27

Wars of Israel and Judah

By 877 BC, in the Kingdom of Israel, the Syrians had laid waste to parts of Upper Galilee. Years of conflict followed as Israel and Judah struggled with interventions and conflict from within.

Baasha, the third king of the northern Israelite kingdom, left his son Elah to reign after him. Elah, however, was murdered by Zimri, a charioteer commander, who annihilated Baasha's family. Elsewhere, the Israelite army was combating Philistines near Gibbethon. The troops proclaimed their leader, Omri, as king and he marched on Zimri's Tirzah. The city fell and Zimri immolated himself in the citadel of the palace there.

Omri not only founded a dynasty but also introduced political and religious change to Israel. Judah became a junior power while Omri attempted to revive the Solomonic state, especially seeking peace and trade expansion with his neighbours. He made a political alliance with the Phoenicians, with his crown prince, Ahab, marrying Jezebel of Tyre and Sidon. Omri also moved his capital west from Tirzah, building Samaria on land bought from Shemer and using Phoenician architects.

Ahab succeeded his father in 869 BC, continuing his father's policies. However, his palace at Samaria was hidden from the city by a wall, shutting away the ruler from the very people who anointed the king. The House of Omri appeared to be moving even further away from its roots. The introduction of the Baal cult by Jezebel was of great concern to the people too. Substantial rebuilding took place at Megiddo and Hazor, the former becoming a base for Israel's chariot force, and the latter emerging as a strong fortress.

The fortifications undertaken by Ahab were possibly a response to invasions by the Aramaeans of Syrian Damascus. A conflict between Ben-hadad of Damascus and Ahab is poorly recorded, but the former besieged Samaria and was soundly defeated by Ahab. The following year, the Aramaeans returned, but Ahab blocked them before they crossed the Jordan. Each side sought to control Aphek, a strategic locale east of the Sea of Chinnereth, where a key route led up to the plateau of Bashan and the road to Damascus. After a week's stalemate, the smaller Israelite force attacked, forcing the Syrians to retreat to Aphek where Ben-hadad surrendered. The defeated king handed back some Israelite cities and allowed Israelite traders into Damascus. In return, he was freed. Among Ahab's Transjordanian interests were the retention of Gilead and the control of Ammon and Moab. Ammon, however, kept its independence, but Moab's King Mesha became a temporary vassal placing Israelites in Moabite territory north of the River Arnon.

Elsewhere, Judah, under King Asa and his son Jehoshaphat, regained control of Edom along with lands lost in Shishak's military promenade and rebuilt Ezion-geber. A merchant fleet was based in the Gulf of Aqabah. New settlements were probably built west of Beersheba and the Wilderness of Judah was occupied with settlements such as the City of Salt, with agriculture being tried out in harsh conditions to its west.

A CHANGING MIDDLE EAST

From the start of the 9th Century BC, the minor states of the Levantine coast continued to engage in a series of wars. Meanwhile, larger states east and west, such as Assyria and Egypt, consolidated and grew in power.

DESERT FORTRESS

Situated atop an isolated cliff at the western end of the Judaean Desert stands majestic Masada, Hebrew for 'fortress'. The cliff overlooks the Dead Sea, where a coalition of Ammonites, Edomites and Moabites crossed the waters and captured En-gedi.

External forces now threatened the two Jewish kingdoms. In 859 BC, Shalmaneser III succeeded to the Assyrian throne. He projected his strength across the Euphrates into northern Syria right up to the Mediterranean. To meet this threat, Syria and Israel allied, fighting the Assyrians at the battle of Qarqar, with Ahab contributing 2,000 chariots. Each side suffered great losses, with the Assyrians claiming victory. However, their progress was stopped for four years. In this interval, Ahab attacked Syria again, intending to strengthen his strategic position in the borderlands, in alliance with Jehoshaphat of Judah. Israelite Gilead was a well-watered, forested area of uplands. Bashan's basalt and limestone plateaus were Syrian. The natural division between the two is the limestone plateau south of the River Yarmuk to the foothills of Gilead. The enemies confronted each other in battle at the strategic point of Ramoth-gilead. Ahab was wounded but stayed on the battlefield to keep up morale. When the combined Jewish forces withdrew, Ahab's dead body was taken to Samaria for burial. Ahaziah succeeded Ahab but died in an accident two years later, the throne then passing to his brother, Jehoram, in 849 BC.

During these events, Mesha of Moab rebelled, his victories being inscribed on a stele at Dibon, the Moabite Stone. According to 2 Kings, Jehoram marched south, being joined by Jehoshaphat and vassal Edomite forces. Passing Arad and using the Way of Edom, they arrived at Zoar. The army then moved along the Dead Sea to outflank Moab's southern defences. A battle near Horonim saw Mesha retreat along the King's Highway to Kir-hareseth. Apparently, Mesha sacrificed his son on the battlements, which caused the Israelite-led allies to lift the siege. However, the Moabite Stone records the devastation done to Israel. Old Israelite communities like Ataroth and the fortress of Jahz were taken; indeed, the tableland around Medeba, Heshbon and the western scarplands to the Plains of Moab were lost.

Judah was also Mesha's target. Together with Ammonites and Edomites, the Moabites crossed the Dead Sea and took En-gedi. They traversed the

A FAMILY IN POWER

King Omri of Israel introduced religious and political change, seeking peace and trade with his neighbours. However, after his death, the dynasty drifted from its Hebrew roots, laying the foundations for future difficulties.

JUDAH IN CLOSE-UP

The hills and valleys of Judah acted as a defence against the assaults of the short-lived coalition of Mesha, King of Moab, together with Ammonites and Edomites.

Wilderness of Judah, coming to the Wilderness of Tekoa, where the Judahites stopped them. The enemy coalition collapsed, with the Moabites and Ammonites turning on the Edomites. Judah was again hit hard when rebellious Edomites stopped and turned back Jehoshaphat's son, Jehoram of Judah, near Zoar. Thus, the Edomites regained the copper mines of the Arabah and Ezion-geber. Then Libnah, in the Shephelah, rebelled. Elsewhere, Jehoram of Israel re-entered the fray against Syria. Wounded, he went to Jezreel, his summer palace, where he was joined by his nephew, Ahazariah, who had become King of Judah.

At this point, Elisha and Jehu enter the story. Elisha was an ecstatic prophet who in a musically induced trance said that there would be much water, as a combined Judah-Israel army marched through a dry wilderness towards Moab. That he was involved in the campaign suggests Elisha was a public figure engaged in affairs of state.

Elisha became an adviser to Jehoram, Ahab's son. Spending much time at the capital, Samaria, Elisha was asked by the Syrian King Ben-hadad to cure his commander Naaman of leprosy. Elisha told him to cleanse and cure himself in the waters of Jordan. Israel and Syria were soon at war again. On one occasion Elisha warned the king of an ambush and on another he told the besieged inhabitants of Samaria that they would soon be fed. Miraculously four lepers approached the Syrian camp causing the soldiers to flee, leaving all their provisions behind.

Elisha next took over the old prophet Elijah's tasks of ending the kingships in Israel and Syria. In Damascus, whilst helping the sick Ben-hadad, Elisha told the king's servant, Hazael, to seize the throne. This servant smothered his master in his bed clothes and usurped the throne. King Jehoram was wounded in a battle with Syrians near Ramoth-gilead. He went to recover in Jezreel at his summer palace, where he was joined by Jezebel and his nephew, Ahaziah, who had just become king of Judah. Among some dissident soldiery, Elisha sent a minor prophet to a commander, Jehu, to anoint him as king with orders to wipe out the entire House of Omri.

Events in Israel had provoked much opposition to the Israelite House of Omri. Despite an improvement in the socio-economic situation in Israel, wealth was spread unevenly and the rich lent money at high interest rates as the poor were forced to mortgage their land or their children as security. The drought in Ahab's reign caused many small farmers to lose their land. The religious crisis started by Ahab's wife, Jezebel, also caused much resentment. Elisha worked closely in his anti-establishment actions with the prophetic orders. They were intense patriots who traditionally rebuked kings if they fell short of their duty. King David, for example, had been criticized by the prophet Nathan over his affair with Bathsheba.

'And Elisha the prophet called one of the children of the prophets, and said unto him, Gird up thy loins, and take this box of oil in thine hand, and go to Ramoth-gilead: And when thou comest thither, look out there Jehu the son of Jehoshaphat the son of Nimshi, and go in, and make him arise up from among his brethren, and carry him to an inner chamber. Then take the box of oil, and pour it on his head, and say, Thus saith the Lord, I have anointed thee king over Israel.'

2 Kings 9:1–3

The Aramean wars had occasioned prophetic activity. Foreign alliances, foreign ways, forgetting covenant law and the introduction of Baal ensured that the Omrides were ripe for an internal revolt by nationalists fuelled by the ancient traditions of Yahwism. That Elisha approached the army to instigate a revolution, and the acclaim given to Jehu upon being anointed, both suggest that the army was dissatisfied with the mismanaged war with Aram and the poor leadership of Jehoram. The soldiers might easily have been contemptuous of the luxury and decadence they observed in the court and among the privileged classes. Adding this to the condition of the poor created discontent, ferment and revolutionary conditions. Jehu's eventual *coup d'état* could not have succeeded if the general populace were not behind him.

Other conservative groups were ready for an uprising. One such element was the Rechabites, whose leader Jonadab physically joined in the revolution that was bubbling away. Some 250 years later, Rechabites took an oath not to drink wine, nor to own vineyards, nor to plough the land, nor to build houses but to live in tents like their ancestors. They clung to the democratic, nomadic ways, standing for a harsher lifestyle than that offered by the softness, vice and corruption of Jezebel and her entourage. These extremists were prepared to excise and sacrifice the cancer in their midst.

The acclaim that Jehu received demonstrates the traditional pattern of kingship by designation and popular acclamation. Jehu mounted his chariot and drove to Jezreel. Jehoram and Ahaziah went to meet him. Jehu drew his bow and shot Jehoram dead. Ahaziah fled but was pursued. Jehu and his men chased him past Beth-haggan, and at the ascent of Gur, near Ibleam, they wounded him. Ahaziah managed to reach Megiddo but died there, being buried later in the tombs of his ancestors at Jerusalem.

Jehu next decided to purge Israel of Ahab's family and his entire court. He entered Jezreel and had Jezebel thrown from the window of her summer palace, splattering her blood around while she was trampled underfoot by horses. Whilst the plotters were eating and toasting their success, dogs came and ate Jezebel's body thereby fulfilling one of Elijah's prophecies. Only her skull, feet and the palms of her hands were left for burial.

Jehu carried his judicial murders further. He jeered at the elders of Samaria, asking them to choose one of Ahab's 70 sons to fight him. The elders killed all 70 and sent their heads in baskets to Jehu at Jezreel. He then advanced on Samaria, meeting 42 of Ahaziah's kinsmen and slaughtering them with much brutality. In Samaria, Jehu assembled all the priests and followers of Baal, conducted the required sacrifices, slaughtered the assembled, razed the temple and turned it into a latrine. The purge was successful in eradicating the cult of Baal, but there were disastrous consequences.

Despite founding a dynasty that lasted for nearly 100 years, Jehu commenced a period of utmost weakness during which Israel nearly lost its independence. He saved Israel from a likely amalgamation into the pagan world but left the country stunned. Ahab's alliance system, so useful in restoring Israel to a position of strength, was destroyed. The murder of Jezebel and her Tyrian retainers, the slaughter of the priests of Baal, and the insult to the god by destroying his place of worship, meant that the friendly relations with Tyre in Phoenicia were ended. The alliance with Judah could not survive after the killing of King Ahaziah along with many of his family and court. Thus, Israel lost the main source of her material wealth and her only dependable ally.

Internally, Jehu had maimed Israel. The slaughter of the entire court and most of officialdom caused feelings of horror. The paralysis that overcame the state lasted for years. Memories of the bloodbath and its excesses brought blood guilt to the house of Jehu thereafter. One hundred years later, the prophet Hosea remarked upon the events: 'And the Lord said unto him, Call his name Jezreel; for yet a little while, and I will avenge the blood of Jezreel upon the house of Jehu and will cause to cease the kingdom of the house of Israel' (Hosea 1:4).

Militarily, Israel had been weakened and was unable to resist Assyrian power as it surged south along the Phoenician coast. Jehu paid tribute to Assyria. After Shalmaneser III's forces returned north to face the hostile kingdom of Urartu, Hazael of Damascus attacked and Israel lost all of Transjordan south to the lands of Moab on the River Arnon. Jehu's son, Jehoahaz (815–801 BC), faced worse problems. Defeated, he was allowed to keep a bodyguard of only ten chariots and 50 cavalry plus a police force of 10,000 infantry. '...for the king of Syria had destroyed them, and had made them like the dust by threshing' (2 Kings 13:7). How had Israel fallen? Ahab had taken 2,000 chariots to the Battle of Qarqar. Now, Israel had all her Transjordan territory, the Valley of Jezreel, the coast and Galilee under Aramean control, essentially reducing the state to a dependency of Damascus. So weak was Israel that Amos describes how its neighbours raided whenever they wanted.

Queen Mother Athaliah, Ahab's daughter, seized the throne of Judah, ruling in Jerusalem 842–837 BC. She killed all the seed royal she could find and continued to worship Baal (2 Kings 11:1–3). Elsewhere, an infant son of Ahaziah, Joash, was saved and hidden by his aunt, the wife of Jehoiada, the chief priest, being kept in the Temple precinct so the Davidic line could continue in Judah. When the child was aged seven, Jehoiada plotted with officers of the royal guard. Joash was brought into the Temple and crowned. Athaliah cried treason, but the guard seized and executed her immediately. The temple of Baal was demolished and the new king was welcomed by his people. The old prophet Elisha outlived Jehu, surviving until the reign of his grandson, Jehoash (801–786 BC).

THE KILLING OF JEZEBEL *(right)*
In an engraving by Gustave Doré, the gruesome remains of Jezebel, the wife of King Ahab, are discovered by followers of Jehu, who had ordered her brutal killing.

TRIBUTE TO ASSYRIA

The year 842 BC saw the end of the house of Omri and the weakening of Israel and Judah by religious unrest. There was also intermittent warfare with Syria and Transjordan. Ammon, Moab and Edom were now independent again and parts of the Negev were lost.

Jehu's usurpation in Israel ended the alliance system that the Omrides had constructed with Phoenicia and Judah. Jehu's purges severely damaged Israel, with a reduction in the standard of living. Simultaneously, Hazael of Damascus (c. 842–806 BC) was expanding his power and pressuring Israelite Gilead to such an extent that Jehu approached Shalmaneser III of Assyria for aid.

Assyria had been looming on the horizon for some time. Ashurnasirpal II handed to his successor a well-organized, highly compact state. Shalmaneser was ambitious, seeking to annex conquered peoples, to integrate them into the empire and to exact annual tribute from a series of vassals. Annual campaigns were launched, especially towards the west. In 858 BC, Shalmaneser III met a coalition of Aramaean kings (Sam'al, Hattina, Carchemish and Bît Adini) at Lutibu. The Assyrian claimed victory although he did not break the allies. In campaigns of 857–854 BC, he captured and annexed Bît Adini, but was stopped at Qarqar, on the Orontes, in 854 BC, by an alliance of Irkhuleni of Hammath, Ben-hadad of Damascus and Ahab of Israel. His western campaigns continued in 849, 846 and 842 BC. The Syrians and their allies were always beaten, but the Assyrians were prevented from moving further south because enemies from the mountains, especially the Caucasus, on the northern border of the state, were raiding. A clay fragment from the period records Shalmaneser III's views:

'In the eighteenth year of my rule, I crossed the Euphrates for the sixteenth time. Hazael of Damascus put his trust upon his numerous army and called up troops in great number, making the mountain Senir, a mountain facing the Lebanon, to his fortress. I fought with him and inflicted a defeat upon him, killing 16,000 of his experienced soldiers. I took from him 1,121 chariots, 470 riding horses as well as his camp. He disappeared to save his life, but I followed him and besieged him in Damascus, his royal residence. There I cut down the gardens outside the city, and departed. I marched as far as the mountains of Hauran, destroying, tearing down and burning innumerable towns, carrying booty away from them that was beyond counting.'

While the Assyrians' attention was elsewhere, Hazael of Damascus attacked Gilead, which generated Jehu's response. Shalmaneser's records showed he assaulted Damascus but failed to breach its walls. He received tribute from Tyre, Sidon and Jehu, son of Omri. The Black Obelisk of Shalmaneser has scenes inscribed showing kings bringing tribute. One panel shows Jehu on his hands and knees making obeisance to the Assyrian king. The inscription states: 'The tribute of Jehu, son of Omri. Silver, gold, a golden bowl, a golden vase, golden cups, golden buckets, tin, a staff for the royal hand, puruhati-fruits.' How low Israel had sunk in ten years. Historians have pondered where the submission took place: at Hazor, Libnath, or Mount Carmel. Some historians claim that the site was at the Dog River near contemporary Beirut.

Israel, Damascus and the other Aramaean states were saved from more suffering because one of

ASSYRIAN EMPIRE BUILDING

Campaigns were launched by the Assyrians, who planned to expand their empire and exact tribute from conquered peoples. This could involve the ruthless destruction of anyone who got in their way. Here Assyrian archers attack a besieged city.

Shalmaneser's sons led a revolt allied to subject mountain peoples beyond the upper Tigris. Wasting no time, Hazael dispatched his armies not just into Gilead but all the way down the King's Highway to Aroer. In 2 Kings 10:33, it says Hazael was victorious – 'From Jordan eastwards, all the land of Gilead, the Gadites and the Reubenites and the Manassites, from Aroer, which is by the river Arnon, even Gilead and Bashan.' Hazael's next thrust was across the Jordan towards the sea. Battles occurred, and the forces of Jehu's son, Jehoahaz, were trounced, with heavy losses. Hazael then marched down the coast along the Way of the Sea to capture Gath. Now, the Syrians could cross the Shephelah and, through defiles and wadis, attack Judah.

When the Omridite usurper, Queen Athaliah, was executed, Ahaziah's only surviving son, Joash, was put on the throne, aged seven. When Hazael marched on Jerusalem, Joash sent him a tribute of Temple treasure. Joash was assassinated by a Moabite and an Ammonite and was succeeded by his son, Amaziah, in 800 BC.

With a new Assyrian threat to Damascus, Amaziah took the opportunity to regain Edom. The Jewish army defeated the Edomites in the Valley of Salt and marched rapidly into Edom to capture Sela, thus gaining the rich copper deposits in the region. However, Amaziah might have taken another road into Edom via the waters of Tamar and to Sela via Punon. If so, the King of Judah would have acquired a trade route as well as copper.

Amaziah used his successes to demand of Jehoash, the Israelite King, that his daughter be wed to his son. However, a contentious issue between the two kings was the behaviour of Israelite mercenaries whom Amaziah had hired for his Edom campaign but sent back before his victory in the Valley of Salt. Deprived of the spoils of war, these men attacked and looted cities of Judah, causing war to break out.

The Israelites moved from Samaria by the Way of the Sea to attack Judah from the west. The clash took place at Beth-shemesh, where Amaziah was taken prisoner. With no king and no army to defend it, Jerusalem fell and the victorious Israelites pulled down much of its northern wall while looting the rest of the city and the Temple. They retreated, taking hostages, but later released Amaziah.

The victories of Jehoash continued elsewhere. Persuaded by the declining Elisha, war was waged upon Damascus and the strategic point of Aphek was captured. Hence, the Aramaean jumping-off point into Israel became an Israelite springboard into Syria, one used by Jehoash's son, Jeroboam II, who eventually took Damascus.

Judah's luck deteriorated further. Amaziah tried to rule from a ruined capital, but time did not lead to repair and recovery. Morale declined and a plot was hatched against Amaziah. He sought sanctuary in the fortress city of Lachish near the Philistine border. The assassins followed and murdered him. His body was taken to Jerusalem for burial by his 16-year-old son, Uzziah, who took the throne in 783 BC. This young man was to change the declining state of Judah and lead it to power simultaneously with the resurgence of Israel under Jeroboam II.

POWER TO THE NORTH

The Assyrians expanded their empire towards Palestine, down the coastal road to Egypt and along the King's Highway on the eastern edge of the Jordan Valley. The Assyrians were not yet ready to occupy the region, but the Palestinian kingdoms began to feel the pressure of Assyrian power. King Jehu of Israel, the northern Hebrew kingdom, bought off the Assyrian King Shalmaneser III with ingots of silver and gold and vessels made of gold, but gained only a temporary respite for his people.

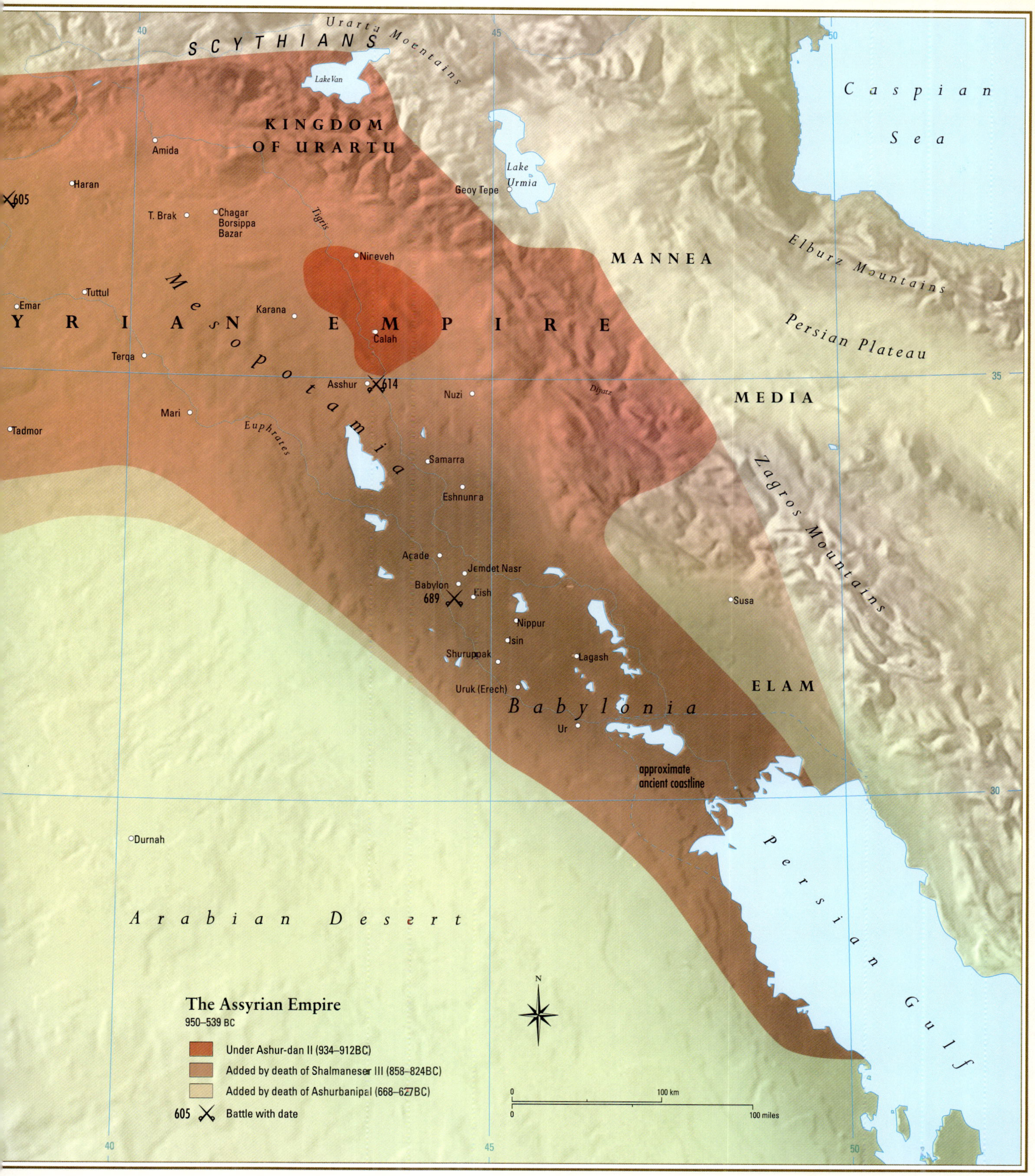
SCYTHIANS
Urartu Mountains
Lake Van
KINGDOM OF URARTU
Amida
Haran
605
T. Brak
Chagar
Borsippa
Bazar
Tigris
Geoy Tepe
Lake Urmia
Caspian Sea
Elburz Mountains
MANNEA
Nineveh
Tuttul
Emar
Mesopotamia
Karana
YRIAN EMPIRE
Calah
Persian Plateau
Terqa
Asshur
614
Nuzi
Diyala
MEDIA
Mari
Tadmor
Euphrates
Samarra
Eshnunna
Zagros Mountains
Acade
Jemdet Nasr
Babylon
689
Kish
Susa
Nippur
Isin
Shuruppak
Lagash
Uruk (Erech)
ELAM
Babylonia
Ur
approximate ancient coastline
Durnah
Persian Gulf
Arabian Desert
N
The Assyrian Empire
950–539 BC
Under Ashur-dan II (934–912BC)
Added by death of Shalmaneser III (858–824BC)
Added by death of Ashurbanipal (668–627BC)
605 Battle with date
0
100 km
0
100 miles
40
45
50
35
30

Renaissance of the Kingdoms

For a period in the 8th century BC, Judah and Israel enjoyed relative peace. Their enemies were in disarray – Syria had been overwhelmed by Assyria, which in turn was in turmoil for nearly half a century.

The fate of Judah and Israel improved in the second decade of the 8th Century BC. Egypt was unimportant militarily, its sole international venture being Pharaoh Osorkon (c. 860–837 BC) sending soldiers to fight Assyrian King Shalmaneser III with Syro-Palestinian allies at Qarqar. Shalmaneser's son, Shamshi-Adad (c. 823–811 BC), had only crushed a revolt with Babylonian aid. He was succeeded by Adad-nirari III (c. 811–783 BC) who came to the throne as a minor. He reimposed tribute on some western states but was being pushed territorially by Urartu. Nevertheless, he managed to capture Damascus in c. 806 BC, taking valuable tribute. Syria recovered from the mauling but engaged in a bitter and unsuccessful rivalry with Hamath. Syria was in no position to maintain a hold on Israel.

Adad-nirari's death led to internal weakness in Assyria. With both major power centres in decline, if only momentarily, Judah and Israel managed to prosper. Two energetic monarchs came to power to exploit the situation. Jeroboam II, son of Jehoash of Israel, ruled from Samaria (786–746 BC). Uzziah (or Azariah) followed his father, Amaziah, as King of Judah, ruling from Jerusalem (783–742 BC). The two monarchs brought Israel and Judah to heights of prosperity and power not known since the times of David and Solomon.

Energetic and thoughtful, Uzziah wanted to rebuild Judah in an efficient and coherent fashion to rival aspects of the Solomonic state. Firstly, he dug new wells and cisterns to support large flocks and herds, allowing agriculture to develop in a systematic fashion. Soil types were tested to establish the best crops per region: grain in the valleys and on the plains, and vineyards on the hillsides. He continued Solomon's scheme for establishing military-agricultural settlements in the Negev to secure and police trade routes in that desolate region. Thus, much Arabian traffic came under his remit. Fortifications were built to a standard military design, with casement walls and a minimum of eight towers, guarding crossroads and strategic points. These towers could be found at Beer-sheba, Hormah and Arad.

Uzziah improved Jerusalem's fortifications by building towers at the corner and valley gates, and at the turning of the wall. He built wooden structures on the city walls to protect his soldiers and constructed war machines to fire arrows and throw rocks. The Bible claims his forces reached 307,500 soldiers, armed with spears, bows and slings. Included in his forces was an elite strike force, which traced its origins to King David's personal guard.

Uzziah engaged in offensive actions against his neighbours (2 Chronicles 26: 6–8). He waged war on Edom, recapturing territory all the way to Ezion-geber, which was rebuilt as a major fortified port and became an important town on the caravan route between Damascus and Egypt. He consolidated Judah's position

A TIME OF WELCOME STABILITY

Two brilliant kings, Jeroboam II of Israel and Uzziah of Judah, succeeded in extending their respective domains, bringing 40 years of stability.

along the trade routes by combating the north-western Arabian tribes, based in Gurbaal and the Meunites in the Edomite desert, who could have threatened Judah's control over the southern portion of the King's Highway. The northern stretches of that highway were held by the Ammonites, who paid Uzziah tribute. His desire for a port on the Mediterranean coast led him to secure the Shephelah and invade Philistia. He constructed a fort at Azekah and destroyed the defences of Gath, Ashdod and Jabneh. Gath and Jabneh were digested by Judah as were some of Ashdod's lands. Uzziah eventually captured Joppa, thereby ensuring that all the dangerous western approaches to Judah were under his control. Cities were built among the Philistine population and inhabited by his people. He had restored the southern part of Solomon's united kingdom to Judah's rule.

In the northern kingdom of Israel, Jeroboam II restored his people's fortunes and laid the foundations for a great increase in prosperity. The king intended to attack Damascus using Aphek as his base. He probably marched to Lodebar, winning victories along the way. After controlling the plateau in that area, which is a route into the Bashan-Gilead region, he captured Ramoth-gilead. Evidence suggests that he next assaulted Karnaim, which lies on a road running northwards to Damascus. Holding both Aphek and Ramoth-gilead, Jeroboam could have attacked Karnaim from both west and south simultaneously. His onslaught tore through Aram, into Damascus and northwards to Lebo-hamath, thereby reaching the furthest extent north of David's and Solomon's domain. Thus, Jeroboam was probably able to impose his authority on both Damascus and Hamath. 'Now the rest of the acts of Jeroboam, and all that he did, and his might, how he warred and how he recovered Damascus, and Hamath, which belonged to Judah, for Israel, are they not written in the Book of the Chronicles of the kings of Israel?' (2 Kings 14:28) Despite the obscure nature of the verse, one might assume that Israel annexed Aramean lands in Transjordan north of the Yarmuk River. In southern Transjordan, Israel's border reached a point along the Dead Sea. The Moabites and Ammonites had been pushed out of Israelite territory and their ambitions checked.

Israel had now regained its rich Gilead lands and tribute from conquered peoples, a sound basis for economic prosperity and the conspicuous consumption it engenders. The population expanded until towns could no longer contain them. Archaeological evidence at Megiddo, a key administrative centre, uncovered many public buildings and stone houses. Excavators there found a wonderful seal bearing the image of a roaring lion, with these words inscribed, 'Shema, servant of Jeroboam'. Shema had probably been the governor of the region, and this was his official seal. Evidence of wealth has been found in Samaria in the form of *ostraca*, pottery fragments. These provide evidence for notations of produce found in Samaria received at the royal warehouse – goods described as 'aged wine' or 'purified oil'. When the jars of liquid were delivered, they were recorded on a pottery fragment and then entered in a ledger.

At Hazor, archaeologists have uncovered examples of some of the finest Israelite houses, dating to Jeroboam's reign. On top of the ruins of Ahab's storehouse there are shops, workshops and houses, built during Israel's 8th Century BC renaissance. All were of a good architectural standard, built with skilled workmanship. One house had a courtyard measuring 9 x 8 metres (30 x 26 ft). Some houses had two storeys and were so well built that the stairs remain in place after 2,700 years. The household goods evidence a degree of wealth. High-grade pottery was used, as were bowls and millstones made out of native basalt. One find was an ivory cosmetic spoon, its handle exquisitely carved in an inverted palmette design, common in the Middle East at that time. The back of the bowl is carved in the shape of a woman's head, with two doves entangled in her hair. Superior ivory objects have been found, but only in the royal palaces. Scenes of luxurious living can also be seen in ivory carvings.

About 760 BC, an earthquake damaged Hazor, allowing for the building of fine, new houses on the site. The scale of material well-being provides evidence for the wealth of Israel at the time. New types of fortification have also been found. Buildings near the edge of the Hazor mound were demolished to enable strengthening of the city wall with offsets and insets to provide stations for flanking fire against any onslaught. A stout rectangular tower measuring 10 x 7 metres (33 x 23 ft) was added to the north-western corner of the mound. Presumably, such fortifications were designed as a defence against a resurgent Assyria.

For some, despite war and earthquakes, life was good. There were, however, growing disparities between the wealthy and the poor, who were ignored by the state. Society was characterized by injustice. Small farmers were squeezed by money lenders and hammered by drought and crop failure, leading to foreclosure, eviction or bond service. The wealthy bought landholdings from the poor, falsified weights and measures and carried out other means of sharp practice. Israel's society had changed. The old unified social structure of the tribal league had dissolved. The advent of monarchy with its subsequent hierarchical power structure, together with the growth of commerce, created classes, destroyed tribal links and broke down traditional society.

Also, the absorption of many Canaanites, not integrated into the tribal system, generated a group of people with no obligation to or understanding of the Covenant. Ancestral strengths were departing.

The Samaria *ostraca* show as many names compounded with Baal as with Yahweh, although some examples of Baal (Lord) might be names for Yahweh. Argument says that many Israelites must have worshipped Baal and that native pagan deities had not been destroyed by Jehu, except for Tyrian Baal. The prophets Amos and Hosea claimed that even the state religion had absorbed pagan rites and pagan rituals of sacrifice were put in place to secure the status quo by appeasing God. What is strange is that the prophetic orders, such strong opposition to the House of Omri, had no rebukes against the current situation, presumably sated by Jehu's purge. The state cult had become perverted. Priests and monarchy alike thought that God's favourable attitude towards Israel had been secured for all time, forgetting that it was conditional upon keeping the covenantal obligations. Elaborate rituals were not enough, as the prophetic protests of Amos and Hosea pointed out.

Hosea described the Covenant bond as wedlock. Yahweh, as Israel's 'husband', expected Israel to be a faithful 'wife'. However, in worshipping other gods, Israel had committed 'adultery' and therefore faced 'divorce', a form of national ruin. Hosea attacked the Baal cult, claiming that Israel was morally rotten and totally impenitent. He saw Israel as being under the Covenant curse and thus faced destruction as a state and nation. Hosea ultimately believed that Yahweh's infinite love would forgive a penitent Israel, but only after an inevitable disaster broke the nation.

Amos inveighed against the decline in morals, drunkenness, injustice and forgotten faith and prophesied that God's judgement would strike Israel. Hosea wailed about the condition of religion and suggested that the ills of society would be punished when Assyria would invade again: '...the wind of the Lord shall come up from the wilderness, and his spring shall become dry, and his fountain shall be dried up: he shall spoil the treasure of all pleasant vessels. Samaria shall become desolate; for she hath rebelled against her God: they shall fall by the sword: their infants shall be dashed in pieces, and their women with child shall be ripped up' (Hosea 13:15–16).

THE HILLS OF SAMARIA

The easily defensible position provided by surrounding hills probably influenced King Omri of Israel in his decision to build his city of Samaria here. For about 150 years the city served as the capital of Israel until destroyed by the Assyrians in 721 BC.

Chaos

The prosperity and well-being of Israel was shattered when Jeroboam died in 746 BC. His son Zechariah lasted six months, when he was murdered by an assassin at Ibleam.

The killer, Shallum, held the throne for a month when he in turn was killed by Menahem, son of Gadi, of Tirzah. Menahem's brutality became legendary – his troops butchered pregnant women at the sack of Tappuah and destroyed the surrounding communities when the people refused him as king. Israel had now been seriously weakened and would soon face the might of a resurgent Assyria.

Meanwhile, Assyria changed its old policy of regarding the Euphrates as its western border, with trans-Euphrates states becoming vassals. Policy modification occurred because Assyria's northern rival, Urartu, had expanded westwards and forged an anti-Assyrian coalition. This alliance of north Syrian statelets, from Melid to Arpad, was a threat to Assyrian trade routes. In 745 BC, Tiglath-pileser III (the biblical Pul) acquired the Assyrian throne and, using his administrative and military skills, sought to expand the empire. A campaign settled the mountain areas, followed by an attack in 743 BC on the Urartian coalition in the west. The Urartian forces were defeated, and Arpad, the major seat of resistance, was taken by siege in 740 BC, when it became the capital of an Assyrian province. Tiglath-pileser next marched on Unqi at the northern end of the Orontes; Kullania, its capital, fell in 738 BC and its name was given to a new Assyrian province. Advances southwards resulted in the creation of the provinces of Simirra and Khatarikka and the payment of tribute by various rulers, including Rezin of Damascus, Menahem of Israel and the kings of Tyre (Hiram), Gubla and Hamath. Assyria wanted to develop provincial government right up to the Mediterranean.

The style of the new Assyrian policies was much harsher than before. These new campaigns did not merely exist to gain plunder, slaves, tribute and the security of trade routes. Now, conquered lands were to be incorporated into the Assyrian empire as provinces, and enemy leadership groups were deported deep into the empire as depopulated areas were settled with Assyrian peoples. The coalition of minor countries also included 'Azriau from Iuda', or Uzziah of Judah, the leper king, whose son, Jotham, served as regent. The tribute paid by Menahem was huge and weighed heavily upon the population of Israel.

'And Pul the king of Assyria came against the land: and Menahem gave Pul a thousand talents of silver, that his hand might be with him to confirm the kingdom in his hand. And Menahem exacted the money of Israel, even of all the mighty men of wealth, of each man fifty shekels of silver, to give to the king of Assyria. So the king of Assyria turned back and stayed not there in the land.'

2 Kings 15:19–20

HIT BY A STORM

After the death of Jeroboam II and shortly after the death of Uzzian of Judah, both kingdoms came under extreme pressure from all directions. The new King of Judah, in his desperation, made an appeal to Tiglath-pileser of Assyria for protection.

WARRIOR KING

A bas-relief from the palace of Tiglath-pileser III shows the Assyrian king capturing the fortified town of Astartu c. 733 BC.

Although the tribute won Menahem a breathing space of seven more years for his kingship, his hold was weakened due to resentment over taxation, his method of achieving the kingship, and his bowing to Assyria. His son, Pekahiah, barely ascended the throne when he was murdered in a military coup by Gileadites.

Elsewhere, Tiglath-pileser confronted Urartian influences: in 739 BC in Ullubu (the Dohuk-Zakho region of north Iraq), in 737 BC in the Median area of north-east Iran and in 735 BC, when he marched on Urartu itself. In 734 BC, Tiglath-pileser again turned westwards, extending Assyrian control into Philistia, taking Gaza and reaching the Brook of Egypt (Wadi el-Arish). He crushed the nomadic tribes and appointed an Arab tribal chief as his warden in Sinai. Relationships were also built with other Arab rulers in northern Arabia and eastern

'So Ahaz sent messengers to Tiglath-pileser king of Assyria, saying, I am thy servant and thy son: come up, and save me out of the hand of the king of Syria, and out of the hand of the king of Israel, which rise up against me. And Ahaz took the silver and gold that was found in the house of the Lord, and in the treasures of the king's house, and sent it for a present to the king of Assyria.'

2 Kings 16:7–8

Transjordan. Now, Pekah of Israel and Rezin of Damascus allied themselves in another anti-Assyrian coalition. It included Tyre, Askelon and some tribes of north Arabia and Transjordan, and sought to persuade Jotham of Judah to join them. He refused, and his son Ahaz, ascending the throne in 735 BC, also refused.

The Israelite and Damascus confederates planned to invade Judah, depose Ahaz, and replace him with someone more amenable – the unidentified son of Tabeel'. However, Rezin of Damascus despatched his troops through Transjordan right down the King's Highway to acquire Ezion-geber. These territorial acquisitions, however, were short-lived.

Rezin also sent forces to join Pekah in an attack upon Israel, probably using the Aphek-Lodebar route. The combined armies crossed the border and besieged Jerusalem, acquiring booty and prisoners along the way. These captives were later freed when the prophet Oded claimed their capture was a transgression against God and that Israel had sinned enough already. Oded was possibly the mouthpiece of opposition growing against Pekah. Ahaz thought an appeal for help to the Assyrian king would be a good idea, but the prophet Isaiah persuaded him otherwise. Reliance on God would see Judah through these difficult times.

However, the Israelite-Damascus armies pushed against Jerusalem and, simultaneously, Judah's old enemies took the opportunity for revenge. Edom recovered its freedom and grabbed the entire mineral-rich Arabah all the way to Ezion-geber; raids were also launched into the Negev. On the coast, the Philistines recovered lands lost to Uzziah, also acquiring the cities of Beth-shemesh, Socoh, Timnah, Aijalon and Gimzo.

The two invasion routes into Judah, the Ways of Beth-horon and Beth-shemesh, were open – leaving Ahaz and Judah insecure. Additionally, the Philistines seized Gederoth and commenced raids into the Negev, destroying Uzziah's system of agricultural-military communities.

The Destruction of Israel and Judah

After several centuries of ruthless domination over Mesopotamia, Assyria forged through Syria and Palestine in the 8th Century BC, going on to conquer the entire Fertile Crescent.

Tiglath-pileser III of Assyria decided to enhance his domains in the west by destroying Damascene independence. However, he realized that it could not be achieved in one campaign. Egypt had always to be taken into account as a potential enemy and a rival empire. Pekah of Israel's alliance with Rezin of Damascus put his kingdom at risk, but not immediately – the Assyrian armies wanted to move through Israel rather than conquer it. Tiglath-pileser mounted three campaigns to achieve his ends: in 734, 733 and 732 BC.

In 734 BC, Assyrian forces began their march along the Way of the Sea towards the Brook of Egypt, the traditional northern border of Egypt. The army moved past Tyre and Acco, travelling inland through the first pass in the Carmel range rather than traversing the route cramped by the Carmel promontory where it meets the sea. The force entered the mountains at Jokneam, emerging east of Dor, and then rejoined the Way of the Sea rather than moving inland and having to encounter fortresses. Along the route, Gezer was torched and the old Solomonic gate destroyed. Evidence of this destruction can be found at the Assyrian king's palace at Nimrud. Tiglath-pileser then captured Gaza and established forces along the Brook of Egypt to prevent Egyptian raids northwards. In fact, a weakened Egypt could never mount more than brief spoiling attacks to retake Gaza and preferred to encourage other states to rebel to divert Assyrian forces.

In 733 BC, the Assyrians re-entered the fray, targeting Israel directly, possibly intending to capture Galilee and Gilead, thereby isolating Syria in the west and south. Assyrian troops passed Mount Hermon, descending into the rift valley guarded by the fortresses at Ijon and Abel-beth-maacah, which were quickly captured. The army then moved to confront Hazor, a massive fortress on a mound 40 metres (130 ft) high. The citadel was stormed, with destruction so massive that only foundations below floor level were left behind. The final incineration left a layer of ash 1 metre (3 ft) thick.

At Hazor, the Assyrians divided their army into three detachments. The first was despatched through Upper Galilee destroying both Kadesh and Janoah and then reaching the coast at Acco. The second and third detachments moved south to Chinnereth on the Sea of Galilee. Splitting here, one unit moved south and east through Pehel to Jabesh-gilead, with a smaller strike force moving on to Mahanaim, while the Assyrians moved throughout Gilead. The final detachment moved out of the rift valley at Adamah and marched westwards through the central area of Lower Galilee, smashing the towns of Rumah, Kahah, Jotbah and Hannathon, then taking a valley route south to the Great Plain to confront Megiddo.

The Megiddo fortress controlled a major pass (Wadi Aria) through the Carmel range and, as an administrative and military base, was one of the most important cities in Israel. Megiddo was now besieged by the formidable Assyrian siege train, possibly reinforced by troops who had crossed Upper Galilee. Archaeologists suspect that Megiddo was flattened, because the Assyrian rebuild followed an entirely different plan, the fortress becoming the administrative capital of the new province of Magiddu. The whole northern part of the Kingdom of Israel was seized by the growing Assyrian Empire. At the same time, the coast from south of Mount Carmel to a border at the Kanah Brook became part of the Dor province.

In Israel, events moved on. Pekah was deposed by Hoshea who became the last King of Israel. Tiglath-pileser's records state that the coup was Assyrian-aided. Israel now existed only as a rump state with precarious independence. Gilead was lost as was territory west of the Jordan. Resources were severely reduced and annual tribute had to be culled from the remnant of the country. Surrounded on three sides by Assyria, Israel was now wide open to attack.

In 732 BC, Tiglath-pileser captured Damascus and moved south to control Bashan. Huge numbers of people were then deported into Assyria. Syria was divided into the Assyrian provinces of Damascus, Karnaim and Hauran Ammon. Edom and Moab remained under loose Assyrian control, paying tribute, but gained Assyrian protection from nomadic raids from east and south. Ahaz of Judah was summoned to the king to abase himself. He was foolish enough to place a copy of a foreign altar in the temple, moving the altar to God into a less significant position. Thus was Ahaz subservient and also a transgressor of God's will.

Tiglath-pileser III died in 727 BC and was succeeded by Shalmaneser V. Hoshea chose this moment to rebel, being assured of help from the Egyptian pharaoh. The Assyrians moved swiftly – Hosea was taken prisoner and Samaria besieged. Shalmaneser died during the fighting, and was replaced by Sargon II. The siege lasted three years, resulting in the Kingdom of Israel ceasing to exist. Sargon claimed to have moved 27,290 inhabitants into Assyria, with Jews being placed near Goran, the Nineveh-Halah region and in Media. The Israel rump state was combined with Dor to create the province of Samaria. New populations were moved in from Babylonia, merging with the remaining poor Israelites and adopting their faith to create a new Samaritan identity.

Sargon claimed that revolts broke out in Hamath, Damascus, Samaria and Gaza in 720 BC, possibly inspired by Hamath. They were quickly defeated as was an Egyptian

MIGHTY MEGIDDO

This model is based on the excavations at Megiddo that have exposed the great walls and gateway built by King Solomon to strengthen Palestine after its capture by the Hebrews.

army seeking to recapture Gaza. Sargon moved south and destroyed Raphia, moving its 9,000 or so inhabitants into Assyria. A later rebellion occurred at Ashdod, encouraged by Egypt and aided by Judah, Edom and Moab, with the latter three rapidly withdrawing their support. Ashdod fell and became a province; Gath, Ekron, Gibbethon and Azekah also fell, leaving the Assyrians controlling the Way to Beth-shemesh. Judah's survival now hung by a thread.

After Sargon II destroyed Israel, the Assyrian king confronted an insurrection in Babylon led by Merodach-baladan. The conflict lasted 12 years, with Sargon forced to withdraw troops from Samaria and its environs to

suppress the rebellion. Consequently, revolts occurred in the newly conquered territories along the Mediterranean coast. Hezekiah of Judah joined in these uprisings (713–712 BC) to try to overturn his father's pro-Assyrian policies. Sargon suppressed all these challenges, and passed an intact empire on to his son Sennacherib in 704 BC.

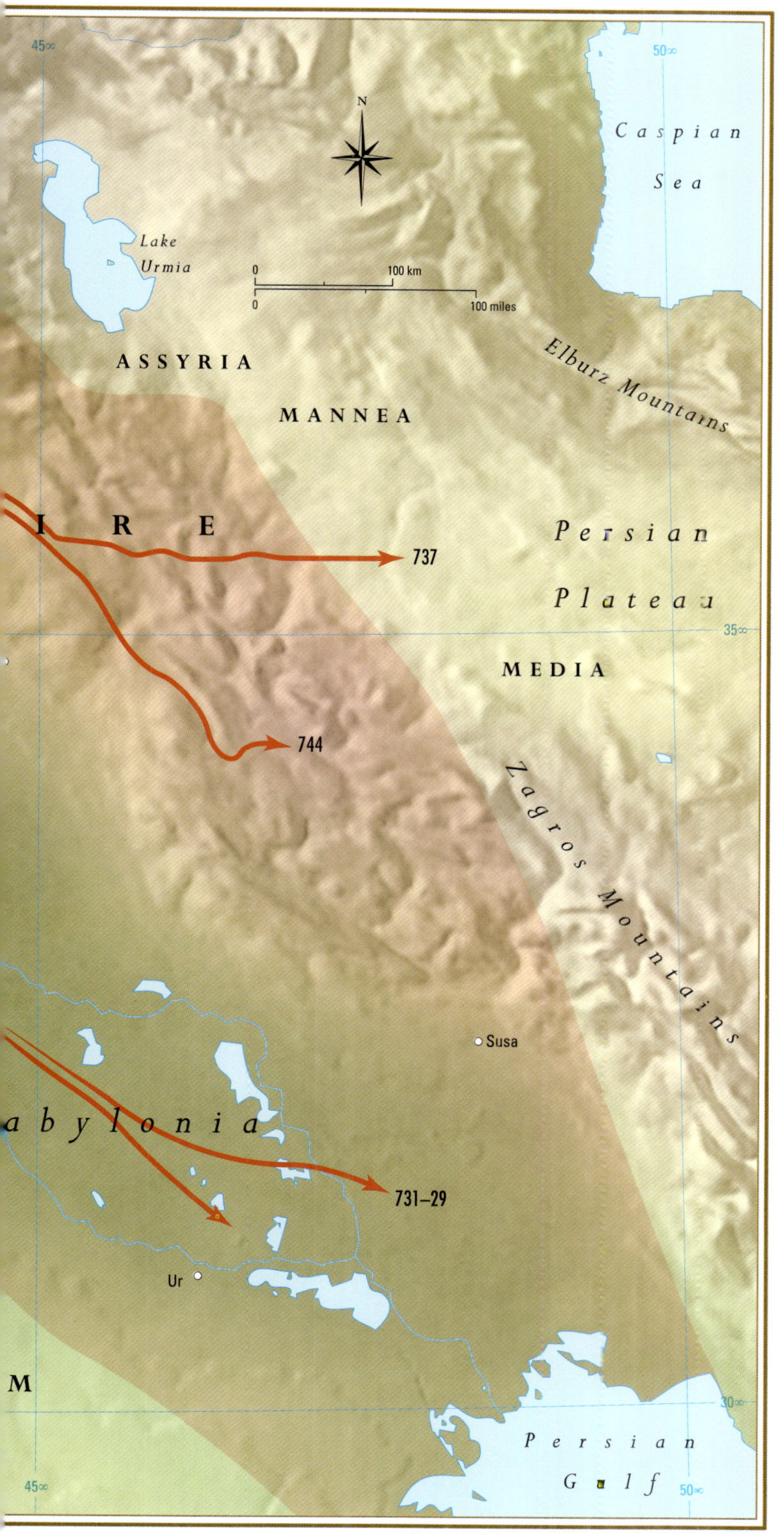

While the new Assyrian king spent time upgrading his capital at Nineveh, Egypt was reunited under the 25th (Ethiopian) Dynasty. As far as Egypt was concerned, any state in Palestine that gained independence would provide a valuable bastion against potential Assyrian invasion. Hence, Judah and the Phoenician cities were important foreign policy targets. Likewise, the states of Palestine could now look to Egypt for support against Assyria. King Hezekiah of Judah took advantage of this foreign policy situation and refused tribute, while preparing his realm for an expected attack by the Assyrians.

War preparations included designating four cities as military depots. Jerusalem, Socoh, Lachish and Ziph were consequently strengthened for this role. One remnant of Hezekiah's preparations was the water tunnel dug under the city from the Gihon Spring in the Kidron Valley to ensure a water supply under siege. This tunnel stretches 533 metres (1,750 ft), chiselled out of solid rock. The width varies from 0.9 to 3.4 metres (3 to 11 ft) and the height from 1.2 to 4.9 metres (4 to 16 ft), and to this day the tunnel pours water into the Pool of Siloam. Springs that might support the enemy were dammed or polluted. Defence works elsewhere are unrecorded, but the hills of the Shephelah and those of Samaria would provide natural obstacles to an invader, as would the compact mountain range, the heartland of Judah.

However, there were weaknesses in Judah's defences. The Shephelah is riven by a series of defiles, especially the Way of Beth-shemesh, which provides a broad road to Jerusalem. Evidently, Hezekiah concentrated his defences here, making it hard for Sennacherib to pass. Sennacherib claimed that he torched 46 cities and walled forts in Judah, thereby providing evidence that Hezekiah had indeed turned Judah into a hedgehog of fortifications. Hezekiah made other preparations. He standardized military equipment, collected huge supplies of spears and shields and rearmed his soldiers. Edom was raided to secure the southern frontiers.

Hezekiah also utilized religious reform as a means of stiffening Judah's resolve. All the Assyrian gods brought in by his father were repudiated and religious values were reintroduced to revive nationalism. The Prophet

SEASONAL CAMPAIGNING

The Assyrians launched campaigns in the summer, after peasant conscripts had brought in the harvest. Their major policy change was to incorporate conquered territories within the Empire rather than arranging a series of dependencies.

ISRAEL IS DEFEATED

The campaigns of 721–720 BC involved the final destruction of Israel as a nation.

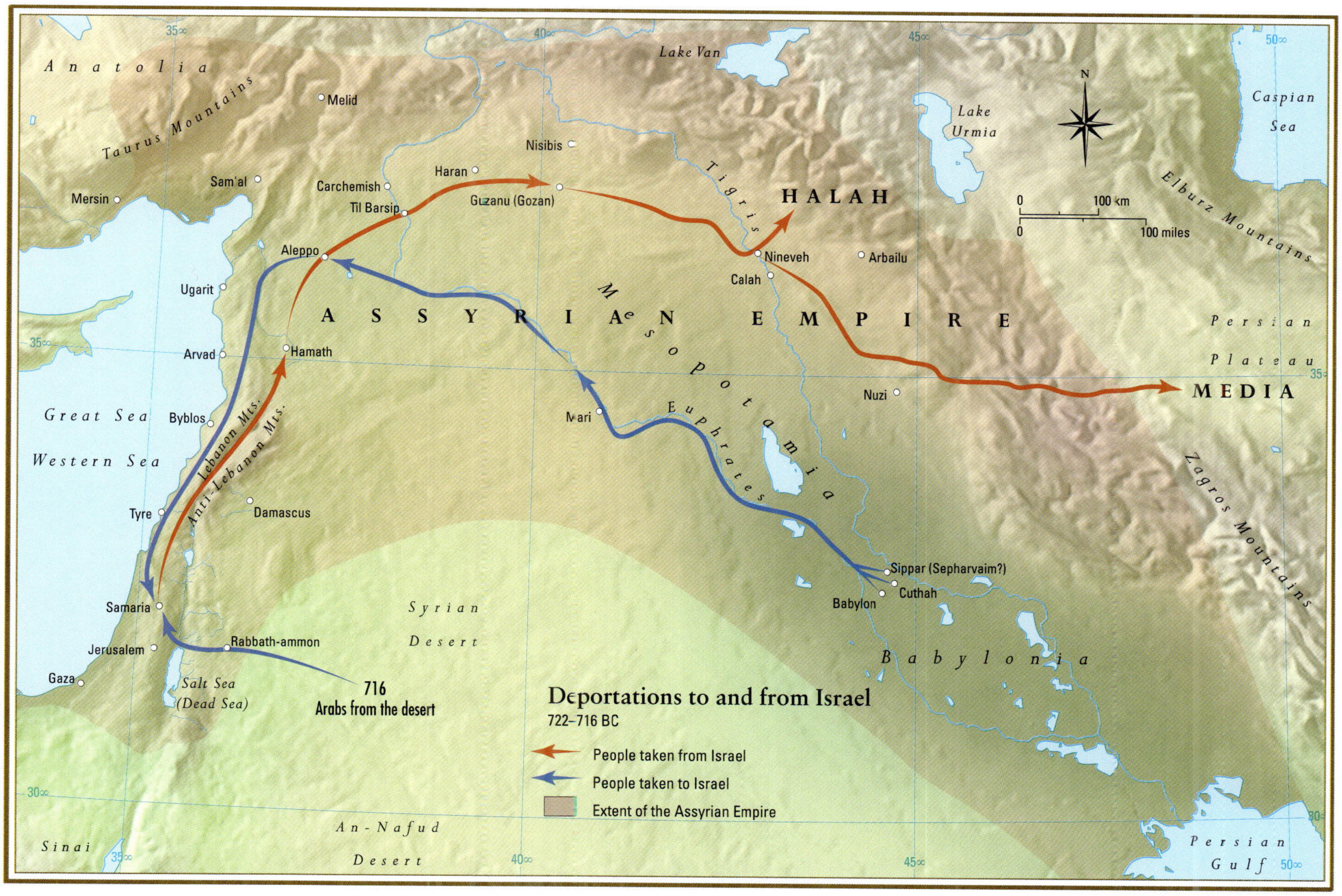

ISRAELITES ON THE MOVE

Assyrian policy involved the movement of conquered peoples. In the case of Israel, people were moved in as well as moved out to far provinces of the Empire.

Isaiah supported Hezekiah. Some the social abuses and economic exploitations were ameliorated, allowing a measure of prosperity to return to Judah, resulting in the doubling or trebling of Jerusalem's population. The king attempted to involve Samaria and Galilee in his adventures, but they refused.

Hezekiah sought support elsewhere, even receiving ambassadors from Babylon's resurgent leader Merodach-baladan. A sizeable anti-Assyrian coalition was built, with the King of Tyre as a ringleader. King Sidqa of Ashkelon joined as did the city of Ekron, which sent its king, Padi, as a captive to Jerusalem, since he remained loyal to Sennacherib. The cities of Ashdod and Gaza did not commit themselves. Pharaoh Shabako signed a treaty with Judah despite the fury of Isaiah, who claimed that Egypt was a paper tiger. Ammon, Moab and Edom might have been implicated in the rebellion. If so, they offered no resistance to Sennacherib.

The year 702 BC witnessed the end of the Babylonian revolt, leaving Sennacherib free to combat the enemy coalition. In 701 BC, a massive Assyrian force marched down the Mediterranean coast in an assault on Phoenicia. Luli, King of Tyre, fled to Cyprus, while Tyre and its inland town of Uzu were utterly devastated. This great port, despite being rebuilt, lost its commercial importance to the Greeks and some of its own colonies, such as Carthage. Byblos, Arvad, Ashdod, Moab, Edom and Ammon swiftly sent tribute to Sennacherib. Only Ashkelon, Ekron and Judah continued to hold out, watching the Assyrian advance down the Way of the Sea. Ashkelon's dependency, Joppa, fell quickly, leaving the Assyrians to turn on Ekron. An Egyptian army, strengthened by bowmen, chariots and cavalry, marched to relieve Ekron and collided with the Assyrians at Eltekeh. The Egyptians suffered a defeat, and Eltekeh was destroyed. However, the Egyptians retreated unharassed by the Assyrians, who wanted to finish off the coalition. Sennacherib then took other Philistine cities, such as Timnah and Ekron, at his leisure.

Judah was the next target. One Assyrian force traversed the Way of Beth-horon intending to strike

Jerusalem from the north. This force fought its way through Bethel, Aiath, Michmash, Geba, Anathoth and Nob. One unit took Ramah, thereby isolating the lynchpin of Hezekiah's northern defences. Sennacherib then surrounded Jerusalem with earthworks so no one could enter or leave the city. While the King of Judah was locked up, the other Assyrian army assaulted the fortified cities of the Shephelah, storming them in turn after taking the key defence of Lachish. The histories of Sennacherib write about earthworks, tunnels, breaches and sappers in the siege. Archaeology shows fire was used as an offensive weapon. A huge pit has been found containing the remains of some 1,500 bodies, covered with pig bones and other Assyrian debris. The populations of 46 cities were executed or deported.

'Your country is desolate, your cities are burned with fire: your land, strangers devour it in your presence and it is desolate, as overthrown by strangers. And the daughter of Zion (Jerusalem) is left as a cottage in a vineyard, as a lodge in a garden of cucumbers, as a besieged city.'

Isaiah 1:7–8

Hezekiah's position was untenable. Judah was being systematically consumed, some of its troops had deserted and even Isaiah told Hezekiah to sue for terms. The king sent some of the Temple's gold and silver to Sennacherib and negotiations were opened, although military operations continued with both Moresheth-gath and Mareshah falling. But then plague afflicted the Assyrian besiegers of Jerusalem, an event referred to by the 5th-Century BC Greek historian Herodotus, who wrote of a plague of mice, possibly a reference to plague-carrying rats. The Assyrians departed.

The punishment meted out to Judah was immense. The King of Ekron was returned and some territory divided between Sennacherib, Ashdod and Gaza. Sennacherib listed the tribute as containing 'Thirty talents of gold, eight hundred talents of silver, precious stones, antimony, large cuts of red stone, couches inlaid with ivory, chairs inlaid with ivory, elephant hides, ebony wood, boxwood and all kinds of valuable treasures, his (Hezekiah's) daughters, concubines, male and female musicians.' Sennacherib also boasted of driving 200,000 people from their homes while seizing their horses, mules, donkeys, camels and big and small cattle. Judah was devastated.

In 687 BC, Hezekiah died and his son Manasseh succeeded him, reigning for 45 years. Being a realist, Manasseh abandoned resistance and abased himself before Assyria. He paid tribute to Sennacherib, placed Assyrian god images in Jerusalem, and, as a loyal vassal, provided troops for Assyrian expansion into Egypt. Here, the 25th Dynasty was destroyed, with only Prince Neco of Sais of the Egyptian princes being spared.

Manasseh remained loyal to Assyria throughout his reign and Judah's religious establishment suffered a return to the earlier policies of King Ahaz. The reformers were repudiated, while pagan practices, both native and foreign, flourished. Astral deities were worshipped as if they were members of Yahweh's court and social injustice returned. Resentment against Manasseh's rule grew, the Book of Kings calling him the worst king ever to sit on David's throne. In foreign policy terms, Manasseh had no choice, nor did his son, Amon, who followed his father's policies until he was murdered in 640 BC. He was succeeded by his eight-year-old son, Josiah.

Externally, Judah saw Assyria's power weaken. Egypt broke away, establishing the 26th (Saite) Dynasty, Babylonia rebelled, while Medes, in the north, pressured the country. However, the Egyptian Pharaoh feared the growth of a new Mede-Babylonian power and gave help to a struggling Assyria to create a buffer. By 609 BC, though, Assyria was finished, leaving Palestine in a power vacuum once Assyrian forces had withdrawn.

When Josiah reached 20 years of age, Judah became free by default, the kingdom enjoying a burst of energy and glory unseen since Uzziah. Josiah pushed for sweeping religious reforms, supported by the prophet Zephaniah, who was outraged by the religious practices under Manasseh. The Temple was repaired and purified, while a consistent purge of foreign cults and practices took place. Assyrian cult images went, as did a variety of solar and astral cults of Mesopotamian origin. Native pagan rites, introduced by Manasseh, were ended and their personnel, such as eunuch priests and prostitutes of both sexes, executed. As Josiah took control of northern lands, reforms were extended into Samaria and the rival temple at Bethel was desecrated, destroyed and its

WEAPONS OF WAR
A detail from a bas-relief at the palace of Ashurbanipal II at Nineveh shows the potent and mobile Assyrian firepower of chariot, archers and spear throwers.

priesthood killed. According to 2 Chronicles 34:6, reforms were extended into northern Galilee. The execution of idolatrous priests was legitimized by a law in Deuteronomy that pronounced idolatry a capital crime. The attack on Assyrian cults can also be seen as eradicating national humiliation in an outbreak of patriotic energy.

The nationalist and religious outburst united the people, fuelling an expansion of Judah's borders. The south witnessed the frontiers being pushed into the Negev, but no one knows how far. There is evidence that Edom attacked Judah in the south as did Nebuchadnezzar. In the west, excavations at Mezad Hashavyahu show that Josiah created a corridor to the Mediterranean Josiah's kingdom developed northwards with the acquisition of Ephraim, Manasseh and Naphtali, suggesting that much of the old Assyrian provinces of Samaria and Megiddo were acquired. Megiddo was rebuilt as an administrative centre and included a large palace fortress.

Events were now to take a turn for the worse. When Nineveh fell to the Babylonians in 612 BC, the Book of Nahum exulted poetically in its destruction and the crushing of the hated Assyrians. 'Thy shepherds slumber, O king of Assyria: thy nobles shall dwell in the dust: thy people is scattered upon the mountains, and no man gathereth them. There is no healing of thy bruise; thy wound is grievous: all that hear the bruit of thee shall clap the hands over thee: for upon whom hath not thy wickedness passed continually?' (Nahum 3:18–19). As the Assyrians retreated towards northern Syria, the Babylonian forces massed to destroy them. This was when Pharaoh Neco II of Egypt chose to reassert Egyptian power in Asia by moving swiftly by the Way of the Sea to help the Assyrians. Neco told Josiah that he wanted to traverse Judah via Megiddo, Galilee, and the ruins of Hazor. Josiah attempted to stop him at Megiddo, possibly acting as an ally of the Babylonians. The Battle of Megiddo saw Josiah wounded, and he was taken to Jerusalem to die. Judah was defeated and Megiddo destroyed. Josiah might have thought that Egypt had designs on the old Assyrian provinces of Samaria and Megiddo, as events proved. Judah experienced much grief at the death of their 39-year-old king, the man who had restored religious and political unity. The prophet Jeremiah's lamentations are evidence of the national emotion. Jehoahaz acceded to the throne of his father in 609 BC.

Neco II's campaign failed, but he secured parts of Syria and the lands south to Egypt. He deposed Jehoahaz, placing his brother, Jehoiakim, on the throne while making Judah a vassal and demanding so heavy a tribute that a head tax was levied on all free citizens to pay for it.

In 605 BC, Nebuchadnezzar attacked, defeating the Egyptian forces at Carchemish, pursuing them south where they were beaten again at Hamath. Southern Syria and Palestine lay wide open. The following year, the Babylonian advance continued into Philistia, where Ashkelon was destroyed. Archaeologists have found a letter written by the King of Ashkelon to the Pharaoh, requesting help. Jehoiakim changed sides, becoming a Babylonian vassal and saving Judah from attack. In late 601 BC, Nebuchadnezzar fought a battle near the Egyptian border. Both sides suffered a mauling, so much so that the Babylonians retreated home to re-organize their army.

Jehoiakim chose this moment to rebel: 'In his days Nebuchadnezzar king of Babylon came up, and Jehoiakim became his servant three years: then he turned and rebelled against him' (2 Kings 24:1). The Babylonian response was to send some of their own units and guerrilla bands of Arameans, Moabites and Ammonites to raid Judah and keep it off balance. Under Jehoiakim, the religious reforms fell apart. Morality sank and high-level corruption increased. The general lack of respect for people was witnessed in the enlargement, by forced labour, of the royal palace at Ramat Rahel. Jeremiah, the prophet, condemned the situation of Judah and railed against the red painted stones used at this palace. He even scorned the king, holding Judah in contempt. In 598 BC, as the Babylonians marched, Jehoiakim died, possibly assassinated. The words of Jeremiah had certainly condemned him. 'Therefore thus sayeth the Lord concerning Jehoiakim the son of Josiah king of Judah; they shall not lament for him, saying, Ah my brother! Or, Ah sister! They shall not lament for him, saying, Ah lord! Or, Ah his glory! He shall be buried with the burial of an ass, drawn and cast forth beyond the gates of Jerusalem' (Jeremiah 22:18–19).

Jehoiachin, the 18-year-old son of Jehoiakim, became king, and within three months Jerusalem surrendered. No further elements of the tale have been found in archaeology or text. However, it seems that the cities of Lachish and Debir were stormed at the time. Leaders of the anti-Babylon party, leading citizens, the king, the Queen Mother and enormous quantities of loot were sent to Babylon. Jehoiachin's uncle, Mattaniah, was installed as king, taking the name of Zedekiah, while portions of the Shephelah and Negev were kept by Nebuchadnezzar.

Zedekiah was a weakling who was manipulated by his nobles. When, in 595–594 BC, there was a rebellion in Babylonia, Jerusalem became a hotbed of conspiracy, involving Edom, Moab, Ammon, Tyre and Sidon. False prophets incited the people, and some of them were executed. In 589 BC, Judah rebelled, accompanied by Tyre and Ammon, while Edom supported Babylon. Nebuchadnezzar surrounded Jerusalem and set about torching Gibeah, Arad, Eglon and En-gedi. Archaeological digs at Lachish, Beth-shemesh, Debir, Beth-zur and Ramat Rahel demonstrate the thorough level of destruction. Ruins at Lachish attest the savagery of the Babylonian assault. Fires against the walls were so intense that mortar between the wall's stones melted and ran down the entrance road in streams, where it solidified and remains to this day. Only Jerusalem survived, while an Egyptian relief force was swiftly turned back near Gaza.

The siege of Jerusalem lasted into 587 BC, its horrors depicted in Jeremiah's Lamentations. Eventually, food ran out, the Babylonians breached the walls, and the fleeing Zedekiah was captured near Jericho and taken to the Babylonian king at Riblah. Some of the leading priests, military and civil officers and leading citizens were executed. Zedekiah's sons were killed before his eyes; he was then blinded and sent to Babylon. Nebuzaradan, commander of Nebuchadnezzar's guard, rounded up thousands for deportation to Babylon, and torched Jerusalem, leaving just some of the poorest people to look after the vines and plough the land.

Judah was organized into the provincial system of Babylon under the governorship of Gedaliah, a nobleman of Judah, whose father, Ahikim, had previously saved Jeremiah's life and whose grandfather, Shaphan, had been Josiah's secretary. The administrative centre was at Mizpah (probably Tel en-Nasbeh). Gedaliah was murdered, and his friends fled to Egypt with Jeremiah. The province of Judah faced a third deportation in 582 BC, probably then being incorporated into Samaria. Judah ceased to exist.

THE PROPHET LAMENTS THE DESTRUCTION OF JERUSALEM

In a painting by the Dutch master Rembrandt (1606–1669), Jeremiah looks inconsolable in the aftermath of the fall of Jerusalem at the hands of the Babylonians. His written thoughts became the Book of Lamentations.

Exile to Babylonia

The region of Babylonia lay near the south-eastern end of Mesopotamia and took its name from the great city of Babylon, on the River Euphrates. Jews were held captive here for decades.

The Babylonians figure prominently in the Old Testament and 'Babylon' became an instantly recognizable symbol of any great oppressive power for both Jews and Christians. However, their actual period of domination after they had defeated the Assyrians lasted only around 80 years, until they were overthrown by the Persians in 539 BC.

The empire of the Old Babylonian period had collapsed under pressure from Kassite tribes to the north-east in the middle of the 2nd Millennium BC. This ended a period of power and splendour, of which the law code of Hammurabi from the 18th Century BC is a fine example. The Babylonians were rebellious subjects of the Assyrians for five centuries, repeatedly brought to heel and at one time ruled directly by Assyrian kings. As with most of the nations of the Near and Middle East, they were a mixture of peoples. During the main part of the Assyrian ascendancy, the dominant Babylonian group were Aramaean nomads from the Syrian Desert who invaded Babylonia during the early part of the 1st Millennium BC and merged with the Chaldeans of southern Babylonia. One of these Aramaen Chaldean chiefs seized power in 721 BC and opposed Sargon II of Assyria. That attempt at Babylonian independence failed, but another Aramaean descendant, Nabopolassar, successfully rebelled in 626 BC and began the war that was to end some 20 years later with the Babylonians in control of the Assyrian Empire.

The destruction of Assyria was assisted by incursions of wild, disorganized mounted tribesmen through the eastern mountains, who fanned out across Mesopotamia and the Near East as far as the Egyptian frontier. These hordes were part of the Scythian migration, which has left its mark on Hebrew and Christian writings as the armies of Gog and Magog (Ezekiel 38–39; Revelation 20:8). Their tombs have yielded delightful gold, silver and bronze figures of wild animals and mounted horsemen. They settled nowhere, but their threat, combined with the Babylonian rebellion, forced the Assyrians to withdraw their troops from Palestine. This gave the Hebrews one of their brief periods of freedom from foreign control, which lasted from 625 to 609 BC, before first the Egyptians and then the Babylonians once more took over Palestine.

The Babylonians, under King Nabopolassar, destroyed the Assyrian capital Nineveh in 612 BC. His successor, Nebuchadnezzar II (605–561 BC), defeated the Egyptian King Necho II (610–595 BC) of the 26th Dynasty, far up the River Euphrates at Carchemish, now known as Cerabulus, on the border of modern-day Syria and Turkey. At first the Babylonians did little to interfere with the only remaining Hebrew kingdom, Judah, and allowed King Jehoiakim (609–598 BC) to continue to rule the country from its capital, Jerusalem. However, the Hebrews intrigued to get the Egyptians to free them from Babylonian rule, but this failed and in 598 BC the Babylonians captured Jerusalem after a siege that had lasted for three months.

The king and his leading officials were deported to Babylon where they were allowed to live in some comfort

CENTRAL BABYLON *(right)*
A reconstruction shows the core of Nebuchadnezzar's great city, including ziggurat, palace, temple and the Ishtar Gate, with the River Euphrates flowing through the middle.

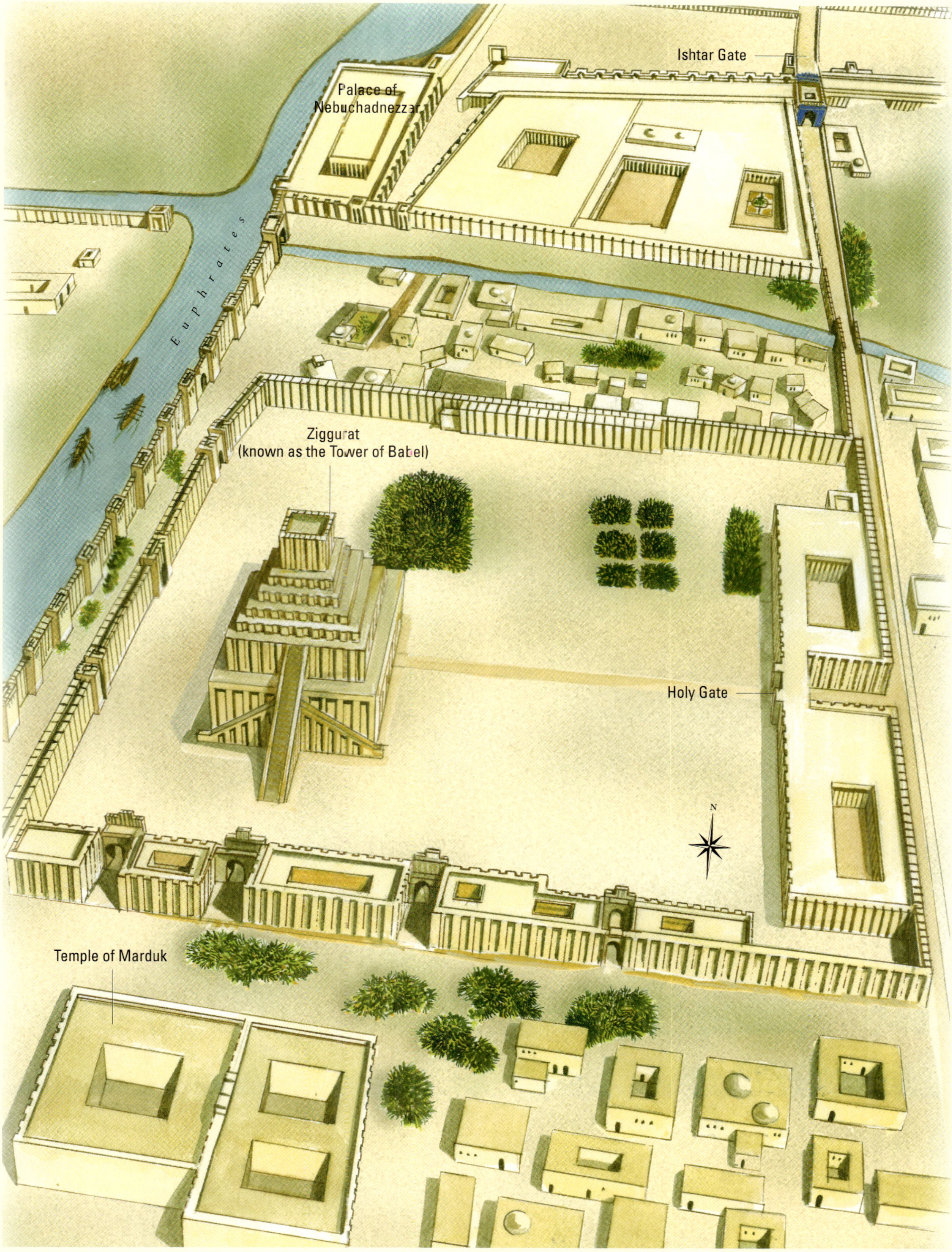
Ishtar Gate
Palace of Nebuchadnezzar
Euphrates
Ziggurat (known as the Tower of Babel)
Holy Gate
N
Temple of Marduk

THE PRIZES OF BABYLON

After vanquishing the Assyrians in Mesopotamia, the Babylonians turned their attention to the Fertile Crescent. At the same time, King Josiah was introducing his religious reforms to Judah, destroying the shrines of foreign religions and giving new life to the old Hebrew laws of the Covenant. Under Nebuchadnezzar II, the Babylonian invaders were a much stronger and more unified force. They captured important towns, including Jerusalem, which they took in 598 BC *and then destroyed almost ten years later.*

Lake Van
KINGDOM OF URARTU
Caspian Sea
Amida
Haran
T. Brak
Chagar Borsippa Bazar
Tigris
Nineveh
Geoytepe
MANNEA
Elburz Mountains
Persian Plateau
Tuttul
Emar
Mesopotamia
Karana
Calah
Terqa
Asshur
Nuzi
MEDIA
Mari
Euphrates
Samarra
Eshnunna
Zagros Mountains
Agade
Jemdet Nasr
Babylon
Kish
Nippur
Susa
Shuruppak
Lagash
Uruk (Erech)
Babylonia
Ur
ELAM
approximate ancient coastline
Durnah
Persian Gulf
N
Arabian Desert
100 km
100 miles
40°
45°
50°
35°
30°

at Babylonian state expense, and another descendant of King David, Zedekiah (597–587 BC), was placed on the throne of Judah. The intrigues with Egypt continued, and in 589 BC the Babylonians again attacked Jerusalem. This time they besieged it for more than two years. There was a brief respite when an Egyptian army tried to relieve the city, but the Babylonians finally destroyed it in 587 BC. The king and people were deported to Babylonia, where the Hebrew monarchy ended. The territory was lost to Hebrew control from the 48 years of the exile until the Babylonians, in their turn, were overthrown by the Persians in 539 BC.

The city of Babylon was capital of the ancient land of Babylonia in southern Mesopotamia. It was situated on the River Euphrates, 80 km (50 miles) south of Baghdad, just north of what is now the modern Iraqi town of Al-Hillah. The name Babylon is a Greek form of the Hebrew name Babel, itself derived from a Sumerian name meaning 'Gate of God'. Genesis 10:10 describes the founding of the city of Babel by Nimrod, a descendant of Ham, son of Noah. Genesis 11:1–9 describes the building of the city and its famous tower, 'whose top may reach unto heaven', and how God punished the people's arrogance by creating a confusion of different languages.

Although Babel and Babylon are probably one and the same, there is not sufficient written or archaeological evidence to establish that Babel was on the same site as Babylon. Though many have attempted to locate the ruins of the original Tower of Babel, no one has succeeded. It is now thought that the legend of the tower refers to a ziggurat, a tower-like temple, built in the 18th Century BC.

Although there is some evidence of occupation from prehistoric times, Babylon was not established as a city until the 23rd Century BC. It was at first a provincial capital ruled by the kings of the city of Ur, but in the late 19th Century BC the Amorite King Sumuabum established a kingdom there. Babylon was enlarged and improved by his successors, particularly Hammurabi, sometimes called Hammurapi (1792–1750 BC), who enlarged his territory to include many of the neighbouring cities, creating a kingdom of Babylonia that stretched over southern Mesopotamia and into Assyria, with Babylon as its capital. It was under his rule that the first ziggurat, the Tower of Babel, was built. Hammurabi is best known for his Code of Laws – not so much a code as a set of legal judgements on 282 different cases that was inscribed on a stone stela, or slab, placed in the temple of the god Marduk. Large fragments of this stela were discovered in 1902 by the French archaeologist Jean-Vincent Scheil in Susa and it now stands in the Louvre in Paris. The judgements cover economic and family law as well as criminal cases, and are in some ways similar to the Hebrew Mosaic Law.

BIG CAT SYMBOL

Lions were so numerous in Mesopotamia that lion hunts were the main sport of kings. They were a favourite feature of decoration in Babylon, as symbols of royal power and courage, particularly to flank processional routes.

Under the Amorite dynasty, Babylon flourished. However, it fell to the Hittites in 1595 BC and then came under the control of the Kassites, who established a dynasty that dominated the region for over 400 years, although often under foreign attack, particularly from the Assyrians and the Elamites. In 1158 BC Babylon was sacked by the Elamites, but soon Elam was conquered by Nebuchadnezzar I, who established a new dynasty in Babylon. This was a time of cultural and literary development when the ancient Babylonian *Epic of Gilgamesh* was rewritten in its finest version.

For several centuries Babylon was a focus of conflict between Assyrian forces and Aramean and Chaldean tribespeople. Assyrian kings dominated from the 9th to the late 7th Centuries BC and it is with reference to that period that the city is first unequivocally mentioned in the Bible. Hezekiah, King of Judah (715–687 BC), was visited by emissaries from the King of Babylon as he lay ill. When he admitted to the prophet Isaiah that he had let these men see the full extent of his wealth, Isaiah prophesied that all the royal treasures would, one day, be carried off to Babylon (2 Kings 20:12–18). In 689 BC, after a period of nationalist uprisings and unrest in Babylon, the Assyrian King Sennacherib ordered that the city be destroyed. His son Esarhaddon rebuilt it, but the city was badly damaged by fire in 648 BC during a war between the Assyrian King Ashurbanipal and his brother, who ruled over Babylon.

The decline of the Assyrian Empire enabled a Chaldean leader, Nabopolassar, to take control of Babylon in 626 BC. He founded a dynasty that began to restore

METROPOLIS OF THE ANCIENT WORLD

At the time it was built, Babylon was the biggest city in the world, covering 10 square kilometres (4 miles²). It was laid out on a grid pattern, with the River Euphrates running almost through the centre, which was enclosed by a series of canals that also irrigated the surrounding field system.

the damaged city. Under his successor, Nebuchadnezzar II (the Nebuchadnezzar of the Bible), who ruled from 605 to 561 BC, Babylon became a great imperial power and the city was splendidly rebuilt, fortified and extended so that it became the largest city the world had ever seen. The River Euphrates flowed through the middle of the city, though it has since changed its course westwards.

Nebuchadnezzar built or restored palaces and temples, the Processional Way, the Ishtar Gate and the ziggurat that was known as the Temple of Babel. If the famous Hanging Gardens, one of the Seven Wonders of the World, ever existed, they were built at this time, possibly a series of terraces covered in trees and plants. Nebuchadnezzar's army conquered Jerusalem, destroyed and plundered the Temple and took the people of Judah back to Babylon as captives (2 Kings 25:1–21). The overweening pride and arrogance of King Nebuchadnezzar is described in the first four chapters of the Book of Daniel.

'... thou shalt take up this proverb against the king of Babylon and say, How hath the oppressor ceased! the golden city ceased!'

Isaiah 14:4

The despair of the Jewish exiles in Babylon and the prediction of the city's fall are conveyed in several Bible passages, particularly Psalm 137 ('By the rivers of Babylon, there we sat down, yea we wept, when we remembered Zion'); Isaiah 13–14, 21 ('Babylon is fallen, is fallen', 21:9); and Jeremiah 50–51 ('How is Babylon became a desolation among the nations', 50:23). Daniel 5 describes the death of Nebuchadnezzar's son and successor, Belshazzar, when the city was sacked by the Persians under Cyrus in 539 BC. Darius the Mede (Daniel 5:31–6:1–28), the 'king' responsible for putting Daniel in the lion's den, was possibly a governor appointed by Cyrus.

Babylon remained under Persian rule for 200 years, diminished in importance but still retaining some of its splendour, until the city was destroyed by Xerxes I when he suppressed a rebellion in 482 BC. In 331 BC, Alexander the Great conquered Babylon. He had ambitions to rebuild the city and make it his capital, but he died there in 323 BC, before he had time to implement his plans. A new city of Seleucia was built on the Tigris and much of Babylon's population moved there in 275 BC. After this, Babylon rapidly declined, eventually falling into ruins.

The New Testament mentions Babylon only in reference to the exile of the Jews (Matthew 1:17; Acts 7:43) or as a symbol for Rome, which had taken over the role as the great but corrupt oppressor of the people of Israel (Revelation 17:5).

Travellers and explorers have been drawn to Babylon for centuries, but serious archaeological research did not start until the mid-19th Century. Almost all that has been discovered on the site relates to the great city built by Nebuchadnezzar II. The change in the course of the Euphrates and a rise in the water-table, combined with the

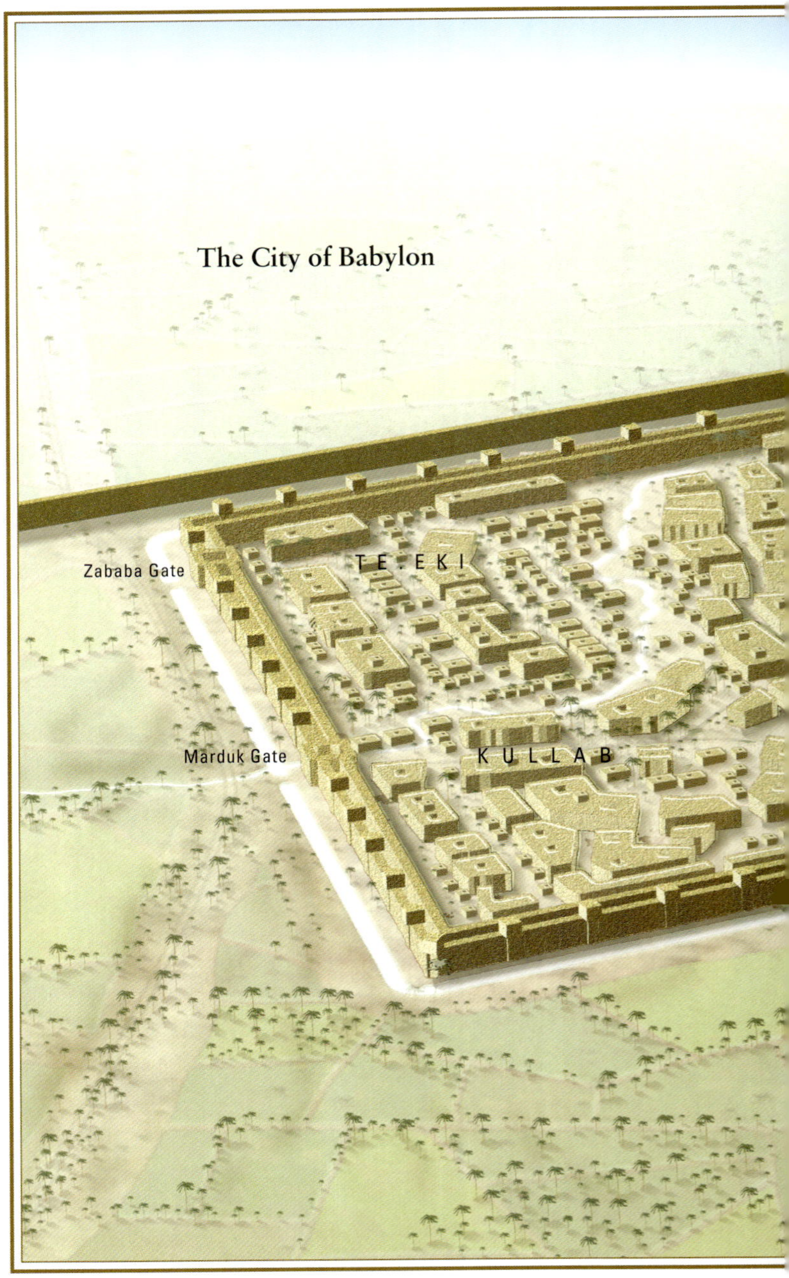

fact that Nebuchadnezzar rebuilt the city so thoroughly, means that little from before his time has been found.

Many inscriptions in cuneiform writing, then in wide use in Mesopotamia, have been found that describe the city. There is also an account by the Greek historian Herodotus, who visited Babylon in about 460 BC. This evidence makes it possible to attempt a reconstruction of Babylon in its prime. There was a vast double wall on both sides of the Euphrates with eight gates, at least one of which, the Ishtar Gate, was faced with glazed bricks depicting bulls and dragons. From the Ishtar Gate ran the Processional Way – a wide paved road flanked by walls decorated with glazed and gilded bricks showing lions and dragons – which led to the Temple of Marduk and the adjacent Temple of Babel ziggurat, 91 metres (300 ft) high. There were four other temples, and west of the Ishtar Gate stood two palace complexes. The German archaeologist, Robert Koldewey, who excavated the site from 1899 to 1917, found vaults in one of the palaces that he identified as the foundations of the Hanging Gardens.

AT THE HEIGHT OF POWER
The city of Babylon, seen from the north, as it may have looked at the time of Hammurabi. The Processional Way led from the Ishtar Gate to the central area where the zigurrat and the Temple of Marduk stood.

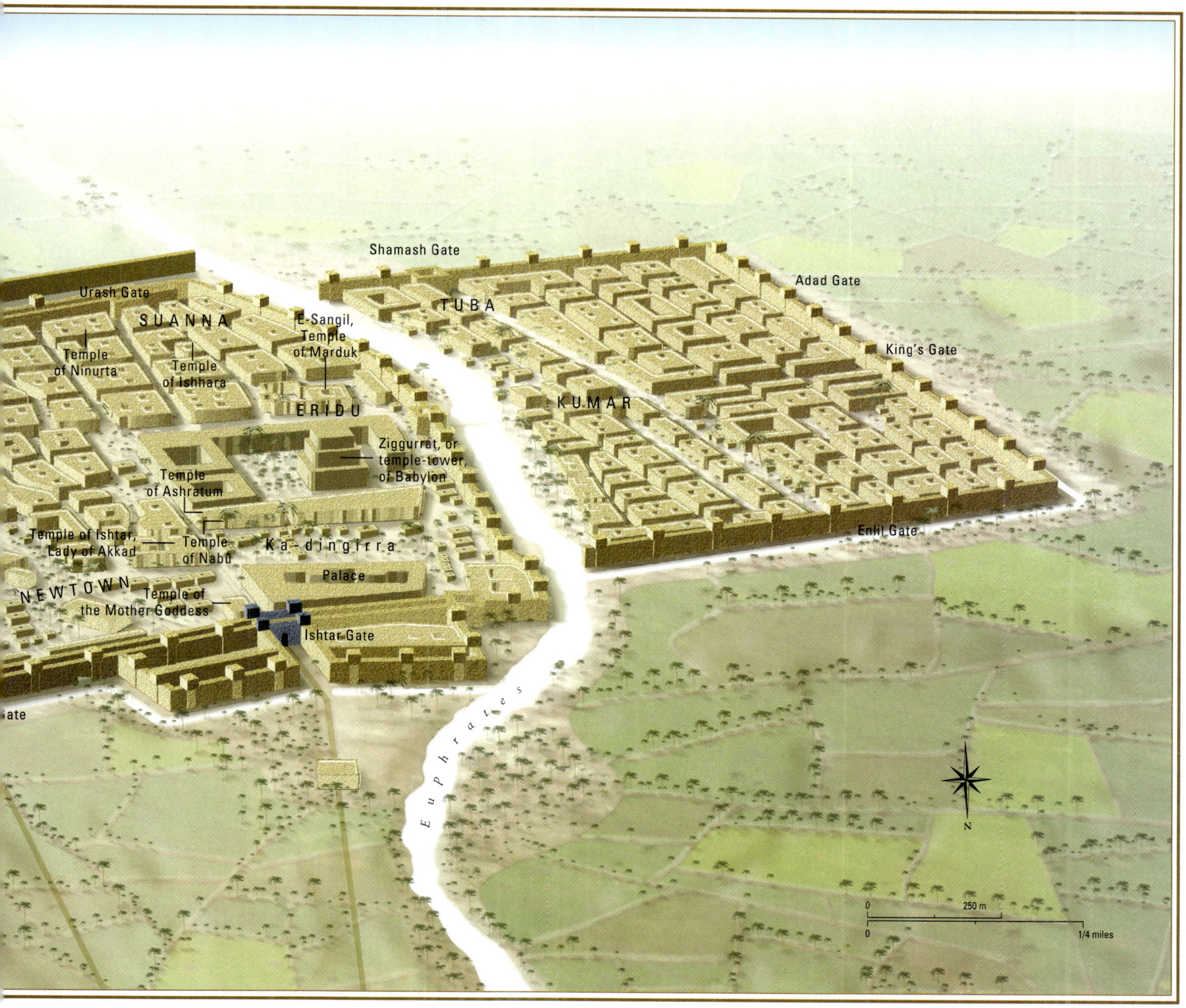

THE RISE OF PERSIA

After a bloodless victory over the Babylonians in 539 BC, the Persian king, Cyrus, went on to build a strong, tolerant empire, which extended as far south as Egypt. The Persians employed unusual military tactics and remained the dominant power in the Near and Middle East for more than 200 years.

In 539 BC, King Cyrus II of Persia (555–529 BC) received the surrender of Babylon without having to fight. This was the climax of the campaign in which the Persian armies had swept across the eastern frontiers of the Babylonian Empire from the Indian Ocean to the Black Sea, and then struck southwards into the heart of Mesopotamia. Tension between King Nabonidus of Babylon (556–539 BC) and the Babylonian priests of the chief god, Marduk, lay behind Cyrus's bloodless victory. Nabonidus had tried to replace the worship of Marduk with the worship of the moon god, Sin, and the Babylonian priests had moved against him.

It was wise of the priests of Babylon to welcome the Persian victor, for Persian rule proved to be remarkably sympathetic and tolerant. Subject races of the Persian Empire had to give military and other kinds of service, but they were treated as equals by the Persian troops and reached high rank in both the army and the civil service. The exiled Hebrews in Babylonia were only one of many exiled national groups that received compassionate treatment at the hands of Cyrus. Such peoples were offered the opportunity of returning to their native lands together with the treasures looted from them by the Babylonians, and were provided with support from the Persian treasury to rebuild their cities and temples. There was certainly taxation and tribute exacted from all parts of the empire, but it was used to benefit the provinces. Although King Cyrus remained faithful to his own gods, it is not surprising that the Hebrews saw the hand of their own God in his victories (Isaiah 44–45).

The army was the key to Cyrus's rise to greatness. The tactics that brought this success depended on fighting at a distance and overwhelming the enemy with a hail of arrows while cavalry harassed the ranks. It was mobile warfare at a time when armies usually confronted each other in ranks, and the Persian bowmen fought with little personal protection so that they were free to move swiftly and fire repeatedly. Hand-to-hand fighting was avoided at all costs. When the Greeks did at last manage to make a Persian army stand and fight at close quarters at Marathon in 490 BC, the Persians were overwhelmed. The Athenians trapped the Persians against their ships in a narrow position, giving them no chance to manoeuvre, and they were slaughtered in close fighting with the hoplites – the Greek infantry.

From his capital, Ecbatana, King Cyrus laid the foundations of an empire that was to last for more than 200 years, until it fell to Alexander the Great in 331 BC. Cyrus was succeeded by Cambyses II (529–522 BC), who extended Persian rule into Egypt. His successor, Darius I (522–486 BC), moved the capital to Persepolis after a year of disorder that followed the succession. By then, the Persian Empire stretched from the north-west of the Indus

SOLDIERS OF THE EMPIRE
Persian official art, like this frieze from the palace of the kings at Persepolis, avoided the Assyrian celebration of barbarity. The Persian Empire achieved a stability that united the various states of the Middle East, ruling the vast lands by using local elites and the common language of Aramaic.

Valley to Asia Minor, and included all of Mesopotamia, Palestine and also Egypt, where the Persian emperors constituted the 27th Dynasty. Control of Egypt was never easy, however, particularly after the Persian defeat by the Greeks at Marathon in 490 BC, and the Persians lost control of Egypt for 60 years during the 28th, 29th and 30th Dynasties (400–343 BC) only to regain it for a mere ten years before Alexander took over.

The Persian Empire was organized in provinces controlled by provincial governors, called satraps, who were relatively independent of the central government, despite a system of separate military commands and a courier system unsurpassed in the ancient world until the Romans. Aramaic – a Semitic language – was adopted as the official language of the Persian Empire and became the common tongue.

The main religion of Persia at the height of its power was Zoroastrianism, which was a monotheistic faith, introduced by the prophet Zoroaster (c 628–551 BC). Its god was Ahura Mazda, creator and lawgiver. In this religion, the world was viewed as a battleground between equal forces of good and evil.

'That confirmeth the word of his servant and performeth the counsel of his messengers; that saith to Jerusalem, Thou shalt be inhabited; and to the cities of Judah, Ye shall be built and I will raise up the decayed places thereof: That saith to the deep, Be dry, and I will dry up thy rivers: That saith of Cyrus, He is my shepherd and shall perform all my pleasure: even saying to Jerusalem, Thou shalt be built; and to the temple, Thy foundation shall be laid. Thus saith the Lord to his anointed, to Cyrus, whose right hand I have holden, to subdue nations before him; and I will loose the loins of kings, to open before him the two leaved gates; and the gates shall not be shut.'

Isaiah 44:26–28; 45:1

THE ALL-CONQUERING PERSIANS

King Cyrus II extended the frontiers of the Persian Empire westwards through Mesopotamia and Asia Minor during the 6th Century BC, *an expansion given greater impetus still and consolidated by his successors, Cambyses II and Darius I. The Persians were defeated decisively by the Greeks at Marathon in 490* BC, *although their empire lasted for two centuries.*

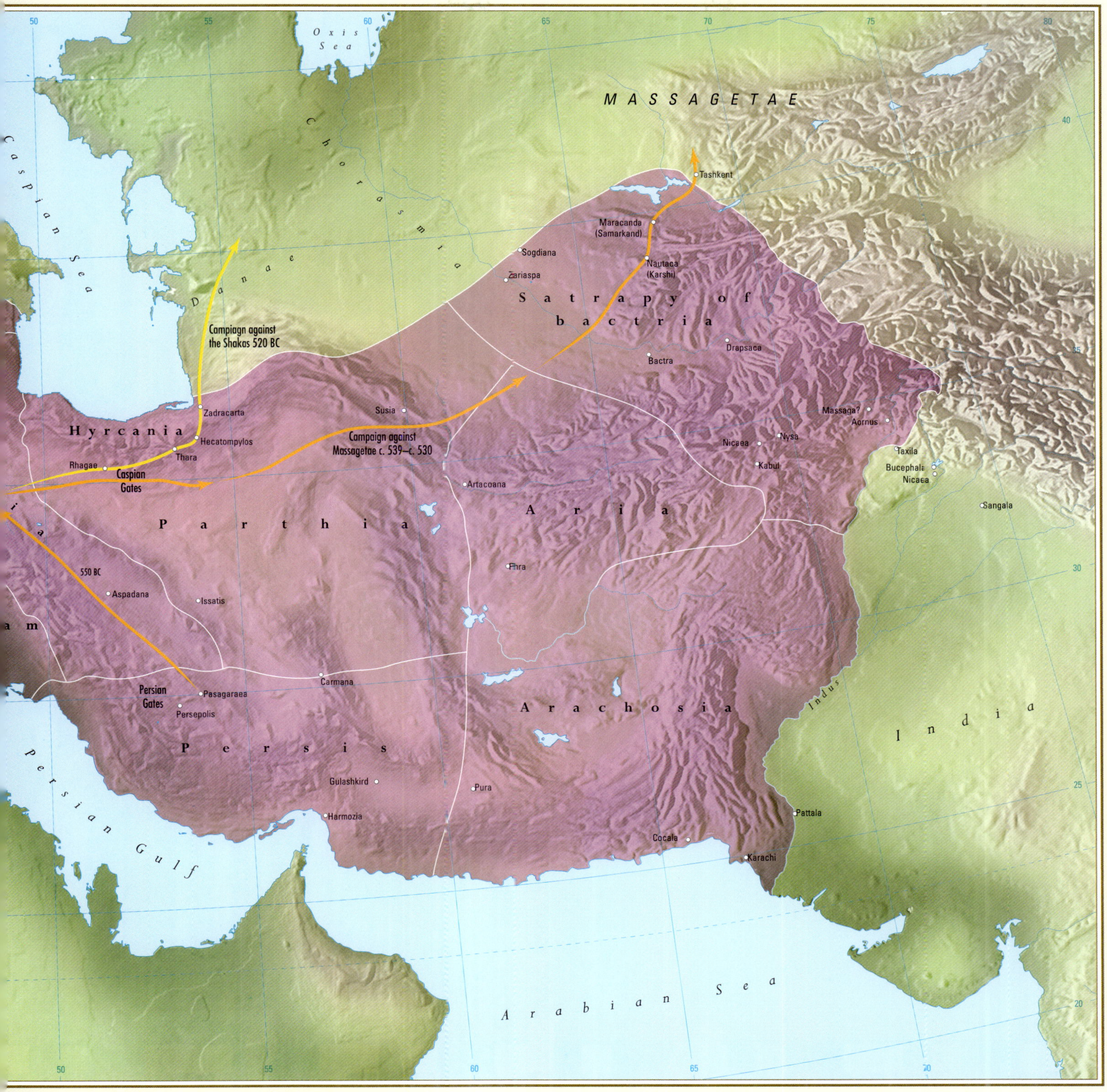
Oxis Sea
MASSAGETAE
Caspian Sea
Chorasmia
Danae
Tashkent
Maracanda (Samarkand)
Nautaca (Karshi)
Sogdiana
Zariaspa
Satrapy of bactria
Campaign against the Shakas 520 BC
Drapsaca
Bactra
Zadracarta
Susia
Hyrcania
Hecatompylos
Campaign against Massagetae c. 539–c. 530
Thara
Rhagae
Caspian Gates
Massaga?
Aornus
Nicaea
Nysa
Kabul
Taxila
Bucephala
Nicaea
Artacoana
Sangala
Parthia
Aria
550 BC
Phra
Aspadana
Issatis
Carmana
Persian Gates
Pasagaraea
Persepolis
Arachosia
Indus
India
Persis
Gulashkird
Pura
Harmozia
Pattala
Cocala
Karachi
Persian Gulf
Arabian Sea

Return from Exile and Resettlement

By the 6th Century BC, the Middle East was entering a new stage of upheaval. In the clash between decaying and new empires, the dream of the exiled survivors of Judah to return to Jerusalem was to be fulfilled.

Nabonidus, the final King of Babylon, fell foul of his priests by introducing new religious practices. This caused him to move his royal residence to Tema, an oasis to the south in the Arabian Desert, while Belshazzar, his son, deputized for him.

Persia, a vassal state of the Median Empire to the east of Babylon, rebelled under the leadership of Cyrus II in 562 BC, capturing Ectabana, the capital, and acquiring the Median Empire in one stroke. Neighbouring states thought that Cyrus would now attack Babylon, considering its proximity to Persia. But Cyrus adopted an indirect approach. Feeling that Babylonia's strength was all bluff with no substance, he pursued a different course. He looked towards Asia Minor, which had been politically weak since the fall of the Hittite Empire. However, by the 6th Century BC, the powerful state of Lydia, ruled by Croesus, had been created. Croesus was legendary for his wealth, much of it based on his conquest of Ionia. Croesus formed an alliance with Nabonidus, while Egypt and Sparta promised to send troops. Invading Cappadocia, he fought an inconclusive battle at Pteria and retreated to build his alliance. Cyrus crossed the Halys River (546 BC), surprised Croesus and stormed the Lydian capital at Sardis. This western thrust meant an ultimate confrontation between western and eastern civilizations during the time of Alexander the Great. Cyrus then turned east, subduing the regions now known as Pakistan and Afghanistan. With his frontiers secure, Cyrus turned on Babylonia and in a decisive battle at Opis (539 BC) on the Tigris River, broke the Babylonian army. Babylon fell without opposition, but was not sacked. Cyrus ordered that people and their property be respected. When Cyrus reached the city, he was welcomed and acclaimed as the deliverer from the oppression of the unpopular Nabonidus.

Cyrus was a tolerant and enlightened king who eschewed the brutality of Assyria and Babylon with their deportation of captured populations. Cyrus also tolerated the beliefs, practices and institutions of all the subject peoples under his rule, thereby unifying these peoples into a great and powerful empire. The inscribed clay Cyrus Cylinder shows that the king gave exiled peoples the chance of returning to countries of their birth. This policy did not mean that nations could regain their independence. Cyrus exerted firmer control over his territories compared with the Assyrians and Babylonians, his Empire being divided into 20 satrapies, or regions, each of which comprised a number of provinces.

Jewish exiles in Persia received an edict (538 BC) allowing them to return to Judah. An Aramaic text of one of Cyrus' decrees states the following:

PROUD SYMBOL OF A PEOPLE

The Star of David, here shown carved as part of the decoration of the synagogue at Capernaum, became a symbol of the new Jewish nation after the exile in Babylon. By that time the Hebrew kings had been replaced by the rule of the priests of the Temple in Jerusalem, but King David remained the ideal Jewish leader. He had given his people victory over their enemies and made Jerusalem the central symbol of Hebrew solidarity. The interlocking star became an expression of hope in God, who would restore the glories of King David's time and give the Jews as great a leader.

'In the first year of Cyrus the king the same Cyrus the king made a decree concerning the house of God at Jerusalem, Let the house be builded, the place where they offered sacrifices and let the foundations thereof be strongly laid; the height thereof threescore cubits, and the breadth thereof threescore cubits; with three rows of great stones, and a row of new timber: and let the expenses be given out of the king's house: and also let the golden and silver vessels of the house of God, which Nebuchadnezzar took forth out of the temple which is at Jerusalem, and brought unto Babylon, be restored, and brought again unto the temple which is at Jerusalem, every one to his place, and place them in the house of God.'
Ezra 6: 3–5

An enthusiastic group of exiles, led by Sheshbazzar, travelled to Judah, from the Nippur region in Babylonia. On arrival in Palestine, they found Judah to be an impoverished, backward place with a poor economy. Jerusalem lay in ruins, witness to the savagery of the Babylonian attack some 50 years before. On the hilltops lived a few poor Jews left behind at the time of the exile; now, the owners of the land, they resented the incomers, as did the Edomites, forced from their lands to make room for Arab tribes who were now living in some districts. The Samaritans claimed authority over Jerusalem, spurning the exiles, especially since the returning exiles, considering the Samaritans to be religiously unclean, would not let them help rebuild the city. Crop failure led to food shortages, which left the returned exiles weak and unable to reconstruct the city.

New energy arrived with a second wave of Babylonian Jews coming to Jerusalem led by Zerubbabel, nephew to Sheshbazzar, and Jeshua, who eventually became High Priest. The Jews settled in an area of the Judaean hill country measuring about 64 km (40 miles) east to west and 48 km (30 miles) north to south. In the

THE WORDS OF THE PROPHET

Ezra had been commanded by King Artaxerxes I of Persia to restore Jewish law. His most important contribution was the codification of the first four books of the Bible. These, together with Deuteronomy, make up the Jewish Torah. In this engraving, by the French artist Gustave Doré from a 19th-Century Bible, Ezra reads from the law to a group of Israelite men and women gathered in a Jerusalem street.

east, they reached into the Jordan valley around Jericho, while in the west they encroached on to the coastal plain at Lod and Ono. In the north, they pushed beyond Bethel and in the south they occupied the strategic site of Beth-zur, but were cut off from Hebron, which was occupied by Edomites. Insecurity faced the population until Jerusalem could be refortified. Zerubbabel became the civil governor, and all were inspired by the arrival of two prophets, Haggai and Zechariah.

Opposition to the Jews emanated from Tattenai, the Governor of Abarnahara – of which Judah (Yehud) was part – who wanted to know who authorized the building work. Cyrus' decree was produced and Tattenai was told to allow building to continue with finance from the royal revenues. In 515 BC, the Temple was reconsecrated; it was no longer the focus of a nation, but the centre of a religious community. The rebuilding had unified the people, but once it was finished, unity collapsed. Religious life deteriorated, mixed marriages were contracted and trade tended to foster assimilation. Existence in the hills was hazardous and agricultural conditions were harsh. The poor condition of the Jews of Yehud was heard of in Susa by Nehemiah, cupbearer to the King of Persia. He requested that he be allowed to travel to Jerusalem and rebuild its fortifications. His wish was granted and he became governor of the province.

The Jewish community in Yehud was now reorganized. Its status was clarified, its religious and physical identity preserved and its laws re-established. Nehemiah, along with a priest called Ezra, implemented these achievements. The former won the political status and administrative reforms for the Jewish community, while the latter reaffirmed the purity of its spiritual life.

Yehud's importance to the Persian kings lay in its position straddling lines of communication to Egypt where chronic unrest threatened the military road and supply bases. A quiescent Palestine would stop unrest spreading, hence the need to end the Samaritans'

Jerusalem as Rebuilt by Nehemiah

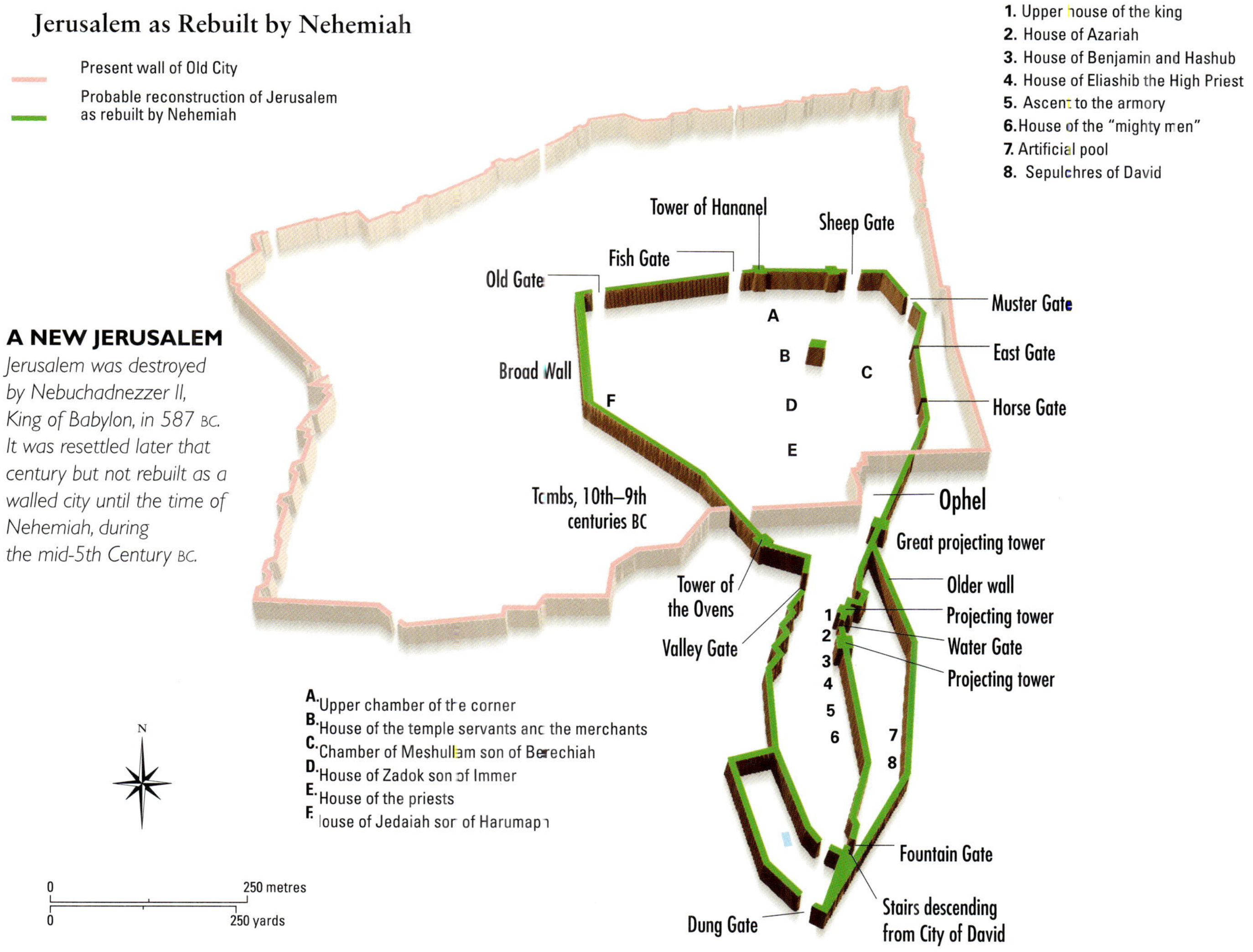

A NEW JERUSALEM
Jerusalem was destroyed by Nebuchadnezzer II, King of Babylon, in 587 BC. It was resettled later that century but not rebuilt as a walled city until the time of Nehemiah, during the mid-5th Century BC.

high-handed treatment of Jews. Therefore, Nehemiah was loyal to his king's interests as well as his co-religionists.

The political environment in Palestine was changing in other ways, particularly in the expansion of international trade, notably with Greece. Phoenicia held the coast from Acco to Gaza, and its ports hosted colonies of Greek merchants. Gaza, now a royal Persian fortress, was becoming a trade outlet for Arabs who had shifted from north Arabia into Edom, the Negev and southern Syria to establish themselves as an important commercial people – the Nabataeans. Dispossessed Edomites were pushed into Yehud, settling in the desert south of Beersheba and Hebron, and later became known as Idumaeans. The Transjordan was ruled by Tobiah, Governor of Ammon, with family connections to the High Priest in Jerusalem, while Samaria, under Governor Sanballat, resented the fact that Yehud had been shorn from the province of Samaria and given to Nehemiah when he arrived. When Nehemiah entered Yehud, he found a demoralized and divided Jewish people with competing interests, all thinking they were the true heirs of Judaism.

On inspecting the city walls, Nehemiah decided that work must commence immediately on rebuilding them. Labour was levied from all Yehud, and the wall was divided into sections with a group responsible for each. Obstacles to the build came from Tobiah, Sanballat, Ashdod and Geshem, the Arabs ruling the desert peoples. The first two men even used a fifth column of their friends and relations in Jerusalem to slow down the build. Eventually, Arabs, Ammonites and Asdodites terrorized Jewish villages, and the historian, Josephus, claims many Jews were killed. Nehemiah divided his building crews into two – one group armed with spears, shields, bows and mail coats, who stood to arms in shifts, while the other group worked with swords at their waists. Jews from the countryside were also drawn into Jerusalem, both for their own safety and to secure the city. The walls went up in 52 days, but the works of wall reinforcement, and finishing the battlement, gates and retaining walls required more than another two years. Nehemiah's task was achieved. After 12 years, he returned to Susa but was reappointed as governor of Yehud.

Nehemiah's second term of office was characterized by uncoordinated religious reforms, finding adequate funds for the Temple and its priests, enforcing Sabbath observance and opposing mixed marriages. To stop the conduct of business on the Sabbath, he ordered the city gates closed on that day, and when he found markets being set up outside the walls, he threatened the traders with arrest. Finding children of mixed marriages who could not speak Hebrew, he became enraged. When he found that a grandson of the High Priest Eliashib had married the daughter of the Samaritan Sanballat, he forced him into exile. Nehemiah's actions in his attempt to advocate religious purity were proving to be purely ad hoc. What was required was a systematic religious policy, and in this he failed. However, Nehemiah did save the Jewish community, bringing an honest administration, ensuring the running of the Temple and providing political status and security, all in the face of considerable opposition.

'Now when Ezra had prayed, and when he had confessed, weeping and casting himself down before the house of God, there assembled unto him out of Israel a very great congregation of men and women and children: for the people wept very sore. And Shechaniah the son of Jehiel, one of the sons of Elam, answered and said unto Ezra, We have trespassed against our God, and have taken strange wives of the people of the land: yet now there is hope in Israel concerning this thing.'

Ezra 10:1–2

The requisite religious policies were provided by the priest Ezra, a man who had secured royal authority over Jewish religious affairs in the satrapy of Abar Nahara. He rode across the desert without military escort, bringing financial contributions from Babylonian Jews, treasure from the king and the Law, which had to be taught and enforced. This religious sheriff had the right to compel all those who claimed loyalty to the Temple cult (those who called themselves Jews) to order their affairs in accordance with the Law brought by Ezra. This 'Royal Secretary for the Law of the God in Heaven' and his deputies used the Feast of the Tabernacles to read out the Law in public and explain it in more than one language.

A WALLED CITY ONCE MORE
The walls of Jerusalem were rebuilt under the supervision of the prophet Nehemiah. This illustration of the rebuilding comes from the John Brown Bible.

Abuses continued, and Ezra was particularly incensed by mixed marriages, in which 'Jewishness' could be lost, or Jews not bred. He made a public confession of the people's sins before the Temple, hoping that the people would acknowledge their delinquency. His plan proved successful and a voluntary covenant was agreed for men to divorce their foreign wives and put aside children of these marriages. On pain of ostracism and confiscation of property, all people were ordered to Jerusalem to receive Ezra's rebukes and to abide by the rulings of a commission investigating cases of marriage. After three months' work, all mixed marriages were dissolved.

Ezra's reforms seem to have been completed within a year. The Law that he delivered originated from what became the Torah, based on the Law of Moses, found in the first five books of the Old Testament – Genesis, Exodus, Leviticus, Numbers and Deuteronomy. Ezra was a spiritual figure of outstanding importance. Moses had founded Israel, but Ezra reconstituted Israel and gave the Jews their faith in a form that would survive into the future. Before Nehemiah and Ezra, Israel had ceased to be a nation and could never hope to regain its national institutions. Ezra helped give the Jews a definable identity based upon the Law as a religious constitution.

Alexander and His Successors

In a decade, Alexander the Great created an empire that stretched from Greece to the Punjab. After his death in 323 BC, his generals divided up the Empire, fought among themselves, and destroyed the prosperity of the great trading ports of Greece. The centre of wealth then shifted to Alexandria, where Jewish culture thrived.

Alexander the Great inherited two things from his father, King Philip II of Macedon in northern Greece: a large and capable army and a plan to conquer Persia. In the spring of 334 BC, he crossed the Hellespont strait between Greece and Asia Minor with 35,000 men. He attacked an army of Persians and Greek mercenaries at the River Granicus, defeating it with little loss to his own forces. His victory ensured the eventual submission of all the states in Asia Minor. Alexander refused to engage the substantial Persian fleet and resolved to defeat it by occupying all coastal cities and ports in the Persian Empire. Accordingly, after reducing Lycian and Pisidian hill tribes in western Asia Minor, he advanced southwards and soon met Darius III and the main Persian army in north-eastern Syria at Issus (333 BC). Macedonian pikemen punched a hole through the Persian forces, generating a complete rout, turned into a disaster for the Persians by the relentless pursuit of Alexander's cavalry. After capturing Darius's family, who he treated with respect, Alexander marched south to Syria and Phoenicia and moved into Egypt, thus securing control of the whole eastern Mediterranean and ensuring strategic control at sea.

On the Nile estuary, Alexander founded the city of Alexandria, which became a centre for science, philosophy and trade. He moved north to attack Babylon. Crossing the Euphrates and Tigris rivers, he again met Darius, defeating him at Gaugamela (331 BC). Darius fled and was murdered by his own generals. When Alexander reached Persepolis, the Persian capital, he burned Xerxes' palace in revenge for the destruction of the Acropolis in 480 BC.

With Darius dead, Alexander could legitimately claim to be the Great King. He only needed to gain the submission of the Persian satraps. His empire now extended beyond the Caspian Sea to present-day Afghanistan and Baluchistan and northwards to Bactria and Sogdiana. Thinking to acquire the remaining oddments of the Persian Empire, Alexander crossed the Indus and fought his last great battle on the Hydaspes River against the kingdom of Porus (in the Punjab). When his troops mutinied and refused to go any further, Alexander followed the Indus to the Arabian Sea and arrived in Babylon in 323 BC. He died of fever in the summer of that year, reputedly in the palace of Nebuchadnezzar II. Alexander achieved much militarily, but he failed to organize his empire or make provision for his succession.

THE YOUNG CONQUEROR
Alexander the Great's campaigns increased the influence of Greek civilization in Judah and its neighbouring states. This detail is from the Alexander Mosaic in Pompeii, which depicts the Battle of Issus and the defeat of Darius III.

Alexander's campaigns between 334 and 323 BC quickened the pace of Hellenization. Alexander worked hard to unite Greeks and non-Greeks, encouraged intermarriage, founded Hellenistic cities wherever possible and named for himself, and settled Greek colonists. The former Persian Empire, including Palestine however, was not flooded with Greek settlers, although Judah did feel Greek influence. During the 7th Century BC, Greek mercenaries had served their Egyptian masters along the Philistine coast. In the 5th Century BC, Greek traders from Tyre made their appearance at Nehemiah's court in Jerusalem and by the next century Judah was using coins originating from Attica (Athens). Graffiti dating from the 2nd Century BC in a tomb in Jerusalem, which shows a Greek warship chasing a cargo ship, brings to life Judah's continuing interest in seaborne trade carried out in a Hellenistic world.

When Alexander the Great died at the age of 32 in Babylon, he was master of an empire spanning the Near and Middle East. After his death, his influence remained in the shape of the many cities he had founded on Greek lines, with Greek architecture and street plans that reflected a desire for clear, rational order. More than 20 cities were named Alexandria, and were scattered from the headwaters of the River Indus to the great new port at the western side of the Nile delta in Egypt. Other cities were named after his companions. Many cities were replanned along Greek lines and given new names, such as Ptolemais for the Palestinian port of Acco. The empire itself, however, collapsed.

With Alexander's death, his generals came into their own for the first time after years of being overshadowed by the towering personality and abilities of their leader. The easternmost parts of the Empire in north-west India survived only briefly as independent kingdoms, although the Greek influence remained. At the other extreme, in Greece itself, the generals fought each other for control of Macedon and of the cities of central and southern Greece. In the process they destroyed the prosperity of the great trading ports, including Athens. Migrating Gallic tribes plundered their way through Greece and on into Asia Minor. Then they created the Kingdom of Galatia, in what is now central Turkey. This was later to become the nucleus of the Roman province of Galatia, which features in the New Testament. By the time some sort of order was restored, after 50 years of chaos, some strong and

The Empire of Alexander the Great
336–323 BC

wealthy ports had emerged in the Aegean Sea, including Rhodes, Ephesus and Smyrna.

Immediately after Alexander's rule, the major part of the Empire was divided among Alexander's main generals – Antigonus ruled Asia Minor, Syria and Palestine; Seleucus ruled Mesopotamia, Persia and the eastern parts to the border of India; and Ptolemy ruled Egypt and Libya. That division only lasted to the Battle of Ipsus in 301 BC, when Seleucus added Asia Minor and Syria to his possessions. Greek became the common tongue of the educated, as the cities established schools, theatres, Greek temples and gymnasiums, while the Persian official language, Aramaic, continued to be used in the countryside – the situation still found in New

Testament times. The Seleucids only managed to hold such a vast expanse of territory for some 50 years before the Parthians took control of eastern Mesopotamia – and eventually of most of the eastern parts of the Seleucid Kingdom around the end of the 3rd Century BC. The Parthian Empire eventually prevented Roman expansion into the east.

AN EMPIRE ACROSS THE KNOWN WORLD

Alexander took the Greek language and civilization to the limits of the known world, across three continents. His ceaseless energy drove him to march his armies more than 16,000 kilometres (10,000 miles) and found more than 70 cities.

Egypt remained under the control of the Ptolemies until the Romans conquered Egypt in 30 BC. Under Ptolemaic rule, Alexandria became the greatest trading port in the ancient world and a centre of learning, with a great library and a community of scholars exempt from taxation and maintained at royal expense. The city became a multiracial society where foreigners could live by their own customs and law within the city's constitution. The Jewish community was particularly prominent.

Officially, Palestine had been allocated to the Seleucids after the Battle of Ipsus, but once again it was a vital frontier area between two great powers and was under Egyptian control until the end of the 3rd Century BC. This helps to account for the growth and influence of

the Jewish population of Egypt in settlements all over the country. By this time, the 'dispersed' Jews far outnumbered those living in Palestine, and Hebrew had become a dead everyday language. To meet the needs of Jews who could no longer read Hebrew, the Jewish sacred book, the Old Testament, began to be translated into other languages, particularly Greek.

AN EMPIRE CARVED UP

After the death of Alexander, his Empire was divided between his senior generals – Antigonus, Ptolemy and Seleucus. It had taken Alexander a little over ten years to forge his Empire. It then took his generals 20 years of battle to fight over who should control the different regions.

THE PTOLEMIES

Ptolemy I Soter (305–283 BC)

Ptolemy II Philadelphus (283–246 BC)

Ptolemy III Euergetes I (246–221 BC)

Ptolemy IV Philopator (221–204 BC)

Ptolemy V Epiphanes (204–180 BC)

Ptolemy VI Philometor (180–145 BC)

with Ptolemy VIII Euergetes II and Cleopatra (170–104 BC)

with Cleopatra II (163–145 BC)

Ptolemy VIII Euergetes II (restored) (145–116 BC)

Cleopatra III and Ptolemy IX Soter II (Lathyrus) (116–107 BC)

Cleopatra III and Ptolemy X Alexander I (107–101 BC)

Ptolemy X Alexander I and Cleopatra Berenice (101–88 BC)

Ptolemy IX Soter II (restored) (88–81 BC)

Cleopatra Berenice and Ptolemy XI Alexander II (80 BC)

Ptolemy XII Neos Dionysus (Auletes) (80–58 BC)

Berenice IV (at first with Cleopatra Tryphaena) (58–56 BC)

Berenice IV and Archelaus (56–55 BC)

Ptolemy XII Neos Dionysus (restored) (55–51 BC)

Cleopatra VII Philopator (51–30 BC)

THE SELEUCIDS

Seleucus I Nicator (305–281 BC)

Antiochus I Soter (281–261 BC)

Antiochus II Theos (261–246 BC)

Seleucus II Callinicus (246–226/225 BC)

Seleucus III Soter (226/225–223 BC)

Antiochus III Megas ('the Great') (223–187 BC)

Seleucus IV Philopator (187–175 BC)

Antiochus IV Epiphanes (175–164 BC)

Antiochus V Eupator (164–162 BC)

Demetrius I Soter (162–150 BC)

Alexander Balas (150–145 BC)

Demetrius II Nicator (145–140 BC)

Antiochus VI Epiphanes (145–142/141 or 139/138 BC)

Antiochus VII Sidetes (138–129 BC)

Demetrius II Nicator (restored) (129–126/125 BC)

Cleopatra Thea (126/25–123 BC)

Antiochus VIII Grypus (126/125–96 BC)

Seleucus V (126 BC)

Antiochus IX Philopator (Cyzicenus) (114/113–95 BC)

Seleucus VI (95 BC)

Antiochus X Eusebes Philopator (95 BC)

Demetrius III Philopator Soter (95–88 BC) in Damascus

Antiochus XI Epiphanes Philadelphus (95 BC) in Cilicia

Twins
- **Phillip I** (95–84/83 BC) in Cilicia
- **Antiochus XII Dionysus** (87 BC) in Damascus

Phillip II (84/83 BC)

LIFE UNDER THE GREEKS *(left and above)*

Following the death of Alexander the Great and the division of the Empire between his generals, Palestine was caught between two new Greek dynasties – the Ptolemies and the Seleucids. For the next 200 years, the Ptolemies controlled Palestine, ruling from Egypt and the great city of Alexandria. In 198 BC, the Seleucids under Antiochus III ('the Great') took control, though this was to last only 30 years.

Maccabean Revolt

Alexander's vast empire was dismembered by his generals. Ptolemy seized Egypt and Seleucus established control of an empire that stretched from the Mediterranean to the River Indus in the east.

Under the Ptolemies, the Jews enjoyed considerable religious freedom, which allowed several Old Testament books to reach their final drafts. However, conflict between the Egyptian and Seleucid empires led to the defeat of Egypt by Seleucid Antiochus III (223–187 BC) at the Battle of Panion (200 BC). Palestine was now acquired by the Seleucids and the Jewish population had to deal with a new ruler, who was not an advocate of religious toleration.

Antiochus sought to rebuild the old Alexandrine Empire. Pursuing territorial claims in Macedonia brought him into conflict with Rome and military defeat at Magnesia in 190 BC in western Asia Minor, followed by naval defeat at Myonnesus. The peace terms required a 12-year financial indemnity and the loss of Asia Minor. Armenia then broke away, as did Bactria. Hostages, too, were taken, including a Seleucid son who later became Antiochus IV. Supporting Carthage's Hannibal did the Syrians no favours. Now, blocked in the west, the Seleucid monarch sought expansion elsewhere, but was so short of funds – to pay Rome and his mercenary armies – that he attempted to recoup his losses by looting wealthy temples. His son and successor, Seleucus IV (187–175 BC), tried but failed to claim the wealth of the Jewish Temple in Jerusalem as the property of the state. His brother, Antiochus IV (175–164 BC), then exacerbated Jewish-Hellene antipathy by using violence.

Different political and religious circumstances affected Antiochus IV. He desired to rid the world of any non-Hellene, non-conformist faith, with Judaism a prime target. The Seleucids wanted to spread and consolidate Hellenism, and Judah was an enclave of religious turbulence that needed to be brought in line. In 174 BC, Antiochus deposed the High Priest, Onias, replacing him with one of his brothers, known as Jason. This new High Priest began to build a gymnasium, an icon of Hellenization. People started to wear Greek dress and the broad-brimmed hat known as the *petasos*, which was the headgear of Hermes, the god of the gymnasium. Jews were forced to use the gymnasium, where all were naked and they could not hide their circumcision. The short Greek tunic incurred horror as it left the legs bare. The Greek obsession with the human body and its physique plunged old and young Jews into unwanted new Greek ideas.

'Now such was the height of Greek fashions and increase of heathenish manners, through the exceeding profaneness of Jason, that ungodly wretch and no high priest; That the priests had no courage to serve any more at the altar, but despising the temple, and neglecting the sacrifices, hastened to be partakers of the unlawful allowance in the place of the exercise after the game of Discus called them forth;'
2 Maccabees 4:13–14

The Jews believed Hellenism to be mere nature worship, a continuation of Canaanite religion with Antiochus as a new Baal, embodying Canaanite god-qualities of hate, lust, anger, greed and envy. This Greek world view conflicted with Israel's *raison d'être* – the requirement to put into practice the revelation of God by building an ordered society that was ruled by God's love and justice, not by man's greed and aggression. Jewish

PALESTINE BEFORE THE MACCABEAN STORM

The actions of Antiochus IV, the Seleucid emperor, provoked an organized rebellion of Jews led by Judas Maccabeus, which ended in defeat for the Greeks and the establishment of Jewish independence in Palestine.

loyalty to a revealed religion and the Word of God was antithetical to Antiochus' "god manifest," the god in human guise. When Jason failed to move beyond cultural affairs, Antiochus deposed him in favor of Menelaus, thereby generating conflict between the supporters of three High Priests—Onias, Jason, and Menelaus—although no rebellion broke out.

Antiochus now felt able to continue his foreign policy plans as Rome in the west and Parthia in the east were not perceived as a threat. In 174 BC, he marched into Egypt and, despite early successes, was forced to retreat when a Roman fleet arrived unexpectedly at the mouth of the Nile. His prestige maimed, Antiochus turned toward Judah. The Egyptian defeat saw Jason depose Menelaus, but the Seleucid king reversed this action and robbed the Temple of its treasures, plundered and burnt parts of Jerusalem, and established a citadel, the Accra, on a hill overlooking the Temple (167 BC). Antiochus next sought to enforce the state of Hellenism. The Temple at Jerusalem was consecrated to Olympian Zeus and the Samaritan sanctuary of Mount Gerezim was given to the worship of Zeus, the Friend of Strangers.

"Now the fifteenth day of the month Casleu, in the hundred forty and fifth year, they set up the abomination of desolation upon the altar, and builded idol altars throughout the cities of Judah on every side; and burnt incense at the doors of their houses, and in the streets. And when they had rent in pieces the books of the law which they found, they burnt them with fire."

1 Maccabees 1:54–56

The rebellion began in the small village of Modin, north-west of Jerusalem. A Syrian official and a Jew were going to offer sacrifice on a pagan altar. The apostasy so angered a priest, Mattathias, and his five sons that they killed the Syrian and the apostate. They then fled into the Judaean wilderness of hills, wadis, and caves, where they might survive attacks from Seleucid forces. The scene was set for guerrilla warfare. Many rebellious Jews fled into the wilderness but were pursued by Syrian forces that attacked them on the Sabbath. The Jews, being uncompromising adherents of the Law, allowed themselves to be slaughtered. This catastrophic event forced the Jews to reconsider the Law—from then on Jews were allowed to defend themselves on the Sabbath.

In 166 BC, Mattathias died and his son, Judas, known as Maccabeus, took over the leadership of the revolt. The meaning of his nickname is debated but may be linked to the Hebrew word for hammer. His family eventually became known as the Maccabees. Judas' military campaigns lasted for a mere six years, but they rocked the Syrian military establishment. Most Seleucid forces faced Rome and Parthia, so the rebellion was first perceived as a local revolt. Initially, Judas engaged in night attacks on villages and towns adjacent to the wilderness, driving out Syrians, punishing apostates and traitors, and destroying pagan altars. His successes stimulated support and his forces grew into a small army.

Apollonius, the Syrian governor in Samaria, attacked Judas but was defeated and killed. Victory brought booty and recruits, but this caused Seron, the governor of the Coele-Syria region, to move against Judas with an army that included many Jewish traitors. Judas enjoyed successful engagements at Beth-horon and Mizpah and an inconclusive skirmish at Beth-zur. When Antiochus heard reports of the defeat, he diverted half his forces from a planned campaign against Parthia, leaving them, under the generalship of Lysias, to subdue Judah. Lysias sent the generals Ptolemy, Nicanor, and Gorgias with some 40,000 infantry, 7,000 cavalry, and war elephants into Judah, where they camped near Emmaus. Traders joined the encampment in the expectation of buying Jewish prisoners of war as slaves. Judas and his brothers assembled their forces at Mizpah, prayed, and then marched on Emmaus (165 BC). Meanwhile, Gorgias led a night expedition of 5,000 infantry and 1,000 cavalry, hoping to surprise the Jewish camp, but it was deserted.

Judas attacked Emmaus with 3,000 men at daybreak, defeated the Syrians, and plundered their camp. When Gorgias returned, his troops fled into Philistia and Judas finished looting their camp. The following year, Lysias mustered 60,000 infantry and 5,000 cavalry and marched into Idumaea, camping at Beth-zur. The Judaean army of 10,000 men under Judas met them and killed 5,000 Syrians. Lysias withdrew to Antioch where he planned to raise a mercenary army for a renewed attack the following year. With the way to Jerusalem now opened,

GREEK AMPHITHEATRE

The influence of Greek dramatic traditions may be seen in the structure of the Old Testament Book of Job. Job's sufferings, the speeches of his 'friends' and God's intervention would have been familiar theatre. It was this kind of influence that the Maccabees resented, together with the high-handed approach of the Seleucids.

Judas found priests to purify and re-dedicate the Temple. The anniversary of Temple cleansing is known as the Feast of Hanukkah, when celebratory candles are lit.

Judas now enjoyed a two-year respite from Syrian attack, using the time to campaign against neighbouring tribes who had started to persecute their Jewish minorities as a response to the re-dedication of the Temple. The Idumaeans were harried at Acrabatene, as were the Ammonites in Transjordan. Simon, Judas' brother, raided Galilee, while Judas and his brother Jonathan campaigned in Gilead. The Jewish minorities were transferred to Judaea, thereby swelling the numbers in the Judaean army.

Antiochus IV died in 164 BC, leaving his son, Antiochus V, under the vice-regency of Lysias. He invaded Judaea, captured Beth-zur and defeated Judas at Beth-zechariah, forcing the Jewish troops back into Jerusalem. The Jews sued for peace, which Lysias granted owing to internecine strife in the ruling Seleucid family. The Jews were granted religious freedom, but the Temple fortifications were destroyed. The subsequent peace was short-lived. Alcimus, renegade leader of the Hellenized Jews, travelled to Antioch to meet a new Seleucid king, Demetrius I (162–150 BC), where he complained about Jewish behaviour. A large Syrian army, under Bacchides, was despatched to Judaea to protect Alcimus and seize Judas and his brothers. Many Jews supported Alcimus since they thought religious freedom was now assured, but Alcimus had many Jews killed and rebellion flared up. A large Syrian army, led by Nicanor, was sent to destroy Judaea and a climactic battle was fought at Beth-horon near Adasa, where Judas enjoyed a great victory and general Nicanor was killed (161 BC). The event has been commemorated as a feast day ever since.

Despite victory, many Jews felt disheartened at the constantly renewed Syrian attacks. Would the Syrians ever desist? Soldiers left the Judaean army, and Judas' forces shrank. He fought his last battle at Elasa against Bacchides, supported by only 800 men. Despite putting the Syrian right wing to flight, he fell fighting and his brothers, Jonathan and Simon, secretly buried him at Modin: '… all Israel made great lamentation for him, and mourned many days, saying: How is the valiant man fallen, that delivered Israel!' (1 Maccabees 9:20–21)

In 159 BC, Alcimus died, weakening the Hellenistic party in Judaea. The Seleucid king was also harassed by other problems in his empire. Additionally, two factions in the Syrian royal house contended for power, with both claimants vying for Jonathan's support, acknowledging him as leader of all the Jews and appointing him High Priest. Jonathan and Simon consolidated their power, ostensibly fighting on behalf of one Syrian pretender, Alexander Balas. Beth-zur and Joppa were garrisoned by Jews, Gaza taken and Seleucid ruler Demetrius II defeated near the Sea of Galilee. Jonathan also began repairing Jerusalem's walls and Judaean fortresses. Trypho, guardian of Balas, feared Jonathan's increasing independence and his sea-outlet at Joppa. He captured Jonathan and his sons at Ptolemais and killed them. Simon took over Jewish leadership, finished rebuilding Jerusalem's walls, seized and fortified Gazara and seized the Seleucid fort, the Accra, in Jerusalem. Judaea was now practically independent, but recent victories had been based largely upon mercenary support rather than Jewish volunteers. Joppa was turned into a military base, a potential springboard for the entry of allied forces. Simon re-established relations with Rome and Sparta, and negotiated away the tribute that was owed to Demetrius II.

Simon commenced building a theocratic state. The Accra was strengthened and became Simon's home, and his son, John, became general of the Judaean forces. Peace allowed agriculture to develop, the towns and cities were provisioned and the people learned to relax. The Law was re-enforced and wrongdoers punished. Diplomatic relations with Rome and Sparta were further strengthened, with the former receiving a gift of a gold shield of a thousand pounds weight to confirm their mutual league. All the Jews and priests were pleased with Simon's achievements and determined that he should be their governor and High Priest until a faithful prophet should appear. Simon accepted and his rank was engraved on brass tablets that were placed in the Temple in conspicuous places.

'Thus the yoke of the heathen was taken away from Israel in the hundred and seventieth year. Then the people of Israel began to write in their instruments and contracts, In the first year of Simon, the high priest, the governor and leader of the Jews.'
1 Maccabees 13:41–42

HEBREW HERO

In a 19th-Century engraving by Gustave Doré, Judas Maccabeus pursues a defeated army. Judas waged a six-year rebellion against the Seleucid rulers of Palestine in the fight for Hebrew independence.

Jewish Independence

For the first time since 587 BC Judah was under the rule of a Jewish king, and the kingdom expanded dramatically. The Seleucid ruler, Demetrius II, exempted Judah from tribute, so granting it virtual independence.

The rulers who sprang from the Maccabee line became known as the Hasmoneans, because the historian Flavius Josephus (c. AD 37–101) claimed that Simon Maccabee's grandfather was called Hasmon. Simon, like so many Maccabees, died a violent death. Abubus, Simon's son-in-law and commander of the Dor fortress, was persuaded by the Syrian king to murder Simon and two of his sons at a meal while visiting him.

This rebellion failed. Simon's third son, John Hyrcanus (134–104 BC), was in Gezer, west of Jerusalem, when the crime was committed. Learning of the murder, he travelled straightaway to Jerusalem, where he was immediately acknowledged as Simon's lawful successor. Meanwhile, Syrian forces arrived to aid Abubus, forcing John, who had been unable to organize his troops, to withdraw into Jerusalem. The subsequent Syrian siege was foiled by intervention from Rome and the Syrians retreated.

Power, therefore, remained in John's hands. Nevertheless, he raised a large army to aid Seleucid Antiochus VII in his campaigns against Parthia to regain Mesopotamia, suggesting that John still owed Syria some kind of tribute. John returned from the fray and was absent when the Parthian ruler, Phraates II, surprised the Seleucid army at Ecbatana, defeating it and killing Antiochus. John renounced his allegiance to Syria and rebuilt the walls of Jerusalem that Antiochus had torn down in the earlier siege. John fortified his position further by renewing the treaty of friendship with Rome, an insurance against possible future Syrian aggression. Again, after 129 BC, John Hyrcanus ruled an autonomous state. Coins were issued inscribed with the words 'Yehohanan the high priest and the congregation of the Jews'. This intimated that Hyrcanus was a typical Hellenistic ruler (his eldest sons bore Greek names), emphasized his High Priesthood, and suggested that he governed with a council rather than as an autocrat.

John then proceeded to attack his weaker neighbours to enlarge his domains. Two main targets were the cities of Samaria and Shechem. These strongholds contained Samaritan worshippers of Adonai, who were making sacrifices at a temple on Mount Gerizim. This alternative temple-cult was anathema to the priests in Jerusalem. Both cities were destroyed and a rivulet diverted over the ruins of Samaria (128 BC). Galilee, occupied by Aramaic-speaking gentiles, was next on the agenda. John forced

'So when Simon and his sons had drunk largely, Ptolomee and his men rose up, and took their weapons and came upon Simon into the banqueting place, and slew him, and his two sons, and certain of his servants.'

1 Maccabees 16:16

AN UNEASY KINGDOM

Despite the victories of the Maccabees, peace did not come to the Jews of Jerusalem during the 1st Century BC. Different factions, centred on Jerusalem, fought bitterly. Although the Jews extended their rule to the borders of the old Davidic Empire, internal tensions brought civil war and appeals to the Romans to restore order.

these Galileans (known as Ituraeans) to Judaize, insisting that males were circumcised. In the south, Idumaea (Edom) was conquered, and its inhabitants were Judaized too. The town of Medeba, east of the Dead Sea, was taken, thereby threatening trade routes used by the Nabataean people to the south. On the northern frontier, cities such as Pella, Dion, Gadera and Hippos, all east of the Jordan (eventually leaguing with others to form the Decapolis), were made tributary. These Greek cities remained intact, and the people were not compelled to Judaize. Instead, trade served to benefit the Hasmonean state, which began to adopt a new religious view that Judaism and Hellenism were compatible.

In 104 BC, John Hyrcanus died and was succeeded by his son Aristobulus I. He ruled for just one year and was followed by Alexander Jannaeus (103–76 BC). Aristobulus suffered from paranoia and imprisoned most of his brothers and even his mother, who allegedly starved to death in prison. His favourite brother was killed by the royal bodyguard by mistake, an event that hastened Aristobulus' death. Alexander Jannaeus was freed from prison by his mother and made king.

Alexander, like his father, was militarily minded and, despite failing in an attempt to capture Ptolemais, in what is now Libya, seized all the port cities of Palestine, taking Gaza with particular brutality. Sensibly, he remained on good terms with the Ptolemaic Egyptian queen, who was quite capable of summoning Roman aid if she felt threatened. Alexander also captured several towns in the regions of Galaditis, Gaulanitis and Syria. However, the southern Nabataeans continued to raid and threaten Judaea and ultimately became involved in Hasmonean internecine family strife. Alexander remained concerned about his southern and eastern borders, evidenced by the forts at Hyrcania, Masada and Machaerus. These were linked to further fortifications at Beth-zur, Gezer, Alexandrium and Dok.

Foreign success did not necessarily make Alexander Jannaeus popular among his own people. Like his father, he used many mercenaries, so the Jews did not particularly feel part of the expansionist plans. Conflict grew with the orthodox religious party, the Pharisees. The latter's devotion to the Law meant spurning the pomp, power and prestige of the Hasmonean dynasty. Further, this family had the temerity to dub themselves kings when they were not part of the Davidic line. The Pharisees also disliked Alexander's behaviour; he was High Priest, but failed to observe the Law. Jannaeus was pelted with lemons at the Feast of the Tabernacles, leading him to massacre his opponents. The Pharisees begged help from Seleucid Demetrius III. This and several scandals provoked resistance and Alexander is said to have crucified 800 rebels in Jerusalem. Flavius Josephus claims that Alexander ordered the rebels' wives and children to be brought out and slaughtered before the eyes of the dying men.

The Pharisees maintained that Alexander, when dying from a wound received while besieging a Greek city, advised his wife, Salome Alexandra (76–67 BC), to mend fences with the Pharisees. Alexandra became Queen rather than a son succeeding Jannaeus. Historians have argued that the older of his sons, Hyrcanus, was impaired, but the Queen did not wish to pass over him to the younger Aristobulus in case of argument and even civil war. Alexandra appointed Hyrcanus High Priest to please the Pharisees, who now felt that their views could be imposed upon the weak-minded Hyrcanus. Since she could not preside over the Sanhedrin, the Jewish high counsel, Alexandra placed her brother in this post. She was now in a secure position: the Seleucids and Ptolemies were both weak and, internally, her détente with the Pharisees won her much popular Judaean support. When places were left vacant in the Sanhedrin, she filled them with Pharisees rather than Sadducees, an extremely conservative group that recognized only the Torah as a religious text. Also, scribes were preferred to priests. In reality, Alexandra was Queen in name only, with the Pharisees holding the real power. However, the country was quiet and her reign was later regarded as a Golden Age.

Peace was shattered when the Queen died in 67 BC. Conflict broke out and the dispute eventually led to the destruction of the entire Jewish state. The Pharisees supported Hyrcanus II as king and High Priest. The Sadducees backed Aristobolus, who was already in control of some parts of Judaea. A civil war ensued; Hyrcanus' defeat resulted in Aristobulus usurping the monarchy and High Priesthood. Hyrcanus accepted his defeat and submitted to his brother's authority. However, a new personality now entered the arena. When Alexander Jannaeus seized Idumaea and forcibly converted the population to Judaism, he appointed a local as governor of the region. This man's son, Antipater, possessed territorial designs and ambitions. Accordingly, he became an adviser to Hyrcanus and persuaded him to seek a restoration of his position in Judaea. So, in 65 BC, the two escaped to the Nabataean capital of Petra. The Nabataeans had schemes of projecting their power into the north-west to gain control of trade routes. Antipater found it easy to persuade Aretas, the Nabataean ruler, to assist Hyrcanus in returning to Jerusalem to recover his kingship. Aristobulus had not yet consolidated his resources and could not counter the enemy advance, having to withdraw inside the walls of Jerusalem.

Judaea's internal affairs were now in chaos. Three parties contested power. Aristobulus was contained in Jerusalem with his coterie of priests and important Jewish families. Outside the walls were Hyrcanus, Antipater and their Nabataean allies. The Pharisees comprised the third party and they ideally sought the eradication of both Hasmoneans and a return to the rule of Law. Aristobulus knew he required outside help to withstand a siege and therefore went to Damascus, which had just been occupied by a Roman army under Pompey. Roman power was emerging from the central and western Mediterranean into the Asian world.

GREEK INFLUENCE – GOOD AND BAD

The fashion for all things Greek was so powerful that even the Jews of Palestine embraced it enthusiastically. In some areas Greek colonies were established, and many of the cities were rebuilt in the Greek style, such as that of Palmyra in central Syria, shown below. Eventually, the Old Testament had to be translated into Greek because the Hebrew language was no longer in everyday use. However, this relationship became strained as Jews considered that their beliefs were infringed by continued Greek interference in the Temple in Jerusalem and their Jewish rights and even by demands that the Seleucid king should be worshipped as a god.

'Now Judas had heard of the Romans, that they were mighty and valiant men, and such as would lovingly accept all that joined themselves unto them, and make a league of amity with all that came unto them. And that they were men of great valour. It was told him also of their wars and noble acts which they had done among the Galatians, and how they had conquered them, and brought them under tribute; And what they had done in the country of Spain, for the winning of the mines of the silver and gold which is there.'

1 Maccabees 8:1–3

The Hasmonean Kingdom had bumped into Rome's foreign policy drive towards the east. Roman ambitions had impinged upon eastern politics during the Second Punic War (218–201 BC), when Philip V of Macedon allied with Hannibal. Two Roman-Macedonian wars followed, with a crushing defeat of Philip at Cynoscephalae in 197 BC. A few years later, Attalos II, King of Pergamon, requested aid against his eastern neighbour, the Seleucid ruler, Antiochus III. The Romans crushed the Seleucid navy at Myonnesus (190 BC) and its land forces at Magnesia (190 BC). These defeats led to the total breakaway of Armenia (under Artaxias) and Bactria from the Seleucid Empire.

The Macedonians returned to the fray under Philip's son, Perseus, and were defeated at Pydna (168 BC). Macedonia was turned into a Roman province. Greece was then swallowed up in 146 BC when Rome destroyed the chief Greek city, Corinth. In 130 BC, the last King of Pergamon died, bequeathing his kingdom to Rome. Thus, Rome acquired its province of Asia, its first territory beyond the Aegean, and its first in Asia Minor. Pamphilia followed in 103 BC and Cilicia was established as a Roman province in 101 BC, as part of the perennial problem of eradicating piracy. Rome continued its policy of seeking to weaken any strong power in the east while bolstering small states. At this point in time, Asia Minor contained other kingdoms such as Bithynia, Pontus and Cappadocia, which were still ruled by Iranian princes, the remnants of satraps holding power under the old Persian Achaemenid royal dynasty.

These states became Hellenized and even founded cities along Greek lines, such as Nikomedia in Bithynia. The most noteworthy independent state was Pontus, ruled by the Persian Mithridates VI. This ambitious king locked horns with Rome when he commenced a campaign of conquest by capturing Colchis and the Crimea from Scythia. He attempted to cement control in Paphlagonia and Cappadocia but was prevented by Rome; his plot to depose Nicomedes III of Bithynia collapsed. In 88 BC, Nicomedes raided Pontus, encouraged by Rome, instigating the First Mithradatic War. Mithradates occupied Roman Asia and marched upon Greece. Between 86 and 85 BC, he was defeated by the Roman generals Gaius Flavius Fimbria and Lucius Cornelius Sulla. The Roman invasion of Pontus in 83 BC during the Second Mithradatic War was repulsed in 82 BC. Rome attempted to seize Bithynia, which Mithradates had occupied, in the Third Mithradatic War and in 73 BC Mithradates was defeated by Roman general Lucius Licinius Lucullus and driven out of Bithynia and Pontus into Armenia. Lucullus also crushed Mithradates' father-in-law, Tigranes of Armenia, who had conquered Mesopotamia, Media, parts of Asia Minor and north Syria, where he was approaching Damascus.

Appointed a Roman Consul in 70 BC, Pompey (Gnaeus Pompeius Magnus), jointly with Marcus Licinius Crassus, was empowered to finally destroy piracy in the eastern Mediterranean. While settling pirates as peaceful farmers, Pompey was given extraordinary powers to take over the command against Mithradates, make peace and war and organize the entire Roman east. A final defeat was inflicted upon Mithradates, who committed suicide in 63 BC. Tigranes surrendered to Rome, was shorn of all conquests and fined 6,000 talents. Pompey was now free to plan the consolidation of the eastern territories and to set up buffer client-states. He established four provinces: Asia; Bithynia-Pontus (excluding eastern Pontus); Cilicia, including Pamphylia and Isauria; and Syria, the area around Antioch. The client kingdoms were eastern Pontus, Cappadocia, Galatia (under King Deitarus), Lycia and Judaea. The buffer states, friends (*amici*) or allies (*socii*) of Rome, were a barrier against Parthia. In northern Mesopotamia, some territory was given to Tigranes. In the south, a Jewish Judaea remained, as did Arab Chalcis (Ituraea) and Nabataea.

FORTIFICATION OF JERUSALEM

Although of much later date, these 16th-Century fortifications in Jerusalem still give an idea of how strong the city could be made in ancient times. Whenever it was vigorously defended, Jerusalem was able to stand long sieges by great military powers.

MIGHTY ROME

Throughout Europe, and particularly around the Mediterranean, there is still visible evidence of Roman civilization. During New Testament times, the Empire was beginning to reach its greatest extent and Rome was at the peak of its power. Palestine was incorporated into a Roman province by Pompey (106–48 BC), who deposed the last of the Seleucid kings in 64 BC, and, in the following year, captured Jerusalem.

SLAVS
IRANIAN PEOPLES
BOSPORAN KINGDOM
CAUCASIAN PEOPLES
DACIA
Danube
Black Sea
Olbia
Tyras
Heraclea
Tomi
Sinope
Trapezus
Salonae
Narona
Stobi
Byzantium
Nicomedia
Heraclea Pontica
PONTUS
ARMENIA
Asia
Thessalonica
Brundisium
Tarentum
Dorylaeum
GALATIA
CAPPADOCIA
SOPHENE
CORDUENE
COMMAGENE
OSRHOENE
PARTHIAN EMPIRE
Demetrias
Pergamum
Smyrna
Antiochia
Iconium
Zeugma
Tarus
Antioch
Syria
Apamea
Patrae
Corinth
Athens
Sparta
Halicarnassus
Attaleia
Side
LYCIA
Rhodes
RHODES
Catana
Syracuse
Melite I.
EMPIRE
Cyprus
Salamis
Gortyn
Great Sea
Western Sea
DECAPOLIS
JUDAEA
INDEPENDENT TOWNS
ARABS
Cyrene
Alexandria
Memphis
EGYPT
NABATAEA
Red Sea
Nile
Thebes

The survival of Judaea and the Arabic-speaking Nabataeans had depended upon the various embassies that the Levantine states had sent to Pompey. Two delegations came from Jerusalem: Hyrcanus II and Antipater were there, supported by the Pharisees, while the other embassy, including Sadducees, claimed that Aristobulus was the more effective of the two brothers and should be recognized as king. Some other Pharisees asked Pompey to abolish the Judaean kingdom and re-establish a theocratic constitution as had existed in the times of Ezra and the Maccabees. Pompey supported Hyrcanus, returned to Jerusalem as King (64 BC). The Nabataeans were instructed to vacate Judaea.

The year 63 BC saw Pompey threatening the Nabataeans by marching two legions south. While the Romans were engaged at Petra, Aristobulus attempted to snatch back the Judaean kingship. Pompey returned swiftly to Jerusalem and laid siege to the Temple precinct, where Aristobulus's followers sought refuge. The siege lasted three months, before the Roman legions entered the precinct and killed the rebels. Aristobulus was sent to Rome. Hyrcanus was re-established as High Priest, but Pompey reinforced his authority by violating the Temple protocols, entering the Holy of Holies, which only the High Priest was allowed to see. Even the Seleucid kings had observed religious scruples, but Pompey trampled over Jewish sensibilities and his behaviour damned him forever in Jewish eyes.

Jewish morale was shattered further when Pompey decided to reduce the area of the Judaean state and to abrogate the title of 'king' in Hasmonean lands. The enlarged Jewish state of Alexander Jannaeus was truncated. The Greek city states in the north-east were placed outside Judaean control and comprised a league known as the Decapolis. The cities on the Palestinian coast from Dor southwards to Gaza were given limited autonomy. Territories in the north were ceded to Ituraea and Ptolemais. These two regions were placed under the loose jurisdiction of the new Roman province of Syria. The Samaritans were allowed a small state around Shechem and the temple on Mount Gerizim. Hyrcanus II received the title of High Priest and Ethnarch. The diminished title demonstrated in no uncertain terms to the people of Judaea that they were now a subordinate Roman client-state, and that their leader kept his title at the whim of the government in Rome.

Antipater became adviser to Hyrcanus and from 63 to 40 BC steered him in his religious and secular duties. Josephus says that the Roman Marcus Crassus seized 2,000 talents of gold from the Temple to finance an anti-Parthian expedition, but Antipater and Hyrcanus prevented the Jews from rebelling. The major problem confronting the two leaders was the support for Aristobulus, who allegedly fostered an anti-Roman feeling after he and his family had been sent to Rome in 62 BC. Here he became a plaything in the contest for power between Julius Caesar and Pompey, and this crisis was not concluded until the period of civil disorder ended in 27 BC. Then, Octavian, Caesar's nephew, received the title 'Augustus' and extraordinary constitutional powers and control over the most important armies and provinces. Rome now had an Emperor.

During the Pompey-Caesar conflict and the civil war between Brutus and Cassius and Octavian and Mark Antony, Hyrcanus continued in his position, becoming a client of Pompey, then Julius Caesar, and of Cassius and then Octavian and Mark Antony. Political decisions, however, were made by Antipater, who consolidated his power by moving his two oldest sons, Phasael and Herod, into powerful political positions.

When Antipater died in 43 BC, Sadducees and opponents to Hyrcanus II sought an alternative Hasmonean candidate in Antigonus II, the surviving son of Aristobulus and nephew to Hyrcanus. He and his partisans were driven from Jerusalem, and Herod was rewarded with the hand of Mariamme, Aristobulus's granddaughter. Antigonus then found backing from Parthia, which wanted to take advantage of the troubled situation and maybe win over the hundreds and thousands of Jews in Mesopotamia, which the Parthians had seized a hundred years before. The Parthians entered Jerusalem, killed Phasael, and arrested Hyrcanus. Josephus claims that Antigonus cut off Hyrcanus's ears, thereby making him unfit to remain High Priest, and sent him to Babylon. Herod escaped to Rome via Arabia and Egypt. In 40 BC, the Roman Senate declared Herod King of Judaea. He was sent with mercenaries and a Roman force under Sosius to Judaea, which he seized, capturing Antigonus in 37 BC and executing him. Herod retrieved the aging Hyrcanus II from Rome, bringing him to Jerusalem. Octavian confirmed Herod as client-king in 31 BC. Hyrcanus, however, became involved in a conspiracy against Herod, was found guilty and executed in 30 BC. This same year witnessed Herod in control of Judaea (with Idumaea), Samaria, Galilee and Peraea. He was also granted rule over Greek cities in Samaria (Hippus and Gadara) and all the coastal cities, except Ascalon.

A NATION LOSES ITS INDEPENDENCE

The Roman General, Pompey, entered Jerusalem in 63 BC captured the Temple that was being defended by the current King and High Priest and made Palestine part of the Roman province of Syria. The brief period of Jewish independence had not even lasted 100 years.

Herod's Kingdom

King Herod ruled Palestine on behalf of Rome from 40 BC and his family remained a major force for the next 130 years. There were deep differences between Jewish factions during the entire period, but they eventually rebelled against the Romans in AD 66.

The politics of Palestine in the 1st Century AD form a complex and changing pattern as different groups manoeuvred and fought for control. The Romans imposed an uneasy peace on the warring factions, having first entered the arena at the request of two groups of Jews locked in civil war, with one group besieging the other in Jerusalem. When Pompey (106–48 BC) captured Jerusalem in 63 BC, he made Palestine part of the Roman province of Syria, ruled by a Roman legate, and limited the religious authority of the High Priest to the parts of Palestine where the Jews recognized the Temple in Jerusalem. Some parts of Palestine, such as Samaria, observed a different form of Hebrew religion.

The brief period of peace was short-lived, as Rome itself slid into civil war again and consequently its rule over Palestine weakened. But then the Roman Senate named the politically astute Herod, who was probably half Jewish, King of Judaea in 40 BC. Herod conquered his kingdom three years later with the aid of Roman soldiers and ruled it for the next 31 years as a puppet king of Rome. He subdued his unruly kingdom and his own treacherous family with ruthless cruelty, backed by his own army, and established fortresses in many parts of his kingdom, where he could find security in times of trouble.

During his uneasy period of peace, Herod built new cities and provided buildings for every kind of different civic need, from baths, theatres and gymnasiums to a temple for emperor worship and, above all, a magnificent rebuilding of the Temple itself, the central symbol of Hebrew religion. It was all done through forced labour and extortionate taxation. The diversity of buildings points to the deep differences between Jewish groups during the whole New Testament period. The Herods and their supporters, the Herodians, remained a major force in Palestinian politics until the Jewish War of AD 66–70, but most of Hebrew Palestine, Judaea and Samaria was put under the direct rule of Roman procurators in AD 6.

The other main groups, who were normally at variance with each other, were the Pharisees, Sadducees and the Essenes. At the extreme of fanatical nationalism

JAR OF KNOWLEDGE
The Dead Sea scrolls made at the Qumran settlement were stored in pottery jars. The jars and the extremely dry climate of the area ensured that the scrolls were still in perfect condition when they were discovered after 2,000 years.

PALACE FIT FOR A KING
Uncovered remains of Herod the Great's magnificent winter palace, built on the Wadi Qilt, south of Jericho, include many features built in the Roman style, such as this bath.

were the Zealots, called 'sicarii' (stabbers) by the Romans because of their reputation for stealthy assassination. The Pharisees believed in meticulous obedience to Hebrew law, which brought every detail of daily life within the province of religion, but they took account of changing circumstances and oral traditions of interpreting the law, which made them more flexible than the other main group, the Sadducees. Paul was a Pharisee before becoming a Christian and this flexibility can be seen in his approach to problems. The Sadducees were violently opposed to the Pharisees and rejected any attempt to adapt the written law to new situations, but their opposition was intensified by their political stance and their religious privileges. Most of the priests in Jerusalem belonged to this party, which tended to support occupying powers such as the Romans for the sake of political stability. Although the High Priest of the Temple had to be chosen from certain priestly families, the appointment was made by whoever ruled Palestine at the time, whether a Herod or a Roman procurator.

There is no mention of the Essenes in the New Testament, because they played no part in mainstream Hebrew religious practices or politics. Similarly, the Samaritans, in the hilly area north of Jerusalem, practised their own form of the Hebrew religion and kept to themselves. After the Jewish War (AD 66–70) the synagogues and their rabbis became more prominent but the mould of Jewish politics in Palestine had been broken.

The Bible sometimes gives the impression that Jewish religion was uniform in practice, closely controlled and strictly regulated by the priests of Jerusalem. However, actual evidence suggests otherwise – and none more so than the Biblical manuscripts and scrolls discovered at Khirbet Qumran, near the northern end of the Dead Sea, in 1947. These changed modern knowledge about religion in Palestine during the 1st Centuries BC and AD. Within the next ten years, hundreds of complete scrolls and fragments of scrolls came to light and the ruins of Khirbet Qumran nearby were thoroughly excavated.

The excavations and the evidence of the scrolls revealed a Jewish community occupying an extensive

complex of buildings on a spur overlooking the Dead Sea and 25 caves in the steep sides of the cliffs nearby. The buildings, with their eight courtyards, included a refectory, kitchen, assembly rooms, a laundry, two potteries and eight water cisterns of various sizes, some of them with steps leading down into them. There was evidence of a dam in a large gully in the cliffs and channels to lead water from the dam to the cisterns. Stone writing tablets that had fallen from an upper storey were also discovered. Objects found in the excavations, especially coins, made it possible to date the occupation periods accurately. The community began at Qumran in the early part of the 1st Century BC and abandoned the site after an earthquake in 31 BC. Herod the Great ruled at the time, and this may be why the community did not return to the site until after his death in 4 BC. It continued there until the summer of AD 68, when the community hid its manuscripts in caves and fled with the arrival of the Roman general Vespasian (AD 9–79) and the Tenth Legion, which destroyed most of the buildings.

The vast collection of writings unearthed at Qumran included books or fragments from the whole Hebrew Bible (except for Esther), other religious writings similar to parts of the Bible and documents about the organization and life of the community itself. The discoveries provided biblical manuscripts many centuries earlier than any that had previously survived, but they differed in many places from the ones authorized by the main Jewish authorities.

A MONARCH MAKES HIS MARK

Herod was a great builder, creating remarkable structures across his kingdom. His greatest work was the rebuilt Temple at Jerusalem, shown here in a model reconstruction.

The community lived a strict life, with joint ownership of all possessions, rituals of purification by water, public prayers and religious meals. It kept a calendar of religious festivals different from the official calendar of the Jerusalem Temple. The members believed that the real meaning of the scriptures had been revealed by a 'Teacher of Righteousness' at the beginning of the community's existence, and that they were chosen by God to be 'Sons of Light' in the conflict with all 'Sons of Darkness' until God finally sent a Prophet and two Messiahs to bring victory and judgement. It seems certain that the members of the community were of the scrict Essene sect. Their beliefs and practices are of first importance for the light they throw on religious attitudes in Palestine during the early years of Christianity.

HEROD PUSHES THE BOUNDARIES

Herod the Great consistently added to the territory under his rule (40–4 BC). To protect his extended kingdom, he built many fortresses, such as Madada and Herodium, and founded a great city at Caesarea,

BIRTH OF JESUS

The New Testament starts with the three 'Synoptic Gospels' (Matthew, Mark and Luke), which give a broad view of the life of Jesus, though there is considerable overlap in the content.

The major sources of information about Jesus's life are the Gospels, compiled in the last half of the 1st Century AD to enable Christianity to spread through Europe, the Mediterranean Basin and the Fertile Crescent. The Acts of the Apostles and St Paul's Epistles also provide information about Jesus. He is mentioned in the *Annals* of Tacitus and by Josephus, the Jewish historian, in *Antiquities of the Jews*, where he mentions the stoning in AD 62 of 'James, the brother of Jesus, who was called Christ'. Other works exist in the apocryphal Infancy Gospels, such as the Protoevangelium of James, which was condemned by St Jerome, along with much other old and authentic early Christian literature, and so came under a Papal ban. Extracanonical literature about Jesus was revealed in the Coptic Gospel of Thomas, written by Gnostic Christians. Found at Naj' Hammadi in Egypt, it contains 114 sayings of Jesus, but no historical context.

Jesus was born at a time when the Jewish people had endured constant foreign domination and loss of political independence. The Romans had divided the kingdom of Herod I among his sons, and by AD 6, the lands of Archelaus – Judaea, Jerusalem, Samaria and Idumaea – were integrated into Roman administration. The Jesus story is concerned mainly with Galilee, where much of his ministry took place. Regarded with scorn by Judaeans, Galilee contained settlements of foreign colonists, while its ruler, Herod Antipas, Hellenized the region. Individual Jewish settlements existed and there was a Jewish urban populace pursuing their own religious traditions. Monitoring the entire region was the Roman Empire, often with the cooperation of Jerusalem's priest-aristocracy.

In religious terms, Judaism was riven by different groups. The Pharisees received a bad press in the Gospels, but, in reality, they originated under the Maccabees, or even earlier, and had sought strict adherence to the Law (Torah) in order to create a pure Israel for God. Scrupulously observing ritual commandments for prayer, fasting, purity rituals and avoidance of the unclean, they desired the promised Messiah of David's line who would take over Jerusalem and destroy pagan power. A second religious party was the Sadducees, a priestly Jerusalem caste. They were extremely conservative, rejecting all written additions to the Torah and having a strong voice in the religious and judicial institution, the Sanhedrin. The Gospels also mention the scribes, a teaching class that interpreted the Law for daily life. Addressed as rabbi, they were carefully trained, engaging in philosophical and religious debates. During the time of Jesus, they were linked to the Pharisees, who controlled religious education in the synagogues.

'Now the birth of Jesus Christ was on this wise: When as his mother Mary was espoused to Joseph, before they came together, she was found with child of the Holy Ghost.'

Matthew 1:18

JESUS QUESTIONING THE TEACHERS
One of the few recorded events from the childhood of Jesus – his conversation with the teachers in the Temple at Jerusalem – is portrayed here by Jacopo Bassano (1517–92).

Two remaining groups deserve mention. The Zealots were an extremely militant nationalist group that wanted a theocracy based on the Law, their political aspirations also looking forward to rule by the promised Messiah. The final religious group was the Essenes, normally identified with the sect living at Qumran. This monastic-style community has sometimes been described as similar in thought to Jesus and John the Baptist, but there are diametrically opposed views, especially Jesus's commandment of love to all, including outcasts and sinners.

The precise date of the birth of Jesus is unknown. Matthew locates it toward the end of Herod the Great's reign (c. 4 BC), while Luke links it to an unrecorded census ordered by the Emperor Augustus, associating this with the tax registration ordered by the Roman governor Quirinius, which occurred in AD 6. There is also evidence of a census implemented around 8 BC. Two Gospels, Matthew and Luke, give us some information about Jesus's birth and childhood, providing genealogies tracing his descent through Abraham, David and his father, Joseph, presumably as proof of Jesus's messiahship. Tradition has Bethlehem – King David's home town – as Jesus's birthplace. In Matthew's Gospel, Bethlehem is considered as Joseph's and Mary's original residence, but they move to Nazareth because of the Herodian threat. Luke, however, has the couple living in Nazareth but travelling to Bethlehem, because Joseph was obliged to register at the Davidic place of origin. Both Gospels, therefore, link Jesus with the Old Testament Messiah as the hope of Israel.

Bethlehem's provenance has an interesting history. The town is mentioned in a prophecy from the Book of Micah, possibly dating from just after the fall of Jerusalem and the Davidic line in 587 BC:

'Now gather thyself in troops, O daughter of troops: he hath laid siege against us: they shall smite the judge of Israel with a rod upon the cheek. But thou, Bethlehem Ephratah, though thou be little among the thousands of Judah, yet out of thee shall he come forth unto me that is to be ruler in Israel; whose goings forth have been from old, from everlasting. Therefore will he give them up, until the time that she which travaileth hath brought forth: then the remnant of his brethren shall return unto the children of Israel. And he shall stand and feed in the strength of the Lord, in the majesty of the name of the Lord his God; and they shall abide: for now shall he be great unto the ends of the earth' (Micah 5: 1–4).

According to the Gospels, Mary was an unmarried woman residing in Nazareth in Galilee, where she was betrothed to Joseph, a carpenter and presumably an accomplished artisan. The archangel Gabriel told her she would conceive a child by the Holy Spirit. Joseph received an angelic instruction to marry her. Mary and Joseph's journey from Nazareth to Bethlehem in Judaea only seems likely if Joseph was originally resident there, with his family being property owners. Matthew has them in a 'house' (Matthew 2:11), and that there was not enough space in the extended family's 'room' or inn (Luke 2:7). Mary placed Jesus in an animal's food trough, which was an object sometimes placed near the entrance of 1st-Century AD houses. Perhaps the animals stayed near the front of the type of cave house known to have been used in Bethlehem at the time.

There may also have been another link with Bethlehem. Extracanonical evidence of a kind can be seen in the early 2nd-Century Infancy Gospel of James, a mainly legendary collection of tales about the origin of Jesus. Mary is the virgin daughter of a prosperous Jerusalem couple named Anna and Joachim. The gospel states she grew up in the Temple, which is possible if she had priestly descent. Her 'relative', Elisabeth, was a descendant of Aaron and married to Zacharias the priest (Luke 1:5).

The virginal conception of Jesus can be neither proved nor disproved. Acceptance of the case affirms the power and glory of God's work rather than dealing with the bitter consequences of an unplanned pregnancy. Interestingly, the doctrine of the virgin birth takes on and mocks an objection from Jesus's opponents. 'Howbeit we know this man whence he is: but when Christ cometh, no man knoweth whence he is' (John 7:27).

Baby Jesus was taken to the Temple at Jerusalem to be presented to God, where he was recognized as the Messiah by two elderly religious people: Simeon, who had been promised by God that he would not die before he had seen the Messiah, and the prophetess Anna.

Herod the Great, that cruel and insecure ruler, learned that wise men (magi) from the East were nearby. They told him that they were following a star, which they believed was a sign that the King of the Jews had been born. Herod's priests confirmed that it was prophesied that the Messiah would be born in Bethlehem. Herod told the magi to go to the village and find the baby because he wanted to worship the child. They travelled to Bethlehem, found Jesus and gave him presents of gold, frankincense and myrrh. Returning home, they were warned in a dream not to report back to Herod. This story is plausible: astrology was highly esteemed in the ancient world, especially Babylonia. A type of Jewish horoscope was found in the Dead Sea Scrolls. We do not know whether Herod went on to kill all the male babies in Bethlehem. There is no evidence of the 'massacre of the innocents'. If it did happen, the number would have been so small that it probably received scant attention.

Jesus, Mary and Joseph escaped Herod's fury by fleeing to Egypt, a logical refuge. Home to approximately one million Jews, this was the largest Jewish diaspora community, with a vibrant life, especially in Alexandria. Returning to Palestine, the family settled in Nazareth. There is little coverage of Jesus's childhood, but Mark

(Chapter 6) describes his family. His brothers have purely Jewish names: James, Joses, Juda and Simon; his sisters are unnamed. Presumably, Jesus was raised in obedience to the Torah, and he certainly took part in annual pilgrimages to Jerusalem as evidenced in the story of the boy Jesus in the Temple.

THE ORIGINS OF JESUS CHRIST

Jesus was born in Bethlehem, about 8 km (5 miles) south of Jerusalem, shortly before Herod the Great died. Strictly speaking,'Christ' is a title, the Greek translation of the Hebrew 'messiah', but it came into use as a surname for Jesus soon after his death and replaced the older 'Jesus of Nazareth'. Jesus lived in Nazareth, in Galilee, during his childhood.

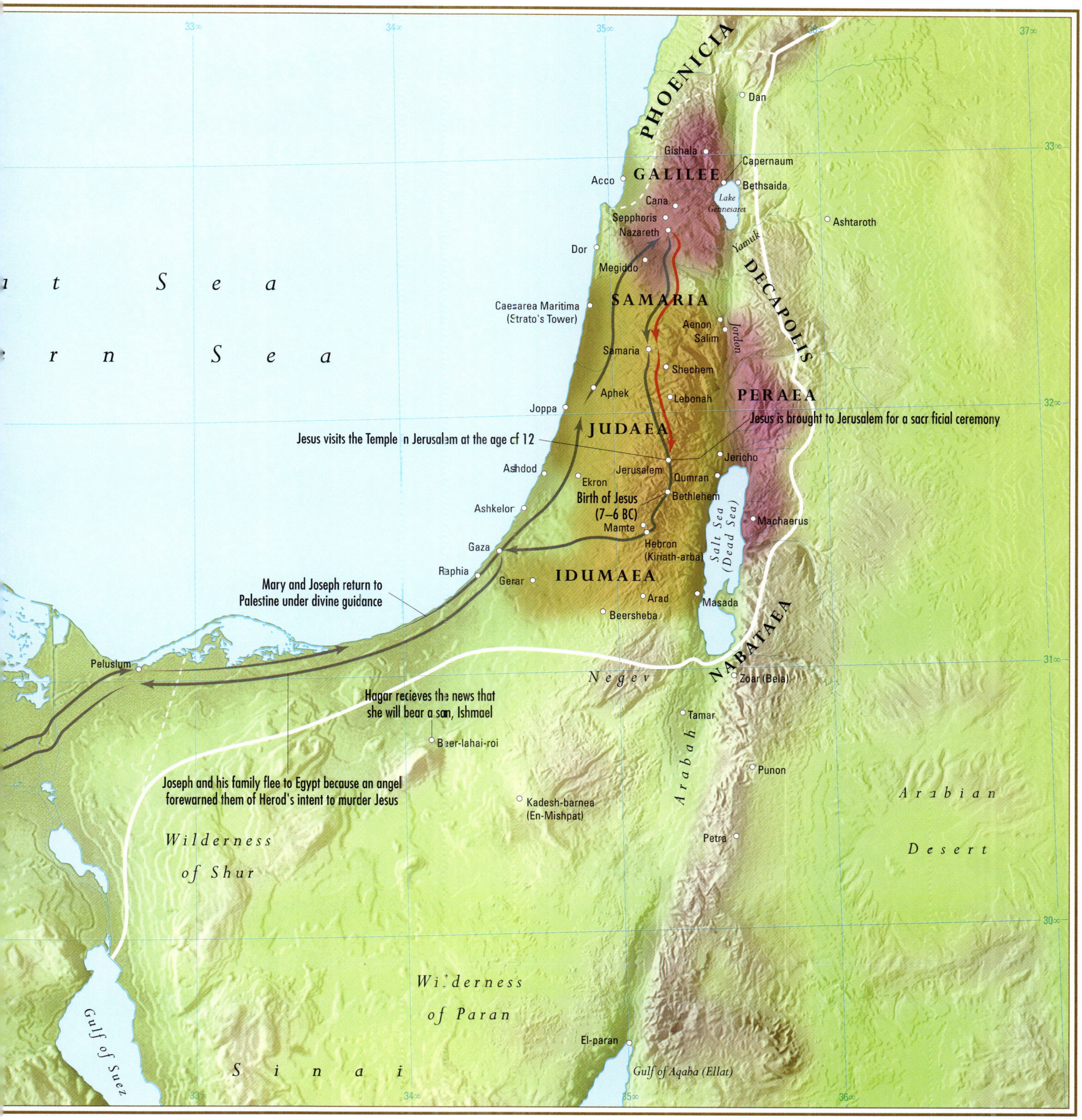

Judaea and Galilee

When Herod died in 4 BC, his will divided his kingdom into three parts. Archelaus, Herod's son by a Samaritan wife, was to be king in Jerusalem over Judaea, Idumaea and Samaria. This region included the Hellenized cities of Sebaste and Caesarea.

Herod Antipas, Archelaus's younger brother, was made tetrarch of Galilee and Peraea, lands separated by the cities of the Decapolis. Their half-brother Philip – son of Cleopatra, one of Herod's Jewish wives (he had ten wives in total) – was made tetrarch of the predominantly gentile areas north and east of the Sea of Galilee, a sizeable but relatively poor area. Salome, Herod's sister, acquired Jamnia, Azotus, Phasaelis and Herod's palace in the free city of Ascalon. The Hellenized cities of Gaza on the coast and the inland cities of Gadara and Hippus in Transjordan were placed under the governor of Syria. This hotchpotch heritage had many political units, but no real power. Overseeing the entire area was Rome.

To have the will ratified by Augustus, Archelaus went to Rome from Caesarea, leaving the region in ferment. In Jerusalem, the inhabitants protested against Herod's recent execution of two rabbis. Archelaus, failing to pacify the crowds, called out troops to stop rioting that left 3,000 of his subjects dead. Even Herod had not managed such a shambles. Philip was left to defuse the situation. Antipas also went to Rome, claiming that a previous will made him the ruler of all Herod's kingdom. Philip turned up in time to support Archelaus and his own interests.

Meanwhile, a riotous Jerusalem fomented trouble in the countryside, forcing Varus, Roman governor of Syria, to impose control and stability. He left a legion to keep the peace when he returned to Syria, but his main financial official, Sabinus, exacerbated the situation by attempting to grab Herod's treasure and hold it in safe-keeping for the emperor. Archelaus's troops prevented this, causing an even more difficult situation. At the Feast of Pentecost, pilgrims from all over Herod's former kingdom flooded the Jerusalem streets and fighting spread through the city. Many of Herod's veteran soldiers joined the rebels, while Roman soldiers and 3,000 auxiliaries, mainly from Sebaste, attempted to crush them.

Violent outbreaks occurred all over the country, which demonstrated its instability. Judaea witnessed 2,000 Herodian veterans driving loyal troops led by Herod's cousin, Achiab,

'But when he [Joseph] heard that Archelaus did reign in Judaea in the room of his father Herod, he was afraid to go thither: notwithstanding, being warned of God in a dream, he turned aside into the parts of Galilee: And he came and dwelt in a city called Nazareth: that it might be fulfilled which was spoken by the prophets, He shall be called a Nazarene.'

Matthew 2:22–23

THE RULE OF THE TETRARCHS

After the death of Herod the Great, his kingdom was divided between his three sons – Antipas, Archelaus and Philip. They became known as tetrarchs of the Tetrarchy of Judaea.

from the plains into the hills. Athronges, a shepherd, claimed kingship, despite having no claim to power, and engaged in guerrilla warfare. In Galilee, a thief named Judas terrorized the population and with other bandits captured Sepphoris, plundering the city and its royal palace. Simon, a former slave of Herod, burned the royal palace at Jericho and was probably responsible for torching that at Beth-ramatha. Simon was caught and beheaded, but violence continued in Peraea and the Amathus palace was incinerated.

Varus returned from Syria with two legions and cavalry, together with a sizeable Nabataean cavalry and infantry force loaned by Aretas IV. He placed his son in command of an armed detachment to liberate western Galilee. Roman forces captured Sepphoris, selling its inhabitants into slavery and burning the city. Varus spared Sebaste, making camp at Arus to serve as a springboard in an attack against Jerusalem. As Varus marched on Jerusalem, his Nabataean allies torched Arus. They went on to the village of Sappho, as Varus burnt Emmaus. He rapidly cleared Jerusalem, liberating Roman troops held under siege inside the city. Rebels were hunted down and captured; 2,000 were crucified. Achiab persuaded 10,000 men to surrender, their leaders being sent to Rome where they were subsequently released unless they were related to Herod.

Meanwhile, in Rome, Augustus accepted Herod's will but reduced Archelaus from king to ethnarch – still a higher rank than that of tetrarch, given to his brothers. Archelaus reigned for nearly ten years, before a delegation of Jews and Samaritans complained to Augustus about his harsh rule. The ethnarch was summoned to Rome, deposed, and exiled to Gaul. Samaria, Judaea and Idumaea were united as the Roman province of Judaea (AD 6).

Antipas then ruled for nearly 33 years, bringing peace and prosperity to Galilee and Peraea. He succeeded in not offending his Jewish subjects and even acquired the support of the Herodians, a pro-Roman group that preferred indirect rule from Rome through their tetrarch. He rebuilt recently destroyed cities, renaming Sepphoris as Autocratoris and Beth-ramatha as Livias in honour of the emperor's wife. He also built Tiberias, renowned for its warm springs.

Antipas divorced his first wife, who was a daughter of Aretas IV of Nabataea, and married Herodias, former wife of his half-brother Herod. The marriage was controversial, instigating a war with Aretas in which Antipas was defeated. John the Baptist criticized his marriage and was beheaded after the manipulation of Antipas by Herodias and her daughter, Salome. After persistent harassment by his wife, Antipas went to Rome demanding that Emperor Caligula make him king. Caligula promptly deposed him, exiling him to Lugdunum (Lyons) in Gaul in AD 39. It is to Herod Antipas that Pontius Pilate, procurator of Judaea, sent Jesus (Luke 23: 7–15).

'And when Herod saw Jesus, he was exceeding glad: for he was desirous to see him of a long season, because he had heard many things of him; and he hoped to have seen some miracle done by him. Then he questioned with him in many words; but he answered him nothing.'

Luke 23:8–9

Philip was the most successful heir to Herod the Great. His land was the rugged north, mountainous, with rough steppe and plateaux. The mainly gentile population was ruled moderately. He enlarged Paneas, making it his capital and renaming it Caesarea Philippi. Near where the Jordan flows into the Sea of Galilee, he turned the fishing village of Bethsaida into a town he called Julias. Bethsaida was the home of Jesus's disciples, Peter, Andrew and Philip. He lived quietly with his wife Salome, the same who was responsible for the death of John the Baptist.

The peace established by Antipas and Philip continued during the first three Roman governors. Caesarea Maritima took over from Jerusalem as the capital, and the only armed force present was 3,000 auxiliaries drawn from the local populations of non-Jewish Sebaste and Caesarea. The comfortable existence was shattered when Valerius Gratus, the first governor of Emperor Tiberias, came to Judaea in AD 15. He deposed the High Priest, Annas, the post eventually going to his son-in- law Joseph Caiaphas. This hostile personality worked with Pontius Pilate, a man who failed to understand the national pride and religious convictions of Jews, and who gave way to the Sanhedrin, sentencing Jesus to death.

JOHN THE BAPTIST PAYS THE PRICE

In a 17th-Century painting from the school of the artist Rembrandt, Salome fixes her eyes on the man who has beheaded John the Baptist. It was her manipulation of Antipas that brought about the violent act.

The Ministry of Jesus

Jesus did not begin his ministry until he was already 30 years old. The way had been prepared for him, however, by the preaching of John the Baptist, who himself baptized Jesus in the River Jordan.

Zacharias was a priest, and he and his wife, Elisabeth, were godly people but elderly and childless. The archangel Gabriel appeared to Zacharias and told him that his wife would have a son, called John, who would be a great man of God. Zacharias did not believe that he and Elisabeth could have a child at their age, and because of his disbelief he was made dumb. This affliction, though, left him after Elisabeth gave birth to John.

John became a preacher, living an ascetic life in the desert. He preached the need for repentance and baptism, and he spoke of a greater one to come after him. John baptized many people in the Jordan, including Jesus. At the moment John baptized Jesus, the Holy Spirit descended in the form of a dove and a voice from heaven said, 'Thou art my beloved son. In thee I am well pleased.'

John's uncompromising preaching made him enemies. He criticized Herod Antipas for marrying his brother's wife, Herodias, and was imprisoned. Her daughter, Salome, danced for Herod on his birthday, so pleasing him that he promised to give her anything she wanted. At her mother's prompting, she asked for the head of John the Baptist on a dish. The promise was kept and John was beheaded.

After his baptism, Jesus went into the desert and fasted for 40 days and nights. The Devil tempted him, suggesting that if Jesus were God's son he could turn the stones into bread, but Jesus resisted him. The Devil then tempted Jesus with power and wealth; Jesus again resisted him. Jesus was led to Jerusalem, to the highest point of the Temple, where the Devil prompted him to throw himself down to test whether God would save him, but once again Jesus managed to resist temptation.

Jesus now began his ministry in Galilee, preaching and healing, and immediately began to attract crowds who recognized his gifts and authority. He started to collect a following and called 12 men to be his particular disciples and accompany him everywhere. The first of these were two pairs of brothers, Peter and Andrew and James and John. These four were all fishermen and Jesus called them from their boats to follow him. Another of the disciples, Matthew, was a tax collector. Although this was a despised profession, Matthew, too, was called.

Jesus delivered his message to many different types and sizes of audience: to individuals, to the intimate group of his disciples, to the congregation in a synagogue, and also to huge crowds gathered in the open air. The content of his preaching also varied widely, but the main themes were the fatherhood and the authority of God and the need for personal righteousness and selfless love. It was not to this wider public but mainly with his disciples that he spoke of his role as the Son of God and predicted his own death and Resurrection.

Probably the most memorable of Jesus's sermons was the Sermon on the Mount, delivered to his disciples and a large crowd. It is a revolutionary sermon, starting with the Beatitudes, where Jesus states that happiness lies not in wealth, health or success, but in humility, mercy, peacemaking and spiritual hunger. He went on to suggest that anger is as great a sin as murder and lustful thoughts as bad as adultery. He urged love for one's enemies, disregard for money and possessions and attention to our own sins rather than condemnation of the sins of others. He warned his hearers to avoid hypocritical, ostentatious

worship and prayer, and taught them the prayer that has come to be known as the Lord's Prayer.

One of the most notable aspects of Jesus's preaching was his conveying of messages through parables: short allegorical stories of everyday life that illustrated his spiritual points. Many striking parables are related in the Gospels, including the stories of the Good Samaritan and the Prodigal Son. The former tells of a man who was attacked and robbed by thieves and left wounded on the road. First a priest and then a Levite came along the road and saw him, but both passed by on the other side. Then a Samaritan man came along. Jews and Samaritans were traditionally hostile to each other, but this Samaritan tended to the injured man, bound his wounds, and paid for him to be cared for at a local inn. The story illustrated the doctrine that we should love our neighbours, and that our neighbour is anyone in need. The parable of the Prodigal Son illustrated the fatherly love and mercy of God with a story of a young man who leaves home and squanders his inheritance on riotous living until he is reduced to penury. When he shamefully returns home, he is joyfully welcomed and forgiven by his father.

BAPTISM OF CHRIST
A painting by Elisabetta Sirani (1638–65) from the baroque church of San Girolamo della Certosa, in Bologna, Italy, shows John the Baptist baptizing a kneeling Jesus, with God the Father looking down from above.

In his three-year ministry, Jesus performed many miracles, and the majority were concerned with the healing of either physical or mental sickness. He restored sight to the blind, speech to the dumb and hearing to the deaf (Matthew 9:27–33; 12:22; 20:29–34). He healed people suffering with leprosy, paralysis and epilepsy (Matthew 8:2–3; 9:2–7; 17:14–18). He delivered people from demonic possession (Luke 4:33–35; 8:27–35; 11:14). He was even able to heal from a distance (John 4:46–54). On three occasions he raised people from the dead: a widow's son and Jairus's young daughter (Luke 7:11–15; 8:41–42, 49–56); and Lazarus, Jesus's friend, who was raised four days after his death and burial (John 11:1–44).

There were also miracles that involved a supernatural mastery over natural forces. Many of these happened on the sea: the calming of the storm (Matthew 8:23–27); Jesus walking on the water (John 6:19–21); two miraculous

catches of fish (Luke 5:1–11; John 21:1–11); and the coin found in the fish's mouth (Matthew 17:24–27). Other miracles in this category include the feeding of the 5,000, when a vast crowd was fed by the multiplication of five loaves and two small fishes (Matthew 14:15–21), and the transformation of water into wine when drink ran out at a wedding feast at Cana (John 2:1–11).

The people who were closest to Jesus, once his ministry had started, were his disciples. The men whose relationship with Jesus was the most intimate were apparently Peter, James and John. John is described as 'the disciple whom Jesus loved'. Besides these, there were several women who were close to Jesus, particularly Mary Magdalene, whom he had healed of demonic possession, and the two sisters from Bethany, Martha and Mary. In his attitude toward Mary of Bethany, Jesus demonstrated his disregard for the conventions of the day, when women were not expected to attend to religious teaching. Martha was annoyed when her sister sat at Jesus's feet listening to his teaching, rather than helping with the domestic chores, but Jesus gently rebuked Martha, and commended Mary's choice (Luke 10:38–42).

Another example of Jesus's disregard for the conventions of sex and race is his conversation with a Samaritan woman (John 4:4–26); it was unheard of for a Jewish teacher to speak to a strange woman, and Jews

JESUS RESISTS TEMPTATION

This 12th-Century fresco shows a black, white-winged Devil tempting Jesus during his time in the wilderness.

and Samaritans did not mix. His concern for individuals is shown again in his encounter with the fraudulent tax collector, Zacchaeus (Luke 19:1–10), who climbed a tree to get a better view when Jesus came to Jericho. Jesus called Zacchaeus down and said that he was going to stay at his house and Zacchaeus repented of his cheating.

Jesus was happier in the company of repentant tax collectors and prostitutes than with the religious leaders and teachers of his day, particularly the strict legalistic sect of Pharisees. He often rebuked them for their hypocrisy and they constantly sought to catch him out in flouting the law. This often involved Jesus's attitude to the Sabbath; traditionally this was a day of rest from work, but Jesus thought that healing on this holy day was legitimate. The story of the woman taken in adultery (John 8:1–11) illustrates Jesus' conflict with the Pharisees and compassion for individual sinners. The Pharisees had caught an adulteress and asked Jesus why she should not be stoned to death, as the law strictly demanded. Jesus's reply was to challenge the Pharisees: 'He that is without sin amongst you, let him first cast a stone at her.' The woman's accusers then left one by one.

THE GEOGRAPHY OF JESUS'S MINISTRY

The Synoptic Gospels represent the ministry of Jesus as being centred on the area around the Sea of Galilee. John's Gospel suggests that the ministry lasted for over a year, including several visits to Jerusalem.

The Last Days of Jesus

Jesus decided to spend his final Passover in Jerusalem, where he could reach the widest possible audience. His last days started with a triumphal entrance into the city and ended with arrest, trial, the journey to Calvary and eventual Crucifixion.

While in Galilee, Jesus had created a movement, allowing a circle of disciples and followers to share in his ministry and wanderings. Tradition has identified the latter group with the Apostles. Their number symbolizes the 12 tribes of Israel. If Jesus did appoint these men, then he made an eschatological claim on the whole of Israel. According to Matthew 19:28 and Luke 22:30, he conferred on the 12 the task of ruling and judging a perfected Israel when the New Age dawned.

Jesus went to Jerusalem probably several times, as John's Gospel alleges, but he decided to go there for what was his last Passover in order to reach a wider audience, calling the people of Israel together to teach of the coming Kingdom of God. Conflict with religious authorities was highly likely, and Jesus must have been aware of this possibility. He, maybe, even imagined his arrest and execution. Possibly, he wished to proclaim his message before being silenced forever.

Jesus would face both Pharisees and Sadducees in Jerusalem, the latter controlling the Sanhedrin and using wide powers under the Romans. They certainly opposed any apparently political activity among the population, seeing such as a threat to the Romans and themselves. Jesus had perhaps locked horns with these groups in Galilee. Certainly, his ministry would have become news. He taught in the city and there are vignettes of him 'that on one of those days, as he taught the people in the Temple and preached the gospel, the chief priests and the scribes came upon him ...' (Luke 20:1).

What is interesting is the violent way in which Jesus sought to cleanse the Temple by driving out the traders and money changers. Mark claims he upset the tables, while John reports he made a whip of cords to lash these people in his drive to clear the building. His actions were an attempt to end the secularization of the Temple. The money changers were there to exchange Greek and Roman coinage for Jewish currency, which would be used to pay Temple dues. Possibly, Jesus objected to the manner

'On the next day much people that were come to the feast, when they heard that Jesus was coming to Jerusalem, Took branches of palm trees and went forth to meet him, and cried, Hosanna: Blessed is the King of Israel that cometh in the name of the Lord. And Jesus, when he had found a young ass, sat thereon; as it is written, Fear not daughter of Sion: behold, thy King cometh, sitting on an ass's colt.'

(John 12:12–15)

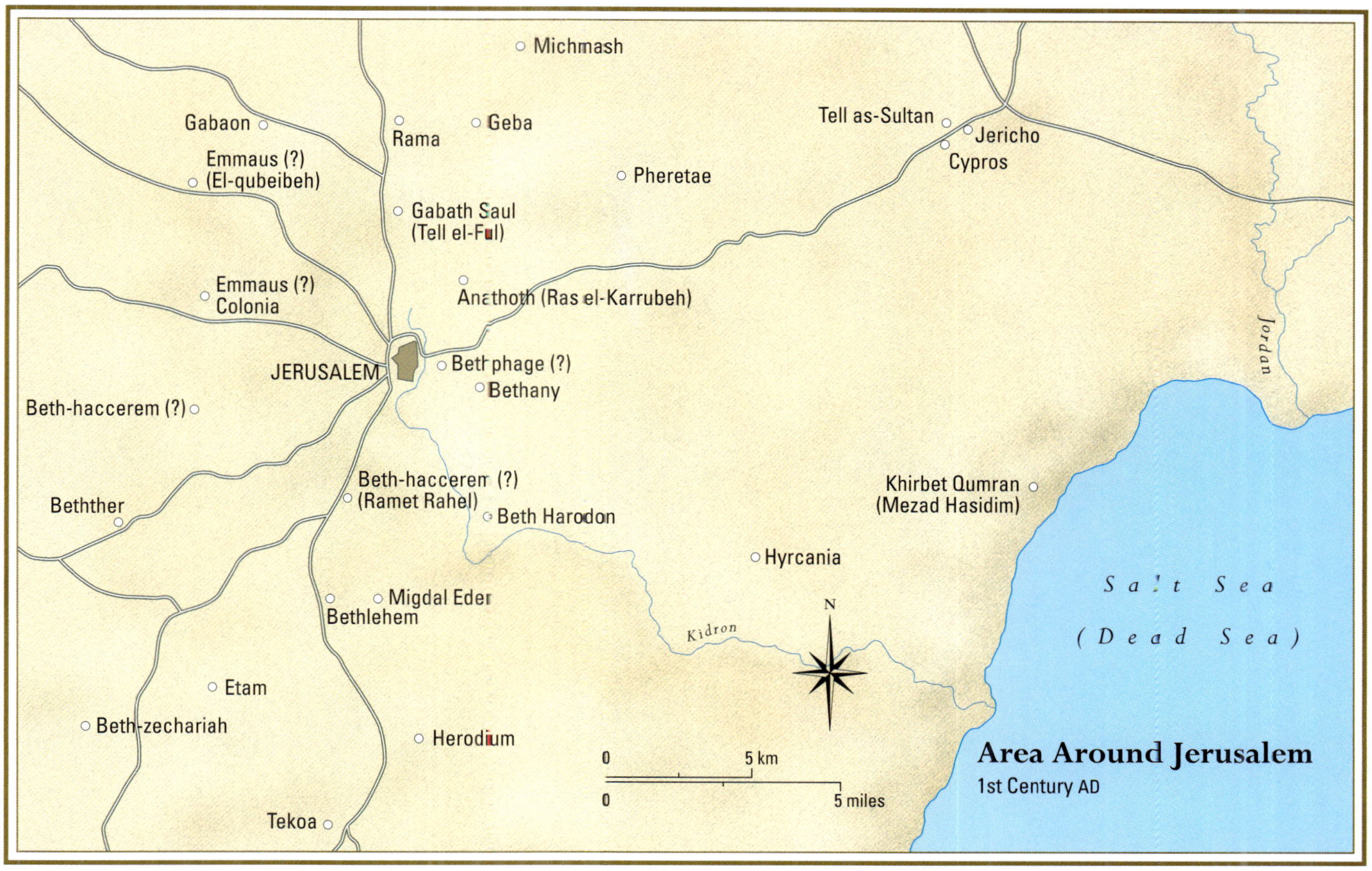

ALL ROADS LEAD TO JERUSALEM
Jesus began his life at Bethlehem, barely 8 kilometres (5 miles) south of Jerusalem, the city where he was to end his days.

of sacrifice. Detailed regulations governed such rituals, with the implication that following rules was sufficient to worship God. Jesus was witnessing the perceived economic and spiritual injustice in the 'corrupt' operation of the Temple. Interestingly, the merchants' business was transacted in the large outer court of the Temple, the only part of the Temple where Gentiles might go. Qumran texts also allude to the Temple as a seat of robbers. There is an accusation reportedly levelled at Jesus's trial: 'We heard him say, I will destroy this temple that is made with hands, and within three days I will build another made without hands' (Mark 14:58). Layered upon this is the prediction of Jesus's own Resurrection after three days, which would signal the New Age and the Kingdom of God.

Whatever the case, Jesus was not arrested because of the people's sympathy. 'And he taught, saying unto them, Is it not written, My house shall be called of all nations the house of prayer? But ye have made it a den of thieves. And the scribes and chief priests heard it, and sought how they might destroy him: for they feared him, because all the people was astonished at his doctrine' (Mark 11:17–18). 'And could not find what they might do: for all the people were very attentive to hear him' (Luke 19:48). Jesus was appealing to the Biblical prophets and their condemnation of moral injustice in the cult of Yahweh, interpreting the present corruption of the priestly caste as doomed to destruction.

Jesus was acting very much like a Jeremiah, causing offence and political liability to the priestly hierarchy, and to many others in Jerusalem whose social and material status depended upon the Temple trade. Jesus also disputed with the questions of the chief priests, the scribes, the Pharisees and the Sadducees about his authority, tribute to Caesar and the resurrection.

'Is it lawful for us to give tribute unto Caesar, or no? But he perceived their craftiness, and said unto them, Why tempt me ye? Shew me a penny. Whose image and superscription hath it? They answered and said, Caesar's. And he said unto them, Render therefore unto Caesar the things which be Caesar's, and unto God the things which be God's' (Luke 20:22–25).

Jesus also told his disciples the signs that would usher in the second coming, the Parousia. He went to Bethany just before Passover and was anointed with spikenard

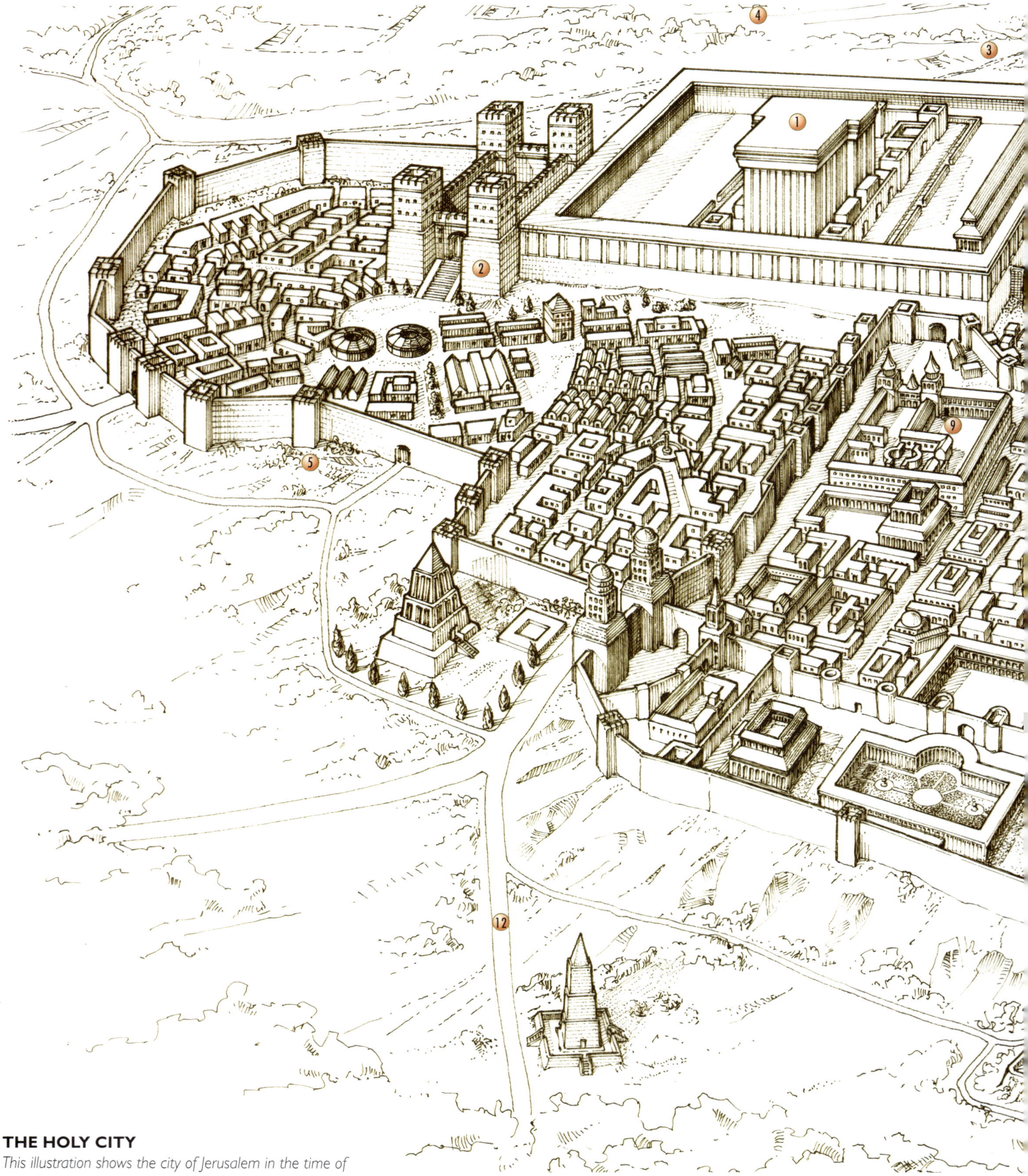

THE HOLY CITY

This illustration shows the city of Jerusalem in the time of Jesus. The impression is based on archaeological finds, though the exact layout of the city will never be known.

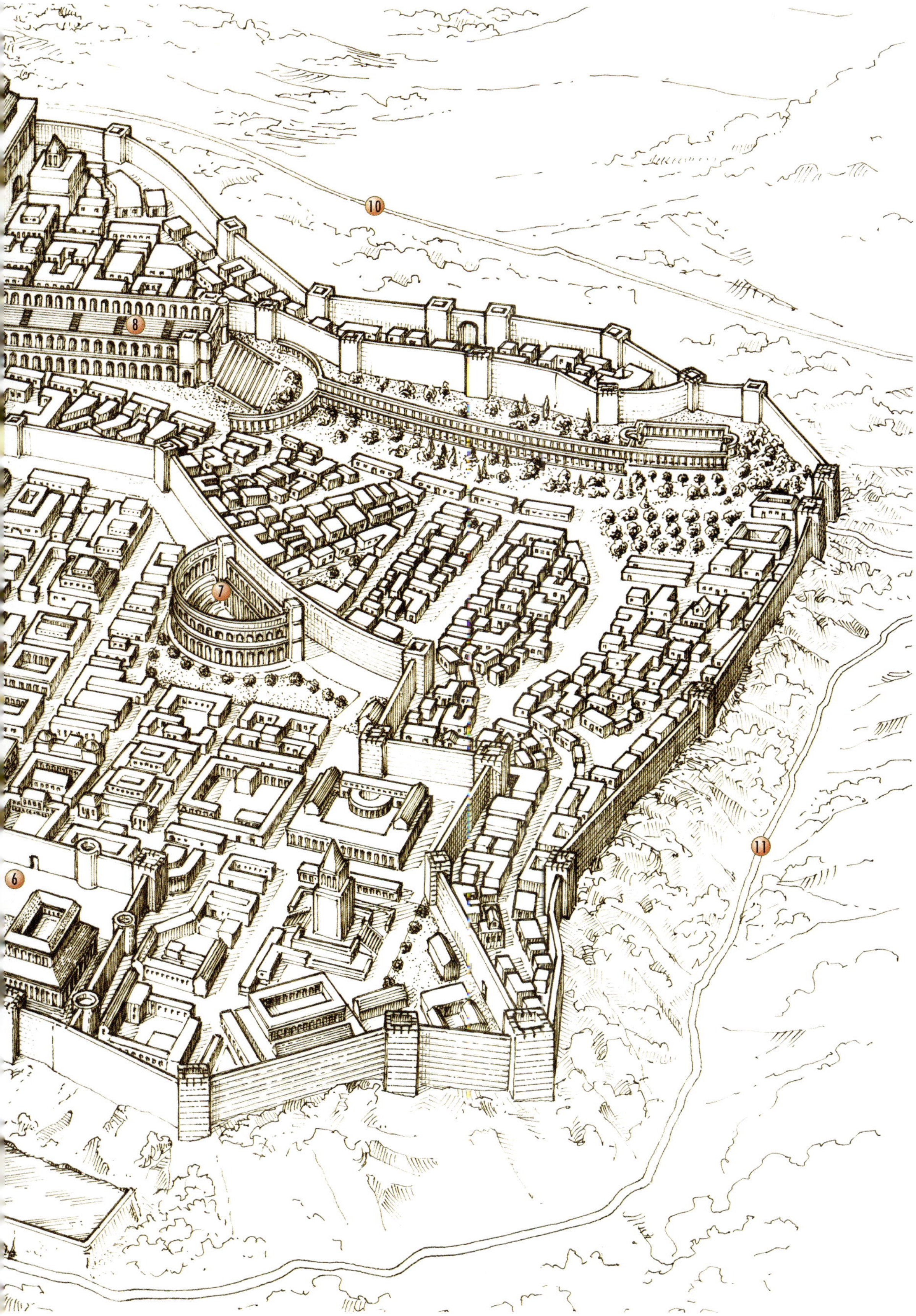

1 The Temple
2 Fortress of Antonia
3 Garden of Gethsemane
4 Mount of Olives
5 Calvary (Golgotha)
6 Herod's Palace
7 Theater
8 Hippodrome
9 Hasmonean Palace
10 Kidron Valley
11 Hinnom Valley
12 Bethlehem Road

oil, a costly fragrant ointment used in ancient times, to prepare for his burial (Matthew 26:6–13; Mark 14:3–9).

When Jesus finally made his triumphal entrance into Jerusalem, the crowds publicly acclaimed him, calling him the Messiah, very much as the old kings of Israel were acclaimed after being anointed. Some even shouted 'God bless the King of Israel'. Despite attempts to disassociate himself from politics, Jesus was increasingly identified with the desired national Messiah, who would free Israel from Roman rule and re-create a Jewish state. Certainly his popular support was visible, volatile and potentially explosive, so the authorities were bound to arrest him for sedition or some trumped-up charge. As Jesus's popularity grew, the chief priests and scribes saw him as increasingly dangerous, and they were determined to kill him. Just before the Passover, they met to plot against him. Judas Iscariot, one of the 12 disciples, went to them and agreed to betray his master in exchange for 30 pieces of silver. Jesus and his 12 disciples then gathered in a room of a house in Jerusalem to eat the Passover meal.

During the repast, Jesus made two predictions. He said that one of the disciples would betray him and that Peter would deny him three times before the cock crowed next morning. Historians have disputed the exact sequence of events, taking into account Jewish Law and the date of the Passover. However, the meaning of events is more significant than an exact chronology, although the chronology of John is perhaps the most likely – that the meal, the trial and the Crucifixion took place on the day preceding the Passover.

While they were all eating, Jesus broke the bread, gave thanks, handing it to his disciples, saying, 'Take, eat; this is my body.' Then he gave them wine to drink, saying, 'This is my blood ... shed for many for the remission of sins' (Matthew 26:28). The testament can be regarded as a new covenant with God and this ritual, the Eucharist, has been repeated by Christians in services ever since, becoming the central sacrament in Christian churches.

The historicity of the Last Supper is uncertain, and not all historians accept that Jesus meant there to be any major ritual meaning in his actions. However, the meal is mentioned in the Gospels and is symbolic of the group's 'communion' with God. Additionally, Jesus knew Jewish religious books, or he would not have used the words of Isaiah and Jeremiah regarding the Temple. Surely, since he publicized himself in prophetical terms, he would cleanse the Temple and enact a new covenant with God as had occurred so often in Jewish history. The Last Supper is part of the Christian tradition and is mentioned by St Paul in his letters (1 Corinthians 11:23–26).

Jesus went with Peter, James and John to Gethsemane, a garden on the slopes of the Mount of Olives. He was in a state of deep sorrow, 'being in an agony' (Luke 22:44), and retreated to pray by himself, begging God to take the burden of suffering from him.

When he returned to the disciples, they had fallen asleep. He spoke to them, and they observed Judas Iscariot approaching, with an armed crowd. Judas went up to Jesus and kissed him, as a sign that this was the man that they were to arrest. Jesus was seized and taken to the High Priest's house; his disciples ran away.

Jesus was accused of blasphemy, physically abused and mocked. Meanwhile, Peter stayed in the courtyard of the High Priest's house to see what would happen. As he sat there, a servant girl approached him and asked if he was one of the men who were with Jesus. Peter denied knowledge of Jesus. Another servant girl asked the same question, and again Peter denied Jesus. One of the men there insisted that Peter was one of Jesus's friends because his Galilean accent gave him away. Yet again, Peter denied all knowledge of Jesus; then, the cock crowed.

The High Priest was Caiaphas, who held the position from AD 18 to 36, although his father-in-law, Annas, deposed from the position, called the shots. The Sanhedrin, sitting in judgement over Jesus, comprised, apart from the High Priest, 70 members drawn from three different groups. The first was known as 'the high priests'. They were priests and laymen directed by the High Priest and in charge of the day-to-day administration of religious affairs. The second group, 'the elders', consisted of the heads of distinguished families. Their contribution gradually diminished because they became increasingly incapable of dealing with religious schisms. The final group – the scribes – had an increasing influence. These men had studied and could interpret the Law and apply it to everyday affairs. In the Sanhedrin, the Pharisees and Sadducees had various supporters, though the Sadducees were dominant. Their supporters were found among 'the high priests' and 'elders', whereas the Pharisees were strong with the scribes who represented the Pharisaic school. The composition of the Sanhedrin boded ill for Jesus – he could expect neither sympathy nor mercy.

Jesus would also face Pontius Pilate, the Roman governor, who understood nothing of Jewish culture or religion. He was merely concerned with the authority of Rome, trampling on everybody's feelings. He allowed

PILATE REMOVES THE BLAME

This famous scene in the life of Jesus is portrayed by a 5th-Century Italian artist, who shows Pontius Pilate, the Roman governor, washing his hands in front of the crowd.

his troops to enter Jerusalem carrying insignia showing the Emperor's image. Octavian, Augustus Caesar, had previously promised the Jews that he would grant Jerusalem immunity from any sign of the cult of the ruler. Pilate would listen to people's demands only when they became highly vociferous. He even took funds from the Temple money chest to pay for a water conduit that led from the pools of Solomon to Jerusalem. In AD 36, when disturbances erupted in Samaria, he used so much brutality and violence that the Emperor had him removed. This, then, was the personality that Jesus would face.

According to John (18:13–24), Jesus was taken before Annas for investigation. The Synoptic Gospels fail to mention this occurrence, stating that Jesus was taken before the Sanhedrin. Here, Caiaphas asked Jesus to say whether he was 'the Christ [Messiah], the Son of God' (Matthew 26:63). Jesus's 'affirmation' (Mark 14:62) caused the Sanhedrin to condemn him to death for blasphemy. However, only the Roman Governor, Pilate, was empowered to use capital punishment. So Jesus was possibly taken to the fortress by the Temple Mount, the traditional site for the trial, near what is now the Ecce Homo (Behold the Man) arch, where Pilate is believed to have shown Jesus to the crowd. Pilate asked him if he was King of the Jews. Jesus replied, 'You have said so' (Mark 15:2). Pilate tried several times to save Jesus but finally left the decision to the priests and rabble. When the people demanded his death, Pilate ordered him to be executed (Matthew 27:24).

Jesus was whipped and mocked by Roman soldiers, who made him a crown of thorns. He was taken to the place of Crucifixion – Calvary, or Golgotha – where he was nailed to the cross and left to die, along with two criminals who were being similarly punished. The traditional route to Golgotha is the Via Dolorosa, and the place of execution was where the Church of the Holy Sepulchre now stands. Crucifixion was the normal Roman punishment for political offenders and criminals. On the cross above Jesus's head was a statement saying 'This is Jesus the King of the Jews' (Matthew 27:37). Later, the body was taken down, and owing to the approach of the Sabbath was quickly put in a nearby tomb by Joseph of Arimathea and, according to John, by Nicodemus.

Early the following Sunday, Mary Magdalene and Mary, the mother of James, went to the tomb to anoint Jesus's body for a proper burial but found the tomb empty. Mark claims that a young man clothed in white was in the tomb, announcing that Jesus had risen. According to John (20:11–18), Mary Magdalene saw two angels and then the risen Jesus. Later on the same day, Jesus apparently appeared to disciples in various places around Jerusalem. Most disciples knew what they had seen, but Thomas doubted. The Resurrection of Jesus became the most compelling doctrine of Christianity because, by rising from the dead, Jesus gave hope of a life after death in the Kingdom of Heaven. All the Gospels state that after the Resurrection, Jesus continued to teach his disciples about the Kingdom of God. He also said, 'Go ye therefore, and teach all nations, baptizing them in the name of the Father, and of the Son and of the Holy Ghost: Teaching them to observe all things whatsoever I have commanded you: and, lo, I am with you alway, even unto the end of the world. Amen' (Matthew 28:19–20). Eventually, according to Luke, Jesus was seen, at Bethany, by his disciples to ascend into the heavens. The Acts of the Apostles states that the Ascension took place 40 days after the Resurrection.

The Gospels of the New Testament were written about 15 years after these events. Previously, Jesus's teachings were transmitted orally by people who had known him. The disciples and witnesses of the Crucifixion and Resurrection saw themselves as the chosen people, who were offering salvation to the world by trying to live as Jesus had done. They continued to worship in the Temple and synagogues of Judaism, but their experience of the Eucharist led them to a new interpretation of the Passover, the new covenant.

The disciples started to preach, as described in the Acts of the Apostles. The general structure and contents of the apostles' sermons and speeches are reflected in the Letters of the New Testament. Those who listened to the apostles heard that God's revelations in the Old Testament had reached their climax and fulfilment in the life, death and resurrection of Jesus. He was the Messiah, the Christ. He had come from God and had now returned to Him to be 'Lord of the whole creation', as both man and God. Through the Holy Spirit, Jesus Christ now shared his powers with the members of the Christian community, which was open to all who were prepared to turn to God, to accept Jesus as Lord and to receive baptism. They were told to act swiftly because God would soon bring his whole plan of salvation to its completion with the second coming of Jesus and a general judgement of all people.

The apostles supported their preaching and teaching with recollections of Jesus's life as they had witnessed it. They told of the things he had done and related, particularly details of his final days in Jerusalem, leading up to his Crucifixion and Resurrection. Christianity was still based on word of mouth, but the people who had known Jesus personally began to die or be killed. Hence, the Gospels were written down to record the apostles' experiences of Jesus. Some of this material may have been written down earlier, but it was not until about AD 65 that the first of the Gospels (probably Mark) was written in the form that is familiar today. This was some 35 years after the death of Jesus. During the next 20 years, the other three Gospels were written. The Gospels differ: the Synoptic Gospels of Matthew, Mark and Luke emphasize the messianic vocation of Jesus and concern themselves with everyday religious and ethical matters. In addition, John states the nature and purpose of Jesus from the start of the Gospel and expresses Jesus's divine nature and relationship to God. The New Testament Letters date from about AD 45 to the end of the 1st Century.

CRUCIFIXION OF JESUS

This representation of the Crucifixion is from an engraving by the French artist Gustave Doré (1832–83).

Conversion of Saul

'And Saul, yet breathing out threatenings and slaughter against the disciples of the Lord, went unto the high priest, And desired of him letters to Damascus to the synagogues, that if he found any of this way, whether they were men or women, he might bring them bound unto Jerusalem.' Acts 9:1–2

Saul of Tarsus, an enthusiastic, youthful Pharisee, was born into a strict Jewish family in the town of Tarsus in Cilicia. He enjoyed Roman citizenship, inherited from his father, also a worthy and committed Pharisee. Saul was considered capable of further education and travelled to Jerusalem to study under the great teacher Rabbi Gamaliel. Saul was an eager student, ready to follow and confirm the ancient faith of his forefathers. The message of Jesus seemed to Saul to undermine all of his beliefs, leading him to oppose Jesus, his teachings, and his followers with extreme ferocity. He was happy to hunt down the followers of Jesus in and around the city of Jerusalem.

SAINT PAUL
In this painting by the Italian artist Bartolomeo Montagna (1450–1523), and in many other Christian images, Paul, originally Saul, is shown holding a book and a sword, which is possibly a reference to his death by beheading.

He was an approving witness to the stoning of Stephen. As Stephen was laid in his grave, Saul continued to ravage the followers of Jesus. While in Jerusalem, Saul was able to secure the necessary authority from the High Priest to travel to Damascus to search out and punish any followers of Jesus found in the synagogue there. With this heartfelt objective he hurried north from Jerusalem.

As Saul approached Damascus, he experienced a blinding vision, 'Saul, Saul, why persecutest thou me?' a voice clearly called out. Saul asked who it was who called him. Saul heard the challenging words, 'I am Jesus, whom thou persecutest … Arise, and go into the city and it shall be told thee what thou must do.' The blinded Saul was led by his companions into Damascus where he lay for three days refusing food and drink.

The disciple Ananias was instructed, in a vision, to lay his hands on Saul in order to restore his sight – 'Something like scales fell from his eyes'. Saul arose and was immediately baptized. In the synagogues of the city, Saul began to proclaim Jesus as the Son of God. There was immediately confusion among Saul's personal followers and among the Jews who knew of Saul's previous anti-Christian fervour. His friends hatched a plot to kill him. Although Saul managed to escape from them, he now had new enemies. Saul was lowered over the city walls in a basket and made good his escape southwards into Arabia, into the hands of the Nabataeans under their king, Aretas. Some three years later Saul, whom we can now call Paul, reappeared in Jerusalem. He was received with some reluctance by the disciples, but he was soon preaching fearlessly and, in so doing, earned the anger of Jerusalem's conservative Hellenists. He fled the dangers of Jerusalem to Caesarea, then by ship to his home in Tarsus. He remained there until he went with Barnabas to Antioch, where they worked tirelessly for a year to build the new Church. By now the disciples were, for the first time, called Christians.

'But Barnabas took him, and brought him to the apostles, and declared unto them how he had seen the Lord in the way, and that he had spoken to him, and how he had preached boldly at Damascus in the name of Jesus.'

Acts 9:27

Some time later, famine struck Judaea, and the church in Antioch decided to send relief, which was taken south by Paul and Barnabas. At about this time, the infant Christian community was subject to various bouts of persecution. Herod Agrippa decided to strike at the Christian leadership, hoping this would destroy the whole community. At Passover, the apostle Peter was thrown into prison and James was killed.

The night before Peter's trial he miraculously escaped, eventually leaving Jerusalem for a safe hiding place. The Christian leadership, with Paul among them, survived. Later, during a public spectacle, according to Josephus, Agrippa was overcome by intense pains and died shortly afterwards. The Christians regarded this as divine judgement for his persecution of their Church.

TRAVELS OF ENLIGHTENMENT

Saul journeyed from his home in Tarsus, in the Roman province of Cicilia, to Jerusalem as a zealous follower of Judaism. It was in Jerusalem that he defended the tradition of his fathers, believing that Jesus's message was undermining his ancient faith. While in Jerusalem, Saul secured authority from the High Priest to travel to Damascus in order to root out any followers of Jesus he found there. The road to Damascus would change his life.

Paul's Missionary Journeys

Soon there were Christian churches in Asia Minor and Greece, where Paul had concentrated his missionary efforts between AD 49 and 58. His letters to his converts were generally in response to specific problems, and he chided, praised, showed anger and even engaged in self-analysis.

The meeting of Church leaders in Jerusalem, which thrashed out the difficulties of non-Jews becoming Christians, took place in AD 48, 18 years after the death of Jesus. Almost all the available information in the New Testament now concentrates on the journeys of Paul into Asia Minor and Europe, until he reached Rome in AD 61. Undoubtedly there was much Christian activity before the war between the Jews and the Romans from AD 66 to 70, which led to the destruction of Jerusalem. By then, there were Christian churches in many places in the Near East and in Rome, only some of which had been founded by Paul on his first missionary journey, to the island of Cyprus and the southern part of Asia Minor. The traditional belief that Peter started the Church in Rome should be seen in this context.

Paul set out on his second missionary journey in AD 49, only intending to revisit the places where he had founded churches on his first journey. He and his companions travelled by land into Galatia, where Paul changed his plans by going to Troas, the busy port near the old site of Troy. From Troas, Paul and his party – including Luke – sailed to Neapolis, on the main land route from Italy to the east, and began their dramatic mission through Macedonia and Greece. Paul's letters show that he succeeded in forming small Christian groups in the towns he visited, but the reception he and his companions received was mixed, and occasionally violent.

At Philippi, where they went after Neapolis, Paul's party ran into trouble, which reveals much about the political problems of provincial towns in the Roman Empire. Paul and Silas were arrested, flogged and imprisoned to await trial on a charge of advocating practices unlawful for Romans. However, the two men were Roman citizens, a status that should have protected them from such treatment, and they were released. Citizenship was an honour that could be given by the Roman state or purchased; Paul had inherited his.

Thessalonica, a later stop, was a free city, where the Romans allowed locally elected magistrates to control affairs. Any hint of disloyalty to Rome would have ended such privileges, and Paul's party fled from the city when his new converts were accused of treason. They were again opposed in the next town, Beroea. As more trouble erupted, Paul journeyed to Athens, while the rest of his companions later left for Corinth. In Athens, Paul changed his methods and presented Christianity in terms of Greek philosophy, but the resurrection of Jesus was too much for most of his listeners, and Paul moved on to Corinth.

PAUL AND BARNABAS
In this painting by the Dutch artist Nicolaes Pietersz Berchem (1620–83) Paul and his companion Barnabas are mistaken for the Greek gods Hermes and Zeus as they preach in Lystra, in what is now modern Turkey.

As a great port and capital of the Roman province controlling southern Greece, and centre of the Aphrodite religion, Corinth was a large and cosmopolitan city. There, Paul and his helpers found the more positive response they had hoped for, and they stayed for 18 months. Paul's two Letters to the Thessalonians, probably written during this stay in Corinth, show that the Christian Church he founded there had a hard time after he left. His Letter to the Galatians reveals a different problem. That Church was insisting that Christians had to keep the Jewish laws as well. Paul feared that all his work among them would be undone. His letter – or epistle – to them is the angriest of all the letters he wrote.

Paul returned to Caesarea, the principal Roman administrative centre for Judaea, by way of Ephesus. It was a logical route for the safest sailing, with busy sea routes available across the Aegean to Ephesus, and round the coast of Asia Minor to Palestine. Paul established contacts among the Jews of Ephesus and promised these people that he would return.

He kept his promise quickly. After a short time at his home church of Antioch, Paul set off again and took the overland route through Galatia and Phrygia once more, but with Ephesus as his main destination. When he reached it he stayed for more than two years. According to Acts 19, Paul met with great success both in Ephesus and among the people of the surrounding area. So great, indeed, was Paul's success that it threatened the trade in silver copies of the famous statue of Diana of the Ephesians, to whom the city's main temple was dedicated. Rioting broke out, and Paul decided to leave for Macedonia, by way of Troas again.

While in Ephesus, Paul had written to the Church he had founded on the other side of the Aegean at Corinth. The consequences also contributed to his decision to move on. Paul's First Letter to the Corinthians starts with a series of rebukes for various matters that had been related to him about his Corinthian Christians. There were factions, law suits, a case of incest and members still worshipping at the Temple of Aphrodite. The letter comments on various questions raised in a letter he had received from Corinth, revealing concerns about marriage, social relationships with non-Christian friends, details of Church order and the Resurrection. The rebukes and the worries throw light on the experience of being a Christian in such a varied and busy city as ancient Corinth. But Paul's response to the situation in Corinth had startling repercussions for him. The Corinthian Christians were so angry that they came close to rejecting him. This may be the deeper reason for Paul leaving Ephesus. The sequence of events is not clear. He may have written another letter and paid a swift visit by sea, which only made matters worse. In the end, he sent his companion Titus to heal the breach and was then so anxious that he crossed from Troas to Macedonia to meet Titus on his way back.

Titus had succeeded, and Paul wrote his Second Letter to the Corinthians to send ahead as he made his way there. It is a very different letter from the first, full of reflection on the experience of preaching Christianity. It reveals more about Paul than anything else he wrote and about the experience of commitment to Christ. The three months Paul now spent in Corinth were the occasion for his most systematic exposition of his beliefs – his Letter to the Romans, in which he sets out his understanding of the Christian faith. He intended to make Rome the base for his next phase of work, and this letter formed his personal introduction to the Christians living there.

Paul and at least six companions retraced their steps through Macedonia to Philippi, and so by stages back

'Now I beseech you, brethren, by the name of our Lord Jesus Christ, that ye all speak the same thing, and that there be no divisions among you; but that ye be perfectly joined together in the same mind and in the same judgment. For it hath been declared unto me of you, my brethren … that there are contentions among you.'

1 Corinthians 1:10–11

to Jerusalem. The Jerusalem to which Paul returned in AD 58 was in ferment. Eight years later it erupted into the disastrous war between Jews and Romans in which Jerusalem was destroyed. Some of this turmoil can be seen in the events that led to Paul's arrest, his long wait

SPREADING THE WORD

Christianity began as a Jewish movement and spread from Palestine through the Hebrew groups dispersed in the main cities of the Roman Empire. Paul was largely instrumental in the success of this new religion.

'And it came to pass, that, while Apollos was at Corinth, Paul having passed through the upper coasts came to Ephesus: and finding certain disciples, He said unto them, have ye received the Holy Ghost since ye believed? And they said unto him, We have not so much as heard whether there be any Holy Ghost. And he said unto them, Unto what then were ye baptized? And they said, Unto John's baptism. Then said Paul, John verily baptized with the baptism of repentance, saying unto the people, that they should believe on him which should come after him, that is, on Christ Jesus. When they heard this, they were baptized in the name of the Lord Jesus.'

Acts 19:1–5

for his case to be heard, and his demand to be tried by the Emperor in Rome. Innocently enough, Paul went to the great Jewish Temple in Jerusalem to pray and to show that he did not encourage Jewish Christians to abandon their traditions. Rumour had it that he had taken a non-Jew into the Temple with him. Such desecration of the Temple carried the death penalty in Hebrew law, recognized by the Romans, and a crowd quickly gathered to lynch him.

Immediately alongside the wall of the Temple area stood the main guard tower of Jerusalem, which had been enlarged by Herod the Great and was now used by the Roman garrison. That, too, was an offence to strictly orthodox Jews. The Roman guard stopped the riot by arresting Paul, and he would have been interrogated under the lash if he had not told them that he held the privileges of Roman citizenship. The next move was a request for Paul, as a Jew, to be tried before the Sanhedrin, the main religious council, but word reached him that there was a plot to assassinate him on the way. The senior Roman officer in Jerusalem decided to move Paul to the safety of Caesarea, the main Roman administrative centre, which was well away from Jerusalem. They sent him there with a strong escort. At Caesarea, Paul could be tried by Felix, the procurator of Palestine, whose harshness towards the Jews under his rule was a major cause of the coming rebellion.

If Paul had been tried by Felix, the charges against him would certainly have been dismissed, but Felix kept him waiting two years, and then he was replaced by a new procurator, Festus. By this time, Paul had had enough. Although Festus was cast in a different mould from Felix, Paul exercised his rights as a Roman citizen to have his case transferred to Rome. Perhaps Paul was influenced by the actions of the current king, Herod Agrippa II (AD 50–c. 100), who had had James executed and Peter imprisoned. Even a Roman citizen might be sacrificed in the jungle of Palestinian politics.

Paul's voyage to Rome, in the charge of a centurion and a detachment of Roman soldiers, took the best part of a year. A coastal vessel carried the group to Myra, where they joined one of the great grain ships that sailed regularly between Egypt and Italy. Headwinds delayed progress and forced the ship down to Crete; then a storm drove them west for a fortnight until they ran aground on Malta, where the ship broke up. It was three months before the voyage could be resumed in another Egyptian corn ship, which called at Syracuse in Sicily and Rhegium on the toe of Italy, before finally reaching Putcoli near Neapolis (Naples). Paul found there were Christians at Putcoli and stayed a week there, then travelled with his escort along the Appian Way to Nero's Rome. It was AD 61, three years before the great fire of Rome and the beginning of Nero's persecution of Roman Christians.

When Paul first reached Rome there were no signs of hostility from any Roman officials towards Christians. Paul himself looked to the Roman administration for protection, so that he could be free to spread his beliefs. In his Letter to the Romans he even wrote that '... there is no power but of God: the powers that be are ordained by God' (Romans 13:1). The Roman Empire was near the height of its power, with control over the whole Mediterranean area, Spain, most of Europe, southern Britain and Egypt. Rome itself was a tightly knit maze of narrow streets and lanes, contrasting with large open spaces and imposing state buildings and temples. Nearly a million people lived in the city, with people from many

THE GREAT SEAT OF EMPIRE

The Forum of Rome, seen here from the Capitoline Hill, was the nerve centre of the most powerful empire in the ancient world. In his Letter to the Romans, Paul gives a clear exposition of the doctrine of justification by faith.

parts of the Empire attracted by the distribution of free food and the public amusements provided by prominent citizens or the state, as well as by the sheer wealth of the city. The final chapter of Romans shows that Paul already knew many of the Christians in Rome when he first arrived there.

The Acts of the Apostles ends with Paul's arrival in Rome and meetings he arranged with leading members of the Jewish community. It says that he spent 'two whole years in his own hired house' (Acts 28 30), where he would be under custody while waiting for his case to be heard, but neither Romans nor Acts says what happened to him. Later Christian writings, some of them very near to New Testament tomes, say that he was freed at the end of the two years mentioned in Acts. If this was the case, he could have carried out his plan to extend his missionary work into the western parts of the Roman Empire, particularly Spain.

Four of Paul's letters mention that he was imprisoned when he wrote them. Even at the time of his Second Letter to the Corinthians, he wrote that he had often been imprisoned, so it is far from certain that his 'captivity letters' were all written from Rome. One of them, Philemon, written to a fellow Christian, gives a vivid glimpse of the change Christianity could bring to human values and social differences. The letter urges Philemon to receive back an escaped slave, whatever wrongs he may have committed. At this time there was no legal restraint on an owner's treatment of his slave, but Paul urges the slave to be received 'as a brother beloved' and to 'receive him as myself' (Philemon 1:16–17). Philippians was written to the Christians in Philippi, which Paul first visited 11 years before his arrival in Rome. The contents of the letter suggest that it belongs to an earlier stage of Paul's thinking. Colossians and Ephesians, on the other hand, deal with the problems that were arising from a new philosophical and religious movement which was attracting Christians. Evidence suggests that Ephesians was written to a number of Christian churches around Ephesus, so the whole area may have been influenced.

The Persecution of Christians and the Shadow of Rome

'I asked them whether they were Christians or not? If they confessed that they were Christians, I asked them again ... If they persevered in their confession, I ordered them to be executed; for I did not doubt but, let this confession be of any sort whatsoever, this positiveness and inflexible obstinacy deserved to be punished.' *Pliny the Younger to Emperor Trajan in* AD *112*

The early Christian community was severely persecuted by Jews well before the well-known attacks by the Romans under Emperor Nero. Originally, Christians were brought up under Judaism, being merely a sect of Judaism. A sectarian conflict began within Judaism, as Jews persecuted other Jews who were Christians. This inter-faith strife might be understood; Christians were preaching about the imminent return of the King of the Jews and the establishment of his kingdom. The Pharisees persecuted Christians because they mistook the kingdom, thinking it political rather than spiritual. The Romans had granted Jews a degree of autonomy, and the Jewish leaders were obliged to collect taxes for Rome and maintain civil order. Jesus appeared to the Pharisees as a seditious political figure who might bring the wrath of the Romans down upon the Jewish leadership. Failure to dampen down or suppress sedition meant that the Jewish leaders would be sent to Rome for trial and possible execution. Therefore, the Pharisees wanted to localize the problem for their own survival.

Whereas other Jewish sects such as the Essenes were left alone, Jesus was crucified, and his followers were persecuted after his death. The Jewish leadership under the High Priest Annas and his family – Caiaphas, John, and Alexander – imprisoned Peter and John after disliking Peter's sermon to a mass outside the Temple, but then released them because they could not find their acts punishable (Acts 4: 1–21). Eventually, all the apostles were imprisoned by the High Priest and Sadducees.

The apostles were brought before the Sanhedrin, where the high priest commanded them not to teach in

MARTYRDOM OF PETER
In a painting by the Italian artist Caravaggio (1571–1610), Peter, the apostle, is prepared for crucifixion in Rome. He was crucified upside down, at his own request.

Jesus's name lest they 'intend to bring this man's blood upon us' (Acts 5:28), a possible reference to the fear of Roman retribution. Gamaliel, a learned Pharisee, and doctor of law, said that the apostles should be given space: 'Refrain from these men, and let them alone: for if this counsel or this work be of men, it will come to nought: But if it be of God, ye cannot overthrow it; lest haply ye be found even to fight against God' (Acts 5:38–39). The apostles were beaten and released, and warned not to speak in the name of Jesus. However, they did, in the Temple and elsewhere.

The first Christian martyr was Stephen, who was stoned to death by members of the Sanhedrin. 'And cast him out of the city, and stoned him: and the witnesses laid down their clothes at a young man's feet, whose name was Saul' (Acts 7:58). This Saul of Tarsus, a Pharisee, implemented a major persecution of Christians. Saul, or Paul as his Greek name, was trained in Jewish Law in preparation to be a rabbi. He excelled in the Law and his zeal in its cause led him to persecute Christians. 'For ye have heard of my conversation in time past in the Jews' religion, how that beyond measure I persecuted the church of God, and wasted it: And profited in the Jews' religion above many my equals in mine own nation, being more exceedingly zealous of the traditions of my fathers' (Galatians 1:13–14). He regarded the Christians as a Jewish sect that should be destroyed, but on his way from Jerusalem to Damascus saw a vision that convinced him that Christ was God's call to all the world, outside of the needs of Judaism itself. His sudden conversion was difficult to accept. People tried to kill him in Damascus (Acts 9: 22–25), and there were other attempts on his life by the Hellenists in Jerusalem (Acts 9: 29).

ROMAN SCOURGE

Under Emperor Nero (as depicted on this coin) Christians would suffer crucifixion or violent death in the gladiatorial arena, as the Roman authorities sought a scapegoat for local unrest

'And laid their hands on the apostles, and put them in the common prison. But the angel of the Lord by night opened the prison doors, and brought them forth, and said, Go, stand and speak in the temple to the people all the words of this life.'

(Acts 5: 18–20)

Persecution by Romans is a well-recorded historical fact. Eleven of the Apostles were killed, murdered, executed or martyred, except for John, son of Zebedee and Salome and writer of the Book of Revelation. Paul was stoned by Jews in Antioch and Iconium, and left for dead (Acts 14:19). Later, Paul and his companion, Silas, were whipped and placed in stocks at Philippi before being freed when an earthquake struck (Acts 16: 22–26). Christian tradition has it that Paul was beheaded in Rome.

Persecution by the Roman Empire commenced under Emperor Nero (AD 54–68). Different forms of execution were used by the authorities, including systematic murder, crucifixion with crosses set alight to provide nightlights in the dark and feeding Christians to lions and other wild animals. The historian Tacitus wrote: 'They were killed by dogs by having the hides of beasts attached to them and worse' (Annals XV: 44). He also states that 'a vast multitude were convicted, not so much of the crime of arson as of hatred of the human race'. The official persecution of Christians in Rome was then taken up by officials in the provinces who wanted someone to blame for local problems. By the middle of the 2nd Century, anti-Christian mobs could be organized with little effort. This was witnessed during persecutions in Lyons in AD 177, during the reign of Emperor Marcus Aurelius (AD 161–180), when there were assaults, robberies and stonings, demonstrating the intensity of anti-Christian feeling.

Records show two more Empire-wide persecutions. The Emperor Decius (AD 249–251) launched a

UNDYING MEMORY

A cross stands on the top of Camlough Mountain in County Armagh, Northern Ireland. The device of torture and pain used by the Romans to crucify criminals became, after the Crucifixion of Jesus, the emblem of belief in Christianity.

systematic attack on Christianity in AD 250, demanding that all citizens signify their willingness to worship pagan gods. Victims of this persecution included Pope Fabian (AD 236–250) and Cyprian, Bishop of Carthage (AD 200–258), who was exiled and later martyred and beheaded under Emperor Valerian (AD 253–260). Church father and renowned biblical scholar Origen (c. AD 185–254) was imprisoned and tortured. Decius had become emperor during a period of imperial usurpations and used the wave of persecutions to shroud the inherent instability of his reign. After he died, Christian leaders argued about the fate of those followers who had accepted the orders of Decius and then wished to return to the fold. Cyprian argued for leniency towards these *lapsi* (Christians who had relapsed into heathenism). The next wave of persecution occurred under Emperor Diocletian (AD 284–305), who ordered all churches and Christian books to be destroyed and followed this with the execution of Christians for the subsequent eight years. Christianity was saved when the joint Emperors Constantine (c. AD 306–337) and Licinius (308–324) gave the faith legal recognition with the bounds of the Roman Empire by the Edict of Milan in AD 313.

Christian churches were hereby recognized as legal corporations. Persecutions still went on, however, when Romans failed to understand Christian rituals, and still considered Christians as corrupt and anti-Roman. However, such hostility gradually diminished.

An explanation for the persecutions reveals a plethora of reasons. Firstly, Christians denied the basis for Roman rule by stating that their God was the only real God. This denied the existence of the Roman pagan gods, including the divinity of the Emperor. This denial, as far as Roman commoners or aristocracy were concerned, was an attack upon the 'peace of the gods' and upon Rome itself. Christians were also accused of corrupting public morals by participating in Mass, mistaken as cannibalism. Christians were also feared for seeking martyrdom. Saint Ignatius of Antioch (c. AD 35–107), when condemned to death, wrote to the Romans: 'Grant me no more than you let my blood be spilled in sacrifices to God, while yet there is an altar ready'. Romans thought that the Christian desire for death was again corrupting public morals. The Romans failed to comprehend the Book of Revelation, viewing it as an attack on Rome because they thought the references to Babylon really meant Rome. Thus, the book was deemed anti-Roman propaganda. A final accusation levelled at Christians was that they failed to honour their ancestors and their authority. Romans continued to worship their own gods, believing that this enhanced social and political stability. The Christians did not acknowledge their Jewish ancestors and the books of the Old Testament. This 'new' approach was a double crime because Christians not only denied their ancestors but the Roman gods, too. Hence, they were oppressed, a policy exacerbated by Roman magistrates who followed public opinion and its antipathy towards Christians.

It was Emperor Nero, though, needing scapegoats for a series of natural and military disasters, who had created the precedent for widespread persecution of Christians in the Roman Empire. The shadow he cast over the fledgling faith was a long one.

Nero, the Roman Emperor to whom Paul appealed, began his 14-year reign in AD 54 with assassinations and executions to secure his power and finance his extravagances. There was, however, no attempt at that time to discredit or suppress Christians. Nero's predecessors had centralized power and increased the efficiency of the Roman civil service until the Emperor's actions were beyond any control – provided the army remained loyal to him. Emperors began to be honoured as divine, and the 16-year-old Nero encouraged the cult. Such absolute power could only be sustained by strong rulers, and Nero was not cast in that mould. A series of natural disasters in Italy and military crises on the borders of the Empire, aroused the suspicion that Nero was out of favour with the gods. In Britain, a rebellion led by Queen Boudicca very nearly drove the Romans out of the province they had only conquered some 18 years earlier. At the eastern extreme of the Roman Empire, the Parthians inflicted a decisive defeat on a Roman army, and Nero had to agree to peace terms. In AD 63, an earthquake destroyed most of Pompeii, anticipating its final destruction 16 years later.

Fire broke out in Rome itself near the Circus Maximus in the summer of AD 64. The congested city was familiar with fires, but this one spread rapidly for six days until all the southern part of the city had been destroyed as far as the Tiber and the Servian wall. Then it broke out again and spread through the northern districts. By the time it finally died down, it had burned through ten of the city's 14 wards. Nero was widely blamed for the fire, which was said to have been started on his orders. Even the rebuilding of the city caused unpopularity, as the rest of Italy and the provinces were squeezed to pay for the

work. A plague in the following year added to the misery. The Christians in Rome were convenient scapegoats, and Nero had as many as could be found put to death with sadistic cruelty, punished both for the fire and on the charge that they were 'haters of the human race' who refused to take part in other religious activities.

THE SPREAD OF ROMAN POWER

From a single city in the middle of the Italian peninsula, the ambitions of Rome spread far and wide across three continents, from Mesopotamia in the east to the island of Britain in the west. This may not have been the largest-ever empire, but it had possibly the greatest influence.

The persecutions of Christians under Nero seem to have been confined to Rome, as a distraction from the suspicions about his own involvement in the fire and other disasters, but it did create a precedent for Roman officials in other parts of the Empire and it ended any possibility of the Christian Church coming to a similar agreement with Rome as that enjoyed by Jews, whose exclusive religion was recognized by the state and respected, without any suggestion that it smacked of treason. There could be no hope of that for Christianity in the foreseeable future, especially as Jesus himself had been condemned by a Roman magistrate on a treason charge and executed. It would no longer be possible for Christians such as Paul to hope that Roman citizenship would provide protection from trouble. This formed the background to the last years of Paul and Peter.

Paul's three Letters to Timothy and Titus are usually called the pastoral letters, because they are addressed to individual leaders of local churches and contain advice about church organization and worship. Timothy was in Ephesus and Titus in Crete. These are the last letters attributed to Paul and show that two of the earlier threats to Christian beliefs had now combined – an insistence that all Christians must express their Christianity in Jewish

SYMBOL OF ROMAN INFLUENCE

The city of Caesarea was founded by Herod the Great in 22 BC and named in honour of the Emperor Augustus Caesar. The port appears in the Bible as the place where St Paul was imprisoned for two years.

form, and belief in a system of secret knowledge that guaranteed salvation and allocated a subordinate role to Jesus. This belief, called Gnosticism, from the Greek *gnosis*, meaning knowledge, dogged Christianity throughout the rest of the New Testament period and beyond.

Information about Paul's last years and death is very sparse, in contrast to the wealth of detail provided by Acts about his arrest in Jerusalem and his struggles to have his case tried properly. Acts ends with Paul staying two years in Rome under house arrest, but does not say what happened to him then. It was still only about AD 63, before Nero began his attacks on Christians, and the charges against Paul would certainly have been dismissed at that time if he had received a fair trial.

If Paul was in fact released he probably went back to Macedonia and to Asia Minor and Crete, where his old companions Timothy and Titus were in charge of churches. He then returned – or was taken – to Rome again after the great fire to a more severe form of imprisonment and to death. This would account for passages in the pastoral letters about Paul's movements and his expectation of death. They would have been written during the second imprisonment in Rome, which ended with Paul's execution near the end of Nero's reign.

Alternatively, Paul might have been executed after the two years of imprisonment described in Acts, with someone else writing the three final letters to give the kind of teaching and advice Paul would have given to leaders of local churches. So it seems likely that Paul was executed before Nero committed suicide in AD 68. He was probably taken outside the southern walls of the city of Rome and beheaded, as befitted a Roman citizen. Early Church tradition asserts that Peter was crucified during the same period in the Vaticanum, west of the River Tiber.

Nero's reign ended in chaos, amid events that created a completely new situation for the Christian churches. His death marked the end of a dynasty and resulted in a year of civil war in Rome. Whatever the Roman constitution said, real power lay with the military – the Praetorian Guard in Rome and the great armies guarding the frontiers of the Empire. During the bloody struggle for political power, Rome itself was stormed by Roman troops, the Capital was burned, three emperors were proclaimed and overthrown, and, finally, Vespasian emerged as victor. He reigned as emperor from AD 69 to 79.

In this period, the situation in Palestine deteriorated swiftly. Even before the death of Nero, war had broken out between Rome and the Jews of Palestine, and this was to have disastrous effects on the privileges Jews enjoyed throughout the Empire, on their economic and political power and on their cultural influence.

Under the corrupt rule of the last of the Roman procurators, Florus, a comparatively small protest grew to open rebellion when Jerusalem Jews compelled Florus and his soldiers to retreat to Caesarea, the Roman administrative centre for Judaea. The Governor of Syria, Gallius, then marched on Jerusalem with the Roman Twelfth Legion and was, in turn, repulsed with heavy losses at the end of AD 66. The rebellion had turned into a war, and Nero sent one of his most able generals, the future emperor, Vespasian, with 60,000 men.

Vespasian began a systematic campaign to subdue Palestine, beginning with Galilee. He drove the Zealots before him to take refuge in Jerusalem, where they murdered Jewish opponents and moderates. By the end of AD 68 all Judaea and Idumaea had been subdued and only such strongholds as Jerusalem and Masada held out. It was at this time that the Jewish community at Qumran hid its library in caves and fled to Masada.

When Vespasian was proclaimed Emperor in AD 69, his son Titus carried on in his place, and began the full siege of Jerusalem early in AD 70. That part of the war was over by September, with the city and its Temple destroyed and the Jews of Jerusalem killed or sold into slavery. Titus celebrated his victory with sacrifices to the standards of the Roman Legion in front of the ruins of the Temple. The following year Vespasian and Titus had their victory proclaimed by a 'triumph' – a huge procession in Rome in which treasures from the Jerusalem Temple were carried and Jewish captives walked in chains. The occasion is vividly portrayed in the carvings of the Arch of Titus, near the Forum in Rome.

Further strongholds fell one by one during the years AD 70–73. These included Herodium, south of Jerusalem; Machaerus, east of the Dead Sea; and, finally, the massive fortress of Masada, where Jewish slaves built a ramp to its summit, more than 300 metres (1,000 ft) above the shore of the Dead Sea. On the night before the final assault, the defenders killed their families and themselves. This marked the end of the war.

The Christians of Jerusalem had fled the city before the siege closed and settled at Pella in the Jordan Valley. This had quite a wide-ranging effect on the early Christian Church. The Christians of Jerusalem could no longer be a centre of authority and stability for the growing number of followers of their faith elsewhere in the Roman Empire. The Jewish Christians who left Jerusalem came under fire from both Jews and Romans, but the only serious persecution that occurred was later, in the reign of Emperor Domitian (AD 81–96).

In the New Testament, three letters that are difficult to date may best be understood as belonging to the period of radical rethinking for Christians, which followed the destruction of Jerusalem. The Second Letter of Peter was probably written after Peter's death to show how he would have guided Christians in the new situation, and it has many similarities to the Letter of Jude, which deals with problems of false teachers and worries about the delay in the expected return of Jesus. The long and remarkable Letter to the Hebrews differs radically from anything else ascribed to Paul, and the authorship has been questioned from very early times. It presents the work of Jesus in terms of the Hebrew priesthood and sacrifices. These are ways that would particularly appeal to Jewish Christians after the destruction of the Temple.

Evangelizing Christianity

After Christ's Resurrection, his followers restricted themselves to evangelizing among the Jewish population – a captive audience. Many converts travelled with the diaspora, spreading the Christian word throughout the Roman Empire.

The spread of early Christianity was aided by several factors. Firstly, a unifying language and culture existed, certainly in an urban sense, from Italy to India. Alexander the Great's empire and its successor states established common Greek, or *koine*, as the main imperial language. A second factor enabling missionaries to travel was the *Pax Romana* (the Roman peace), founded by Augustus Caesar. Safe travel had been possible by sea, since Pompey's eradication of piracy turned the Mediterranean into a Roman lake, and via a network of brilliantly engineered roads.

A third major factor was the extent of the Jewish diaspora, which created target audiences for the new Jewish message being spread by Jesus's supporters. Large communities of Jews had existed outside Palestine since the fall of the kingdoms of Israel and Judah. However, the greatest Jewish diaspora occurred after the Alexandrine conquest of the Persian Empire freed up movement in the Fertile Crescent. Whatever the causes of the diaspora, trade certainly played a major part in establishing Jewish communities in many of the cities along the east Mediterranean coastline. This massive movement was enhanced when Jewish captives were sold into slavery after the two Jewish revolts of AD 66–70 and 132–135. By AD 100, the philosopher Philo claimed there were a million Jews, either by birth or conversion, in Egypt.

The New Testament, especially the Acts of the Apostles, constantly mentions Jews, often Christians, living in Syria, Asia Minor and Greece. Evidence about Jews in Egypt is extant, owing to surviving papyri and some archaeological excavations of synagogues, although the majority originates from later centuries. The exiles' religious worship remained constant to Judaism, with its notion of ethical superiority. Concern was mainly expressed over the Temple and the Law. The latter was most important, all Jews preserving the traditional food restrictions and observing the Sabbath as a rest day.

The Law became the focus of life as did the local synagogues, which became sacred buildings, often of architectural note, since the Temple was in Palestine. Leaders of synagogues were not only important in religious life but often acted as magistrates within their congregations, settling disputes without reference to Gentile authorities. In some cases, the local sovereign power would acknowledge this autonomy as convenient or consider that the community was more likely to control its deviants and rebels through excommunication rather than official local sanctions. Such self-concern often led to isolation, the requirement of the Law in dietary terms and hostility towards mixed marriages occasionally causing resentment in some cities. Endemic anti-Semitism became vicious in Alexandria, where local Greeks were

THE MESSAGE ON THE MOVE

The Gospel seems to have spread into Samaria and then along the coastal plain. Philip, one of the seven deacons of the early Church, travelled from Jerusalem into Samaria, then from Jerusalem to Gaza, before turning north. In his travels, Peter proclaimed the Gospels to Gentiles as well as Jews.

angry at Jews seeking full city citizenship while refusing to join in local pagan cults or allow city authorities to police their religious community. Alexandria in the 1st Century was prone to communal fighting, culminating in a Jewish uprising in AD 117–119, as in Cyrene and Cyprus.

Christianity commenced as a movement within Judaism. Jesus was a Jew, as were his Apostles. He was accepted by his adherents as the 'Christ' sent to fulfil God's promise to Abraham, Isaac and Jacob. Jesus's message was awaited, since Palestine was in turmoil after the formal annexation by Rome in AD 6, with a variety of contending sects such as the spiritual Essenes or nationalists (like the later Zealots). Enter Christ, the Messiah, a liberator? In this situation, Jewish authorities regarded Jesus with suspicion, as another troublemaker, and more so as his adherents increased after the Resurrection. The good news of God's reigning power was first presented in an exclusive Judaic context. A major issue confronting this situation was whether Gentiles would be allowed to pursue Christ's doctrines without accepting Judaic Law.

After Christ's Resurrection, his supporters restricted themselves to evangelizing among Jews. Thousands of Jews surged into Jerusalem for the most important religious festivals – a captive audience. Undoubtedly, many converts then returned to their homes in the diaspora, spreading the Christian word throughout the Roman Empire. However, some Jerusalem Christians were more progressive, seeking to spread the new teachings beyond orthodox Jewry. Hellenized Jews were quick to digest the new message as compared with Aramaic-speaking Jews. While the Apostles were out preaching, they required people to administer Church funds. Seven men were ordained as deacons for this purpose. One, Stephen, thought the faith was for all people, and not just orthodox Jews or Pharisees. His views attacked conservatism and led to ideological conflict within Judaism. Stephen was seized by the High Priest and the Jewish Supreme Court and accused of blasphemy and disavowing the Temple cult and the Jewish claim to be the sole authority in religious belief. He was condemned to death by stoning, becoming a martyr and eventually a saint.

The expansion of the early Christian Church in Palestine can be laid at the feet of Philip, Peter and John as shown in the Acts of the Apostles (4–11). Philip, another Hellenist, went to the city of Samaria and began evangelizing among these despised, unorthodox Jews. Samaritan scriptures consisted of Moses' five books, and that of Joshua, but not the prophets, their temple on Mount Gezerim, near Shechen, claiming to possess legitimate Zadokite descent. Mass conversions resulted, causing Peter and John to travel to Samaria to confirm new disciples in their faith. Philip also preached along the road from Jerusalem to Ascalon, where he baptized a court official from Ethiopia. His ministry took him to Ashdod, Lydda, Joppa, Antipatris and Caesarea Maritima, which became his home and base. Philip, later known as the Evangelist, was neither an apostle nor a prophet but an immensely spiritual person. He turned Caesarea – the most important city in Palestine after Jerusalem, and centre of Roman government in the country – into a new missionary district, developing the Hellenized form of Christianity. Here, he preached and raised his four daughters, all allegedly prophets, and entertained Paul on his last journey to Jerusalem.

Several other events in Acts demonstrate that missionary activities outside Jerusalem were successful. Peter made extensive travels through Palestine, healing Aeneas, a paralytic, at Lydda. While there, he was called to Joppa and raised Tabitha (Dorcas), a disciple, from the dead. At Joppa, he lodged with a tanner whose calling was deemed unclean by virtue of touching dead animal skins. Peter's sojourn with the tanner showed that at least one disciple of Jesus no longer considered himself bound by Pharasaic laws of official Judaism. Next, Peter received a message from a Roman officer called Cornelius, requesting that he come to Caesarea. That Peter went marks a crucial turning point in the ideas of the early Christian Church. Cornelius was God-fearing but uncircumcised. Peter baptized Cornelius and his entire household. Disciples in Jerusalem were shocked, but Peter defended his actions in baptizing a Gentile. His views were accepted, recognizing that observance of the Jewish Law was not necessary for baptism, nor was circumcision, thereby implying that belief in Jesus's message was no longer a continuation and extension of Judaism. Those Christians who had shared Stephen's ideas, fleeing to Cyprus, Phoenicia and Antioch on the Orontes on his martyrdom, had only preached the Gospel to Jews. News of Peter's stand meant that they could now widen their proselytizing to Gentiles too.

The New Testament includes a letter (1 Peter) sent from Rome to the Christians of Asia Minor, possibly during Nero's persecutions (AD 65), or maybe when pressure was being applied to the Christians of Pontus and Bithynia (AD 11–112 or somewhere in between). It seems that the Roman Church was now responsible for congregations in Galatia and Asia.

Other apostles have been credited with spreading the faith. Mark helped found the Church in Alexandria, as did Thaddeus in Edessa, and Thomas is traditionally believed to have taken Christianity to India.

The seven Churches of pro-consular Asia – Ephesus, Smyrna, Pergamum, Thyatira, Sardis, Philadelphia and Laodicea – are addressed at the beginning of the Book of Revelation, allegedly written by John on the island of Patmos in the Aegean Sea. The Revelation is addressed to the seven Churches that were at the borders of evangelism as prophets and evangelists pushed westwards and northwards. The book criticizes the Churches for a variety of faults, such as self-satisfaction and openness to strange doctrines. Pergamum had some who held the idea of Balaam, who taught the Jews 'to eat things sacrificed unto idols, and to commit fornication' (Revelation 2:14). So, the seven Churches were exhorted to mend their ways and remain steadfast, possibly because a crisis of faith brought on by Roman persecution was occurring.

Another visitor to Asia (AD 110) was Ignatius (c. AD 35–107), Bishop of Antioch-in-Syria, and, possibly, a disciple of St John the Evangelist. During the reign of the Emperor Trajan, he had offended the Roman authorities and was condemned to be devoured by wild beasts. His

REACHING THE EPHESIANS

One of the destinations on Paul's evangelizing travels was the great Roman city of Ephesus, in present-day Turkey.

route from Antioch is unknown, but it is probable that he traversed the Cilician Gates to Troas. He wrote five letters to the Christian communities of Ephesus, Magnesia, Tralles, Philadelphia and Smyrna in Asia. He addressed a personal letter to Polycarp, Bishop of Smyrna, and another to the Christian community in Rome. From Troas, he sailed to Neapolis. Possibly, he was taken from Philippi along the Egnatian Way to Italy. Ignatius warned against heretical writings, thereby providing detailed summaries of Christian doctrine. He also depicted Church organization as a community of love surrounding a presiding bishop, assisted by a council of elders (presbyters).

From Alexandria, Christianity spread into Egypt to both Coptic- and Greek-speaking communities. An example of the latter was Oxyrhynchus. Papyri unearthed there include writings that show a Christian presence, which ultimately spread to Nag Hammadi. Dating from the 4th Century AD, a complete collection of Christ's sayings has been translated (1945) from the original Greek into Coptic, the so-called Gospel of Thomas.

Jewish Revolts Against Rome

The first revolt was a direct challenge to the harsh Roman rule and reflected nationalist aspirations for independence. The second revolt was the result of Emperor Hadrian's decree on circumcision and his desire to build a Roman city on the site of Jerusalem.

The first Jewish revolt grew from resentment at the conquest of Judaea in AD 6, which humiliated nationalist aspirations. Also, Roman administration was harsh and the combination of nationalism and civic hostility along with religious fervour against Rome was triggered by the venality, corruption and brutality of the last two procurators of Judaea, Albinus (AD 62–64) and Gessius Florus (AD 64–66).

A minor incident pre-dating the revolt happened in AD 62, when the Romans deprived the Jews of citizenship after a fight between Jews and Syrians. The real spark that lit the fire of revolt was in late spring AD 66 when Gessius Florus seized a large sum of money from the Temple, and then brought in Roman soldiers who were ordered to kill anyone who jeered at them. The Jews, under Eleazar, son of the High Priest, refused to continue offering the usual daily sacrifice for the Emperor, which was considered to be treason by the Roman authorities. Another immediate action by the revolutionaries was the occupation of the fortress of Masada. King Agrippa II, together with the civic leaders, proved unable to subdue the insurgents by persuasion, resorting to force, which also failed. This internecine strife was accompanied by mixed Jewish-Gentile Palestinian cities, like Caesarea, Ptolemais, Gabe, Samaria and Ascalon, and even some in the Decapolis, Syria and Egypt, erupting in communal massacres.

Cestius Gallus, the Syrian legate (AD 63–66), failed to crush the revolt in Jerusalem and, on his return, was defeated by the Jews near Beth-horon. In Jerusalem, the moderate pro-peace party of the Jews was hustled into joining the revolutionaries, leaving leading Pharisees and Sadducees to direct the initial stage of the war. Evidence concerning the insurrection can be found in *The Jewish War* by Flavius Josephus, in which he said the country was divided into revolutionary military districts. Jerusalem was placed in the hands of its former High Priest, Ananus, son of Anunus, and Joseph, son of Gorion. Idumaea was entrusted to two chief priests, Jesus, son of Sapphias, and

THE UPRISING BEGINS

(far right and map overleaf left)
The Jewish-Roman War of AD 66–70 began with disturbances near Caesarea, the Roman administrative headquarters, then spread throughout the country. The war was a severe test of the Roman occupation of Palestine; isolated pockets of resistance held out for more than three years. Many patriotic groups, such as the Zealots, were ready to commit suicide rather than surrender. These groups provided the main Jewish resistance to the Roman occupation. The Zealots' last stand was the royal stronghold of Masada, which they held for nearly six years before it fell to the Romans in AD 73. The Romans overran Jerusalem in stages, and the Temple, held by the Zealots, was the last place to be captured. The burning of the Temple and destruction of Jerusalem marked the climax of the war.

The First Jewish Revolt
AD 66–68
Non-hostile troop movements
Cestius Gallus AD 66
AD 67
AD 68
Primarily Jewish population
Primarily Samaritan population
Rebel military district
Major Roman camp
Hasmonean or Herodian fortress used by rebels
Major siege
Site possibly fortified by rebels
Site probably fortified by rebels
Tyre
Cadasa
UPPER GALILEE
Lake Huleh
Gischala
Meroth
Jamnith
Sepph
Seleucia
GAULANITIS
Sogane
Acchabare
Bersabe
Ptolemais
Selame
Gamala
Gabara
Chabulon
Mt Asamon
Jotapata
Tarichaeae
Arbela
Sea of Chinnereth (Sea of Galilee)
Caphareccho
Tiberias
Hippus
Sepphoris
Garis
LOWER GALILEE
Geba
Dium
Japha
Mt. Tabor
Gadara
Dora
Strato's Tower (Caesarea)
Scythopolis
Narbata
Pella
Great Sea
Western Sea
Samaria
SAMARIA
Shechem
Jordan
Gerasa
Mt. Gerizim
Zarqa
Apollonia
Antipatris
Acrabeta
Gerasa
Alexandrium
Joppa
Aphek
Gedor
Adida
Gophna
Ephraim
PERAEA
Lydda
Bethel
Philadelphia
Beth-horon
Shucib
Bethennabris
Jamnia
Gabaon
Cyprus
Jericho
Herodion
Emmaus
Abilia
Julias
Hisban
Azotus
Hierosolyma (Jerusalem)
Esbus
Beisimoth
Bethletepha
JUDAEA
Medeba
Hyrcania
Ascalon
Herodium
Capharab s?
Capharatobas
Chebron
Salt Sea (Dead Sea)
Machaerus
Gaza
Adora
IDUMAEA
Mujib
N
Masada
0
20 km
20 miles
Negev

The First Jewish Revolt
AD 69–70
Non-hostile troop movements
AD 69
AD 70
After AD 70
Primarily Jewish population
Primarily Samaritan population
Rebel military district
Major Roman camp
Hasmonaean or Herodian fortress used by rebels
Major siege
Site possibly fortified by rebels
Site probably fortified by rebels
Great Sea
Western Sea
Tyre
Cadasa
UPPER GALILEE
Lake Huleh
Gischala
Seleucia
GAULANITI
Meroth
Jamnith
Sepph
Sogane
Bersabe
Acchabare
Gamala
Ptolemais
Selame
Gabara
Chabulon
Taricheae
Arbela
Sea of Chinnereth (Sea of Galilee)
Mt Asamon
Jotapata
Capharecchō
Tiberias
Hippus
Sepphoris
Garis
LOWER GALILEE
Dium
Geba
Japha
Mt. Tabor
Gadara
Dora
Scythopolis
Caesarea (Strato's Tower)
Narbata
Pella
Samaria
SAMARIA
Shechem
Jordan
Gerasa
Mt. Gerizim
Zarqa
Apollonia
Acrabeta
Antipatris
Gerasa
Alexandrium
Joppa
Aphek
Gedor
Thamna
Gophna
PERAEA
Adida
Ephraim
Lydda
Philadelphia
Bethel
Beth-horon
Shueib
Bethennabris
Jamnia
Gabaon
Cyprus
Jericho
Abilia
Herodion
Julias
Emmaus
Hisban
Azotus
Hierosolyma (Jerusalem)
Esbus
Beisimoth
Bethletepha
JUDAEA
Medeba
Hyrcania
Ashkelon
Herodium
Capharabis?
Betogabris
Salt Sea (Dead Sea)
Machaerus
Chebron
Gaza
Adora
Mujib
IDUMAEA
Masada
N
0
20 km
0
20 miles
Negev
35°
36°
33°
32°

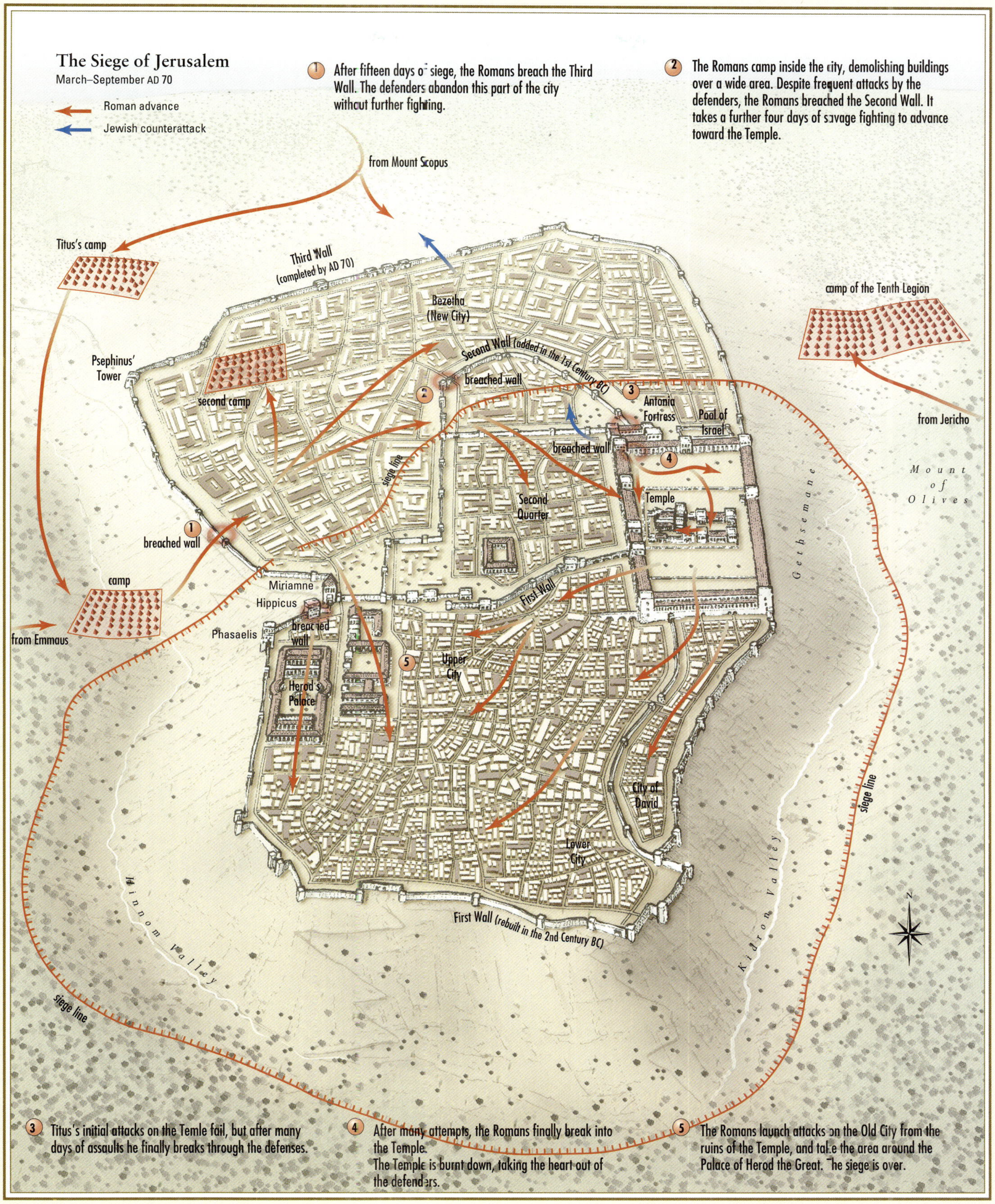

JERUSALEM UNDER FIRE

Vespasian's son, Titus, took over the siege of Jerusalem when his father was proclaimed Emperor and captured the city in AD 70. Jerusalem was levelled and its surviving citizens sold into slavery. The Romans rebuilt Jerusalem, but they forbade Jews to live there.

Eleazar. Jericho was placed in the hands of Joseph, son of Simon, and Peraea (Transjordan) under Manasseh. The west and north of Judaea (the districts of Thamna, Lydda, Joppa and Emmaus) were governed by John the Essene. John, son of Ananias, led northeastern Judaea (Gophna and Acrabeta), and both Galilee and the area of Gamal in Gaulantis were given to Josephus, son of Matthias.

Josephus, then Joseph ben Matthias, immediately began to organize the defence of his command, despite fierce armed opposition from an extreme nationalist, John from Gischala. In Gaulantis, Josephus agreed that the walls of Gamla should be repaired and Seleucia and Sogane fortified in Upper Galilee. Meroth, Jamnith and Acchabare were circumvallated and the three cities of Taricheae, Tiberias and Sepphoris were fortified, together with several villages: the Cave of Arbele, Bersabe, Selame, Jotapata, Capharecho, Japha, Sigoph and Mount Tabor. A few of these fortifications were intended to be obstacles blocking the roads from Roman bases at Ptolemais (Sigoph, Capharecho) and Scythopolis (Mount Tabor), or from Phoenicians (at Bersabe, Selame, Meroth) and from Agrippa's base at Caesarea Philippi (Jamnitj, Seleucia, Sogane). Others defended large population centres (Tarichaea, Tiberias, Sepphoria and Japha). The remainder of the fortresses were major strongholds (Jotapata, Acchabare and Gamala).

In December AD 66, Emperor Nero sent Vespasian to restore order. Vespasian acted cautiously and assembled troops in Syria, while his son, Titus, was sent to Egypt to seek reinforcements. In spring, AD 67, Vespasian marched on Galilee from Antioch via Ptolemais, where Titus, with his Egyptian force, joined him. In total, the two generals commanded 60,000 legionaries and auxiliary troops. Galilean resistance cracked. Sephoris joined the Romans immediately, but Jotapata was besieged for two months and its garrison slaughtered. Josephus's army at Garis fled and all of Lower Galilee fell, with Josephus retreating to Tiberias and then Jotapata. The latter was captured and Josephus surrendered. The end of AD 67 witnessed the conquest of northern Palestine. Vespasian then sent his legions to winter at Caesaria and Scythopolis, thus keeping Galilee cut off from the area still resisting Rome.

The next phase of the war saw civil unrest between various Jewish factions, between the fanatical supporters of John of Gischalla, allied to the Idumaeans, and the aristocratic leaders of the revolt, who were accused of dragging their heels in the fight against Rome. Vespasian chose to let the Jerusalem factions destroy each other while turning on Peraea, where he soon occupied the whole area as far south as Macherus. By late spring, Antipatris, Lydda and Jamnia were taken. A legion was stationed outside Emmaus and, after travelling through Samaria, the Romans entered Jericho.

While Vespasian's forces were travelling to Caesarea to prepare the siege of Jerusalem, Nero's suicide was announced. Vespasian ceased military activity while the political situation settled down. Finally, in the summer of AD 69, the armies in the eastern part of the Empire proclaimed Vespasian as emperor. Faced by the rise of a new rebel leader, Simon bar Giora, Vespasian completed the subjugation of Judaea, controlling Acrabeta, Bethel and Ephraim, together with Hebron in the south. Only Jerusalem, Macherus, Herodium and Masada still held out against Rome. He then journeyed to Rome via Alexandria, leaving Titus to end the rebellion.

The Jerusalem civil war continued. One faction of aristocratic patriots, of whom Josephus had been one, controlled a hill in the south-west of the city, while the Zealots under John of Gischala held the eastern city and a major area of the Temple court. The aristocrats requested Simon bar Giora's help, but he conducted a reign of terror among the aristocrats, killing anyone who mentioned surrender. In the spring of AD 70, Titus marched on Jerusalem, breaking into the city and driving out final, fanatical resistance by fire, including torching the Temple. Within a month the Romans occupied the city, capturing Simon bar Giora and John of Gischala. These two men formed part of Titus's triumphal procession in Rome in AD 71. The event was commemorated on the triumphal Arch of Titus, which still stands in Rome.

Lucilius Bassus, Palestinian governor, began the final clearing-up operation against the remaining Zealot strongholds. Herodium, near Bethlehem, surrendered. Macherus on the Dead Sea followed after some resistance. Masada, Herod's awesome palace on its high rock plateau, remained under the leadership of Eleazar, son of Jair, a descendant of the Zealot founder, Judas the Galilean. The new governor of Judaea, Flavius Silva (AD 73–81) started the siege. The fortress sat on a steep, craggy outcrop rising from the western shore of the Dead Sea. The only route to the top was a narrow trail, known as the 'snake path', zigzagging its way to the top for two miles, and a shorter, much steeper, path. The plateau rim was surrounded by a wall 5.5 metres (18 ft) high, 4 metres (12 ft) broad, and with 37 towers. The Romans built fortifications around the 396-metre (1,300 ft) high

MOUNTAIN FORTRESS
The fortress of Masada stood on a spur of rock overlooking the Dead Sea. Its position made it practically impregnable.

rock to prevent escape or reinforcement. They then built a siege ramp and mound on the west side where a battering ram could be brought into play. The wall soon collapsed, and the Romans entered. The insurgents decided to die rather than surrender. The men killed their wives and children first then drew lots to kill each other. Some 960 died; only two women and five children escaped this terrible fate.

Jewish resistance continued intermittently. About AD 116, during the reign of Emperor Trajan (AD 98–117), a revolt occurred. Little is known about the uprising, but it was probably crushed quickly. Elsewhere, between AD 115 and 117, the Jews of Egypt, Cyrenaica, Mesopotamia and Cyprus rose, the latter uprising commencing with a massacre of the ruling Greeks, which was crushed by the Romans. The Jews next rose again during the reign of the Emperor Hadrian (AD 117–138). He had attempted to ban circumcision in the Empire in all subject nations, irrespective of their faith. Perhaps more importantly, he planned to build a new city, Aelia Capitolina, on Jerusalem's ruins. Hadrian was in Syria and Egypt between AD 129 and 131, and his departure signalled the beginning of an uprising. The second Jewish revolt erupted in AD 132.

The leader of the revolt was known as Simeon bar Kokhba ('son of the star') to his friends, and Simeon bar Kosiba ('son of the lie' – false Messiah) to his enemies. When the revolt began, Jerusalem was not a fortified city and was faced by the camp of the Tenth Legion. Jerusalem was easily captured from Tinneius Rufus, the Roman governor, and the rebels held out against the Romans for two years. The insurgents minted coins in the first year of the rebellion with legends such as 'liberation of Israel', 'liberation of Jerusalem' and 'the priest Eleazar', the latter suggesting a possible revival of the Temple cult. Hadrian then called for Julius Severus, from Britain, to command forces against the rebels.

The main concentration of rebels was in the Judaean desert, centred around Herodium, Tekoa, Qiryat Arabayya, En-gedi and the unidentified Beth Mashko, the last three being centres of rebel government. Papyri have ascertained the names of several rebel leaders: Joshua ben Galgula, Judah bar Manasseh, Jonathan bar Ba'ayan and Masabala bar Simon. One Roman historian, Cassius Dio, stated that the Roman soldiers could not fight the Jews in open combat owing to the rough countryside. Guerrilla warfare ensued, with the Romans hunting down the insurgents in small groups, ferreting them out of caves, or holding areas to intercept supplies, thereby starving them to death.

ARCH OF TRIUMPH

Titus' victory in the Jewish-Roman War and his conquest of Jerusalem in AD 70 are commemorated by this triumphal arch, erected by his brother, Domitian, at the old entrance to the Palatine in Rome. It still stands today.

Archaeological and manuscript evidence has been discovered in numerous caves the length of the Judaean desert, at Wadi Murabba'at, Nahal Hever, Nahal Mishmar and Nahal Ze'elim. Four caves discovered in the northern wall of Wadi Murabba'at, just over 19 kilometres (12 miles) south of Qumran, have offered up Hebrew, Aramaic, Greek and Latin papyri fragments together with lamps, jars, weapons, tools, domestic objects, sandals, cloth and dresses, as well as coins dating from the revolt. The best-known letter from the uprising leader, Simeon bar Kokhba states: 'From Simeon ben Kokhba to Joshua ben Galgolah, and to the men of your company, peace! I call heaven to witness that if one of the Galileans whom you have taken under your wing should cause us any trouble, I will clap your feet in irons, as I did with the son of Aplul. Simeon ben Kokhba, ruler of Israel.'

In four caves on the northern side of Nahal Hever, domestic vessels and bones of sheep and goats have been found. In the fifth, the Cave of Letters, were preserved papyri fragments and 19 human skeletons. The south side Cave of Horrors indicated that 40 men, women and children starved to death. This cave also held food containers, cooking pots, lamps and the remnants of the scroll of the Twelve Minor Prophets in Greek. These victims could not escape since some caves were overlooked by a Roman camp on each side of the defile. A leather bag containing papyri texts and one text on a strip of wood provides letters to two men at En-gedi, called Jonathan and Masabala. They were commanded, in a very dictatorial fashion, to provide Simeon with provisions and troops.

Two caves in the south wall of Nahal Mishmat were used as hiding places by several families, while a third was a store containing papyri fragments, glass vessels and good-quality lamps and stone utensils. The single occupied cave in the south wall of Nahal Harduf contained a water cistern and pottery but no human remains. On the north face of Nahal Ze'elim, the Cave of Skulls revealed seven skeletons, with pottery and a coin of Trajan; the Cave of Arrows produced arrows and pottery; and the Cave of Scrolls yielded fragments of a leather scroll, papyri and a phylactery (a small leather box containing Hebrew texts worn by Jewish men at morning prayer).

In AD 135, Bether, a mountain fortress south of Jerusalem, where Simeon bar Kokhba was killed, witnessed the final battle of the insurgency. The siege lasted nearly a year, while the entire war went on for three and a half years. Roman losses were so severe that Hadrian ignored the traditional phrase 'I and the legions are well' when he reported to the Senate. The historian Cassio Dio recorded the disaster overwhelming the Jews. 'Fifty of their most important outposts and nine hundred and eighty-five of their most famous villages were razed to the ground. Five hundred and eighty thousand men were slain in the various raids and battles and the number of those who perished by famine, disease and fire was past finding out. Thus, nearly the whole of Judaea was made desolate.' Reports show that, with the marketplace swamped by Jewish prisoners, the price of a Jew in the Hebron slave market fell below that of a horse. Surplus captives were removed to Gaza, then Egypt. Little wonder a Roman coin from Hadrian's reign was inscribed, 'Judaea Capta', with the depiction of an enslaved woman.

After the revolt was crushed, Jerusalem was rebuilt into a Roman provincial city named Colonia Aelia Capitolina, a pagan city inhabited only by Gentiles, Romans, Greeks and other peoples from the Empire. Jews were forbidden to live there on pain of death. Only on the anniversary of the destruction of the Temple were Jews allowed in to bewail the loss of their Temple. The southern gate of Jerusalem, facing towards Bethlehem, portrayed the carved image of a pig. On the Temple hill, a sanctuary rose to Jupiter Capitolinus and the province of Judaea was renamed Syria Palaestina. In Judaea, the Jews were apparently exterminated, but they survived in Galilee, which, like Samaria, seemed not to have been involved in the revolt. Tiberias, in Galilee, became the residence of Jewish patriarchs, who there completed the Mishnah, the Talmud and other early rabbinic texts.

THE ROMAN ADMINISTRATION OF JUDAEA—Emperors, Governors and High Priests

ROMAN EMPERORS

Augustus (16 January 27 BC–19 August AD 14)
Tiberius (17 September 14–16 March 37)
Gaius (16 March 37–24 January 41)
Claudius (24 January 41–13 October 54)
Nero (13 October 54–9 June 68)
Galba (10 June 68–15 January 69)
Otho (15 January 69–14 April 69)
Vitellius (2 January 69–20 December 69)
Vespasian (1 July 69–24 June 79)
Titus (24 June 79–13 September 81)
Domitian (14 September 81–16 September 96)
Nerva (16 September 96–25 January 98)
Trajan (25 January 97–8 August 117)
Hadrian (11 August 117–10 July 138)

ROMAN GOVERNORS OF JUDAEA (AD 6–135)

Prefects or Procurators, subject to supervision by the Imperial Legate in Syria (AD 6–66):
Coponius (c. 6–9)
Marcus Ambibulus (c. 9–12)
Annius Rufus (c. 12–15)
Valerius Gratus (15–26)
Pontius Pilate (26–36)
Marcellus/Marullus (36–41)
King Herod Agrippa (41–44)
Cuspius Fadus (44–46)
Tiberius Iulius Alexander (46–48)
Ventidius Cumanus (48–c. 52)
Antonius Felix (c. 52–c. 60)
Porcius Festus (c. 60–62)
Lucceius Albinus (62–64)
Gessius Florus (64–66)
(Jewish Revolt 66–70)
Commanders of the Legio X Fretensis with praetorian rank (AD 70–c. 120). Only isolated names are known:
Sex. Vettulenus Cerialis (70–71)
Lucilius Bassus (71–73)
L. Flavius Silva (73–81)
Cn. Pompeius Longinus (80)
Sedx. Hermetidius Campanus (93)
Atticus (c. 100–c.103)
C. Iulius Quadratus Bassus (c. 103–c. 105)
Q. Roscius Coelius Pompeius Falco (c. 105–107)
Tiberianus (c. 114)
Lusius Quietus (c. 117)
Governors of consular rank when the Legio VI Ferrata was also stationed in Judaea (c. AD 120–135):
Q. Tineius Rufus (132)
C. Quninctius Certus Publicius Marcellus (?)
Sex. Iulius Severus (235)

HIGH PRIESTS

Appointed by King Herod the Great (37–4 BC):
Ananel (37–36, and again from 34 BC)
Aristobulus III (35 BC)
Jesus son of Phiabi (to c. 23 BC)
Simon son of Boethus (c. 23–5 BC)
Matthias son of Theophilus (5–4 BC)
Joseph son of Ellem (one day)
Joazar son of Boethus (4 BC)
Appointed by the Tetrarch Archelaus (4 BC–AD 6):
Eleazar son of Boethus (from 4 BC)
Jesus son of See (to AD 6)
Appointed by Quirinius, Legate of Syria (AD 6–12):
Ananus/Annas son of Sethi (AD 6–15)
Appointed by Gratus, Procurator of Judaea (AD 15–26):
Ismail son of Phiabi (c. 15–16)
Eleazar son of Ananus (c. 16–17)
Simon son of Camithus (c. 17–18)
Josephus Caiaphas (c. 18–37)
Appointed by Vitellius, Legate of Syria (AD 35–39):
Jonathan son of Ananus (two months in 37)
Theophilus son of Ananus (from 37)
Appointed by King Agrippa I (AD 41–44):
Simon Cantheras son of Beothus (from 41)
Matthias son of Ananus (?)
Elionaeus son of Cantheras (c. 44)
Appointed by Herod of Chalcis (AD 44–48):
Joseph son of Kami (?)
Ananias son of Nedebaeus (47–c. 59)
Appointed by King Agrippa II (AD 50–c. 93):
Ismael son of Phiabi (c. 50–61)
Joseph Cabi son of Simon (61–62)
Ananus son of Ananus (three months in 62)
Jesus son of Damnaeus (c. 62–63)
Jesus son of Gamaliel (c. 63–64)
Matthias son of Theophilus (65–?)
Appointed by people during the Revolt (AD 66–70):
Phannias/Phanni/Phanasos son of Samuel (?)

THE JEWISH DIASPORA

'By the rivers of Babylon, there we sat down, yea, we wept, when we remembered Zion. We hanged our harps upon the willows in the midst thereof. For there they that carried us away captive required of us a song; and they that wasted us required of us mirth, saying, Sing us one of the songs of Zion. How shall we sing the Lord's song in a strange land?' *Psalms 137: 1–4*

The spread of Christianity was aided by missionaries targeting Greek-speaking Jewish communities outside Palestine. This Jewish Diaspora, or 'exile', was a dispersion of Jews throughout old Babylonia and the Roman Empire, with the numbers of Jews increasing by further migrations or conversions. The first dispersion took place after 931 BC, when Jewish tribes in the north split from their southern kin and formed the Kingdom of Israel, while the southerners established the Kingdom of Judah. Israel collapsed in 722 BC, when King Shalmaneser V of Assyria attacked and deported some of the tribes to Khorasan. In 597 BC Nebuchadnezzar II, King of Babylon (630–562 BC), attacked Judah and laid siege to Jerusalem, which left the city and the Temple in ruins. He deported a portion of the Jewish population, including King Jehoiachin, to Babylon and the valley of the Euphrates.

Many Jews fled to Alexandria and Elephantine in Egypt, with the former turning into a major Jewish centre. Jews moved about freely in Greek colonies and settlements, including Kallatis, Tyras, Olbia, Tanais, Phanagoria and inland in Asia Minor at Trapezunt and Gerasus. The Jews also played a key role as traders in the Carthaginian Empire, establishing vibrant communities. In 536 BC, King Cyrus of Persia (c. 576–530 BC), who conquered Babylonia, allowed the exiles to return. Many did, but some chose to remain in exile. The end of the Babylonian captivity is captured in the words of Ezra, below.

Nevertheless, some Jews rebelled against Persia in the regions of Babylon, Cutha and Sura. The failure of the revolt witnessed some Jews flee ng north to Hycarnia on the Caspian Sea and towards the Caucasus, while

'... Thus saith Cyrus king of Persia. The lord God of heaven hath given me all the kingdoms of the earth; and he hath charged me to build him an house at Jerusalem, which is in Judah. Who is there among you of all his people? His God be with him, and let him go up to Jerusalem, which is in Judah, and build the house of the Lord God of Israel (he is the God), which is in Jerusalem.'

Ezra 1: 2–3

JEWS EJECTED
A 15th-century engraving shows the expulsion of Jews from Jerusalem in the reign of the Roman Emperor Hadrian in the 2nd Century AD.

others fled east towards India. By 175 BC, Jews were established in Mumbai. In 320 BC, Egyptian rulers settled 30,000 Jews on the Sinai and Cyrenaican borders, and in Cyprus to protect Egypt from attack. Jews were also active in converting tribes to Judaism in 200 BC at Sale and Volubilis, in modern-day Morocco.

Under Greek Seleucid rule and the later Hasmonean princes, Jews dispersed throughout the known world, as they did under Roman rule after Pompey invaded Jerusalem in 63 BC. As early as the middle of the 2nd Century BC, a Jewish author in the third book of the Oracula Sibyllina recognized that the Jews were present in every land. Works by the period's greatest writers – Greek historian, geographer and philosopher Strabo, the Greek-speaking Jewish philosopher Philo, the Roman philosopher Seneca and Josephus, the Jewish historian – all bear witness to the dispersion of the Jewish people.

In a letter to Emperor Caligula (AD 12–41), King Agrippa I of Judaea (c. 10 BC–AD 44) stated which Roman provinces were Jewish communities, but ignored the settlement in Rome and Cyrene. Josephus maintained that, after Palestine and Babylonia, Syria, particularly Antioch and Damascus, was host to the densest Jewish population. Philo claimed that one mill on Jews inhabited Egypt, comprising one-eighth of the population. Alexandria was the most important Jewish community in Egypt, inhabiting two out of five quarters in the city, according to Philo. The large Jewish community was classified as Politai (citizens) and therefore enjoyed the protection of civil laws. The Jews were a distinct group – below the Greeks but above the native Egyptians. Alexandrine Jews had not been citizens of the old Greek polis, nor did they wish it. Retention of their status was essential; citizenship would have meant losing their Jewish identity. Considering the number of Jews massacred in 115 BC, the numbers living in Cyrenaica, Cyprus and Mesopotamia must have been large. At the accession of Caesar Augustus (Octavian) to the imperial throne in 27 BC, 7,000 Jews were known to be living in Rome. Tax records also show 45,000 Jewish males paying taxes in Asia Minor. Estimates from the 1st Century suggest that five million Jews lived outside Palestine, four-fifths of them within the Roman Empire.

Roman rule over Palestine was shaken by the Jewish revolt of AD 66–70, led by the Zealots and finally crushed with the capture of Masada. One outcome was the destruction of the Temple, the focus of the Temple cult and centre of national and religious life. Another result was the creation of Greek and Roman colonies in Judaea, an attempt to dilute Jewish national aspirations. Titus, the Roman victor, exterminated a quarter of the Jewish population and enslaved a further tenth, reducing the Jewish population to such an extent that they were almost a minority in their own land. Despite the destruction of the military power of the Zealots, the Jewish faith remained a powerful unifying force. In the villages and towns of Judaea and the Diaspora communities, the teachings and rituals of Judaism continued and a Jewish underground grew. Many Jews hoped a messianic leader would restore their independence and plotted for that eventuality.

A major Jewish exodus then commenced, with Jewish elites fleeing to Mesopotamia, then part of the Parthian Empire. In AD 114, Emperor Trajan attacked the Parthians, invading Mesopotamia. The Roman legions smashed the Parthians but faced fierce resistance from the large Jewish settlements. These settlers were enraged that the destroyers of the Temple were now attacking them again. Jewish troops were recruited at Nisibis. Queen Helena of the semi-independent Kingdom of Adiabene, who had converted to Judaism, both supported the revolt in Judaea and allowed Jewish forces to be recruited in her lands.

The conflict in Mesopotamia signalled a general Jewish revolt in the Roman Empire. Risings began in Cyrene, spreading to Alexandria and Cyprus. Judaea saw unrest but no actual rebellion. The Romans crushed the revolts with great difficulty, exterminating the Cypriot Jewish community and burning the main synagogue in

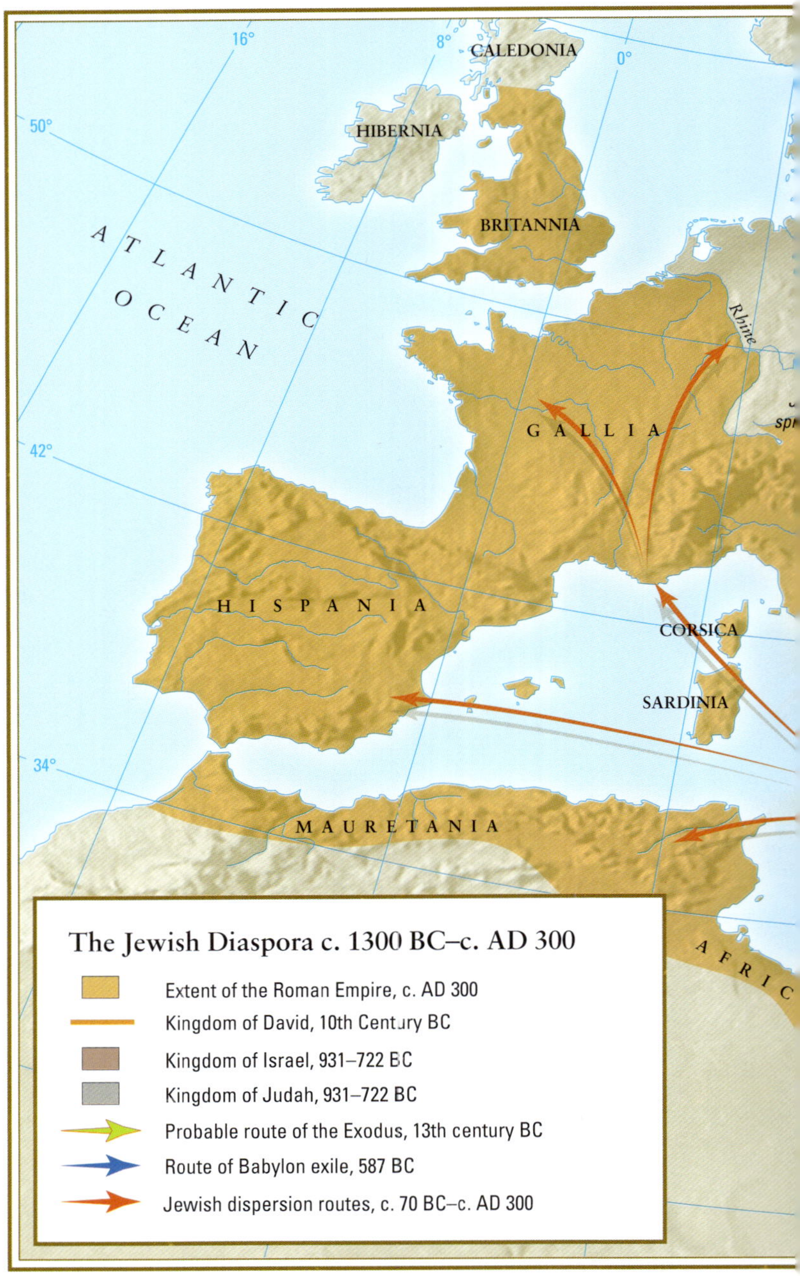

Alexandria. Trajan's successor, Hadrian, withdrew from Parthia allowing peace for the Mesopotamian Jews.

A second Jewish revolt (AD 132–135), under Simeon bar Kokhba, ended in defeat. Some half a million Jews were massacred during this war and thousands sold into slavery. Judaea became known as Syria-Palaestina, and Jerusalem was dedicated to Jupiter. Even so, Jewish communities remained in the Negev, Galilee and the Jordan Valley. Gamaliel III became head of the Jewish community and leader of the Sandedrin, while he established an academy at Usha in Lower Galilee. He and his successors compiled part of the Torah, comprising the Psalms and Proverbs, the Song of Songs and the Books of

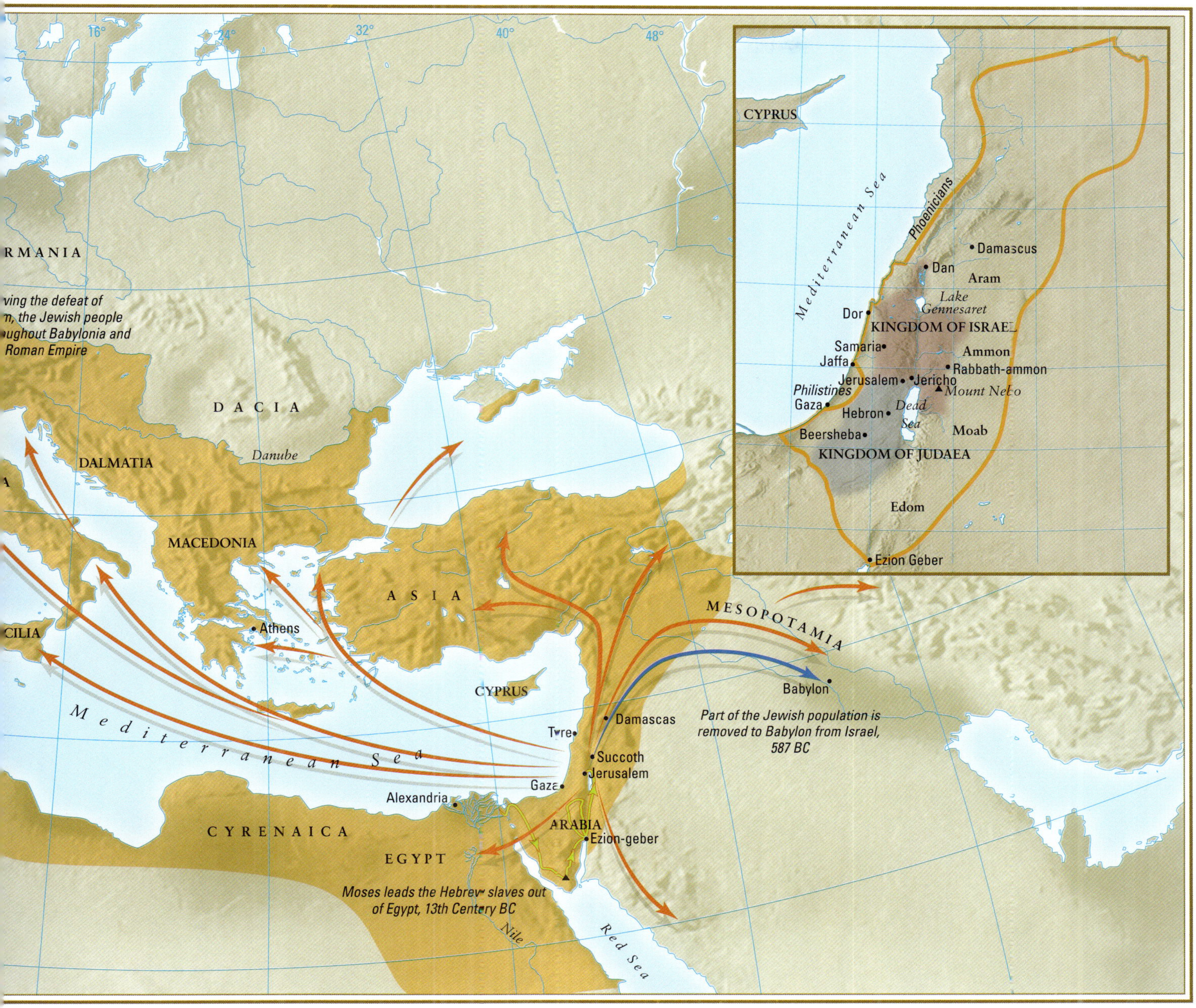

Job, Ruth, Lamentations, Ecclesiastes, Esther, Daniel, Ezra, Nehemiah and the Chronicles – collectively known as the Writings or Hagiography (Ketuvim).

The destruction of the Temple saw the final dispersion of the Jews throughout the world. Jews sold as slaves ended up everywhere. Diaspora Jews were eventually accepted into the Roman Empire. Other Jewish communities were expelled from Judaea and despatched to Roman provinces in the Middle East, Europe and North Africa. With the rise of Christianity, however, came restrictions, especially as Jewish communities became a focus of Christian missionary work. Jews in Babylon enjoyed a different life, becoming the centre of Judaism. In the 3rd Century AD, a religious academy was established in Babylon, with another founded at Pumbetia in Mesopotamia. These centres became significant in creating the most important version of the Talmud and Sua and Pumbetia became the major centres of Judaic thought until the 9th Century. These eastern Jews enjoyed relative autonomy, whether living under the rule of the Assyro-Chaldeans, the Persians, the Parthians, or, eventually, the Muslims.

ROUTES OF DISPERSAL

The main diaspora of the Jews began in the 8th–6th Centuries BC. The number of Jews that were dispersed was greater than that living in Israel. After this period, Jews were scattered broadly throughout the Roman Empire and the world beyond.

The Spread of Christianity

Beyond the time of the Bible, Christianity, despite persecution, expanded rapidly, was given Roman legal status in AD 313 and was helped by the monastic movement. However, about 750, it faced a new challenge, Islam, which recognized Allah as the only god and began to spread into the Mid and Near East.

The Greek culture and language that dominated the eastern Mediterranean region assisted the spread of Christianity. The dispersed Jewish communities in towns dispersed throughout the Middle East spoke Greek, possessed a Greek translation of the Old Testament and provided the first Christian missionaries with points of contact with the local population. The initial, speedy expansion of Christianity during New Testament times was northwards into the Greek cultural zone of Syria, Asia Minor and Greece, and into the Greek-speaking areas of North Africa, particularly Alexandria and Cyrene. Until the end of the 2nd Century, the lists of the Bishops of Rome show them to be Greek-speaking, and the New Testament was first written in Greek.

Syrian Edessa was the portal through which Christianity would spread beyond the borders of the Roman Empire into Mesopotamia, where Syriac became the language of Christian worship and devotion. From there, Christianity reached slowly into Persia and India. Once it had spread into the western, Latin-speaking areas of the Roman Empire, Christianity advanced swiftly. By the 3rd Century AD, there were more than 100 bishops in Italy, while Christianity established itself in Gaul and Spain. After the Romans gave Christianity official recognition in AD 313, there were at least three bishoprics in Britain, with St Patrick's mission to Ireland starting about AD 432.

During this expansion, Christians engaged in the holy meal of bread and wine – the Eucharist (thanksgiving) – which was regarded as a sacrament, a conduit for divine grace to permeate the recipient with the spirit of Christ. Converts were initiated into the Church via baptism, through which God's grace washed away all sins. For obscure reasons, the wide range of written texts telling the story of the Christian faith had been whittled down

'We believe in one God … and in one Lord, Jesus Christ, the only son of God, eternally begotten of the Father, God from God, light from light, true God from true God, begotten, not made, of one being with the Father …'

(Nicene Creed)

to those ascribed to Matthew, Mark, Luke and John, which became the core of the New Testament. Christians were also inspired by the lives of saints, whose written tradition is known as hagiography.

Initially, Christian communities met in private homes, but eventually purpose-built churches became the norm. A distinction grew up between the clergy and laity. The former governed the Church and administered the sacraments, while the latter were the recipients. The clergy became ordained into the priesthood and became divided into ranks: the priests administered the Eucharist,

HOLY SETTLEMENTS

Christians at first met in private homes, but in time began to construct chapels for worship and entire religious communities based around the church, such as Iona, a small island off Scotland, which was founded as a Celtic monastery in AD 563 by Columba.

while the bishops supervised priests and led Christian urban communities. Archbishops supervised the bishops and were sometimes known as metropolitans. The most important bishops were those of the greatest and most influential cities, such as Rome, Antioch, Alexandria, Jerusalem and Constantinople. These bishops were known as patriarchs. Of these, only one lived in the West, and claimed to have pre-eminence – Peter. The most important of the apostles, Peter lived out his last years in Rome and was martyred there. He was held to be the first pope, and later popes considered themselves his successors. However, the other patriarchs refused to acknowledge Rome's authority until centuries later.

The Christians were convinced that they possessed the absolute truth and totally rejected all other religions. This certitude and arrogance resulted in intermittent waves of persecution, which finally ended when joint Emperors Constantine and Licinius granted Christians official toleration and protection in 313. The Roman emperors nourished Christianity, and several councils of bishops were held in the 4th Century to iron out doctrinal disputes and set out rules of behaviour. Magnificent and awesome Christian churches were built. The emperors ended gladiatorial combat in the arena and replaced it with chariot races. The abandonment of babies was prohibited, but slavery continued for so-called economic reasons. Constantine's activities won him the support of the Church, which led to imperial legitimation.

The Christian faith won over masses of converts and became the dominant religion in the Mediterranean, but its character changed. The Church became controlled by the wealthy, aristocratic families, thereby diminishing its initial equality, and women's roles were curtailed that weakened their earlier role in church formation. The institutionalized Church became ever more patriarchal and rigid, and much spirituality withered on the vine.

The Church now switched its fight against paganism and Roman gods to enemies within the fold. Issues of doctrine became paramount, with disagreements between schools of thought being fought out as conflicts between orthodoxy and heresy. The most noticeable confrontation was between orthodox Trinitarianism and Arianism. The latter was condemned at the Council of Nicaea in AD 325 and the reign of Emperor Theodosius I (AD 379–395) witnessed the state adding to the ban on Arianism by outlawing its teachings and making Christianity the official religion of the Roman state. Arians based their views on those of Arius, a Libyan who studied at the school of Lucien of Antioch. Despite his views being outlawed, they survived amongst the Germanic tribes into the late 6th Century.

Arius contended that God was unbegotten and without beginning, whereas Christ was begotten and could not be God in the sense of God the Father. Christ the Son was not created from the divine substance of the Father; he did not exist from all eternity, but was formed out of nothing like all other creatures, and existed by the will of the Father. In other words, the relationship of the Son to the Father was not natural but adoptive.

The Council of Nicea formulated the Nicene Creed, which remains intact and is still used by Roman Catholic, Orthodox, Anglican and some Protestant services. The Creed affirms that Father and Son are of one being. Arius was exiled as were the Libyan bishops Theonas of Marmarica and Secundus of Ptolemais. These events failed to end controversy. Constantine wanted leniency to exist for Arius and his Arians. Arius was rehabilitated and his main accuser, Athanasius, Bishop of Alexandria, banished. Constantine's son Constantius II (AD 353–361) attacked adherents of the Nicene Creed, preferring Arianism. However, supporters of Arius splintered into various groups, who sought to reconcile their differences in 18 councils. Theodosius sought to end all confrontation at the ecumenical council at Constantinople in 381. Henceforth, the Nicene Creed was accepted by the Roman peoples, excepting the Germans.

As Arianism began to flourish in Constantinople, a Goth convert named Ulfilas was despatched as a missionary to the Gothic tribes across the River Danube, to convert them and thereby diminish the Goth threat. Ulfilas was incredibly successful in teaching, preaching and converting the Germanic tribes to the Arian brand of Christianity. These Germans, having now been Christian for over a century, eventually entered the Roman Empire and founded successor states in the western part, such as Lombardy in Italy. In these Arian Germanic kingdoms, the Germanic Arian élite co-existed with their Nicene subjects. Parallel Church hierarchies worked with the elites, holding on to Arianism in order to keep their identity amid the majority Nicene peoples. The Germans tolerated Nicene beliefs, except in North Africa, where the Nicene clergy and their institutions were persecuted. The Arian German kingdoms included the Ostrogoths, the Visigoths, Vandals, Burgundians and Lombards. The Franks converted to Nicene Christianity immediately, and their leader, Pepin, supported the Pope in his search for

CHURCHES SPREAD THEIR WINGS

Hagia Irene Church, above, was the first church to be built in Constantinople. It was commissioned by Emperor Constantine I, who had guaranteed the acceptance of Christianity within the Roman Empire in AD 313.

RESURRECTED CHRIST

The first appearance of the resurrected Christ was to Mary Magdalene, who had come to visit his tomb. This painting of the scene is by the Dutch artist Rembrandt (1609–69).

secular lands to protect Rome and in turn was anointed King of the Franks. By the beginning of the 8th Century, these Germanic kingdoms had been either converted or conquered by their neighbours, or, like the Visigoths and Lombards, they had accepted Nicene Christianity.

Elsewhere, a division within Nicene Christianity occurred that mirrored the divisions of the old Roman Empire into East and West. Western Christians looked to the Pope in Rome for authority as he claimed authority over all Christians, using the term catholic (universal) to categorize his faith. Eastern Christians rejected this claim, and regarded the Byzantine Emperor and the patriarch of Constantinople as their leaders. This division between Catholic and Eastern Orthodox Christians developed over several centuries, with various issues being disputed, but the year 1054 is usually accepted as the date of the schism between East and West, when Pope Leo IX (1049–1054) and Patriarch Michael Cerularius (1043–1058) excommunicated each other.

The Western Church is particularly important in another sense. It digested Roman political organization, administration and law. The Pope assumed the ancient Roman title of pontifex maximus (supreme pontiff) and kept going much of the ritual of the late imperial courts. Canon law, that is Church law, is modelled on Roman civil law, and in this sense the early medieval church was a spectre of the Roman Empire. However, the Church allowed the masses to participate in common rituals, providing a sense of involvement and identity, which had never happened under the Roman Empire.

During the early days of Christianity, the authors of the New Testament saw the rapid spread of the new faith as miraculous. It provided direct evidence of the divinity of Jesus. The final phase of God's plans to save the world must have begun, clearly shown by the Christian groups that sprang up and survived in the towns from Palestine to Rome. The movement was helped by a number of factors, particularly the peace imposed by Rome on her Empire, which by now included all the peoples of the Mediterranean and Black Sea areas, the whole of Europe as far east as the River Rhine and most of Britain. Wherever the Romans gained control, they created safe, efficient communications by both land and sea, in order to move administrators and troops swiftly and to supply the needs of Rome's teeming population.

The official religions of the Empire were extensions of Roman power that tended to confirm and justify its rule and the divine authority of the Emperor. Christianity, on the other hand, offered its members a sense of freedom, equality and community, which transcended all differences of race, social class and legal status. The destruction of Jerusalem by the Romans in AD 70 helped to free Christianity from its Jewish origins so that it could make a more universal appeal and meet the needs of non-Jewish converts without the restrictions of the Hebrew religious laws.

From the time of Alexander the Great's triumphant reign (336–323 BC), Greek culture and language had dominated the eastern Mediterranean region, and this also assisted the spread of Christianity beyond the confines of Palestine. The scattered Jewish communities in towns throughout the Near East spoke Greek, had a Greek translation of the Old Testament and provided the first Christian missionaries, with convenient points of contact with the population. The first rapid expansion of Christianity during New Testament times was northwards into the Greek world of Syria, Asia Minor and Greece, and into the Greek-speaking areas of North Africa, particularly Alexandria and Cyrene. The lists of the early bishops of Rome show that until the end of the 2nd Century they were all Greek-speaking and, indeed, the New Testament was originally written in Greek.

Edessa in Syria was the gateway for Christianity to reach beyond the borders of the Roman Empire into Mesopotamia, where Syriac became the language of Christian worship and devotion, and from there Christianity spread slowly into Persia and India. Once it had penetrated effectively into the western, Latin-speaking areas of Roman rule, Christianity made rapid advances. By the 3rd Century AD, there were more than a hundred bishoprics in Italy, and Christianity was firmly established in Gaul and Spain.

Persecution of Christians by the Roman authorities was usually spasmodic and localized, typified by Nero's

A NEW FAITH SPREADS *(see overleaf)*
From its centres in the Greek- speaking world, Christianity spread into Mesopotamia, Persia and India. Soon it was also firmly established in western Europe, including Britain, and Christians were largely allowed to practise their religion without interference, even though there are records of two widespread persecutions by the Roman authorities in AD 250 and 303. In AD 313, the joint Roman Emperors, Constantine and Licinius, gave legal recognition to Christianity. When Constantine moved the capital of the Roman Empire from Rome to Constantinople in AD 331, he hoped that Christianity would unite all his subjects, for the Empire was beginning to disintegrate. The differences between Greek-speaking Christians and those that spoke Latin had become more serious. In AD 325, a council held at Nicea tried to close the widening breach with a creed that set out the basic beliefs of Christianity. Six more ecumenical councils during the following four and a half centuries would try to establish a form of Christianity faithful to its founder and agreed by all Christians.

The Spread of Christianity
Christian by AD 45
Christian by AD 100
Christian by AD 185
Christian by AD 325
Roman Empire c. 300
CALEDONIA
HIBERNIA
BRITANNIA
Ebaracum
Londinium
OCEANUS GERMANICUS
Mare Suevicum
OCEANUS ATLANTICUS (ATLANTIC OCEAN)
GERMANIA INFERIOR
GERMANIA
BELGICA
Durocortorum
Augusta Treverorum
Agri Decumates
Lugdunensis
GALLIA
Burdigala
Aquitania
Lugdunum
Narbonensis
Massilia
RAETIA
NORICUM
PANNONIA
Mediolamum
ALPES COTTIAE
ALPES MARITIMAE
ITALIA
Ravenna
ILLYRICUM
DALMATIA
Salanae
CORSICA
SARDINIA
Rome
Capua
MACEDO
Apollonia
Tarraconensis
HISPANIA
Lusitania
Emerita Augusta
Baetica
Corduba
Hispalis
Tarraco
Carthago Nova
Tingis
Caesarea
MAURETANIA
Tingitana
Caesariensis
Hippo Regius
Carthago
SICILIA
Syracusae
Melite I.
Atlas Mountains
AFRICA
Leptis Magna
Cyrene
CY
Sahara Desert

S A R M A T I A
Maeotis Palus
Pontus Euxinus
Black Sea
Caucasus Mountains
Mare Caspium
Caspian Sea
Sinus Oxianus
MOESIA
THRACIA
Byzantium
Sinope
Trapezus
Artaxata
ARMENIA
BITHYNIA AND PONTUS
Nicopolis
CAPPADOCIA
ASSYRIA
A S I A
GALATIA
CILICIA
Tarsus
Antiochia
SYRIA
Ephesus
LYCIA
CYPRUS
Creta
MESOPOTAMIA
Babylon
PERSIAN EMPIRE
Damascus
Tyre
Bostra
Jerusalem
JUDAEA
Gaza
ARABIA
Alexandria
Heliopolis
Memphis
A E G Y P T U S
Antinopolis
Thebes
Sinus Arabicus
Arabian Desert
Sinus Persicus

notorious cruelty to them in Rome following the great fire of AD 64. However, the martyrdoms at Lyons in AD 177, during the reign of the Emperor Marcus Aurelius (AD 161–180), show how intense such local persecutions could be. There are records of two more universal persecutions – Emperor Decius (AD 249–251) mounted a systematic attack on Christianity in AD 250 and a subsequent period of tolerance ended abruptly in AD 303 when the Emperor Diocletian (AD 284–305) ordered all churches and Christian books to be destroyed and followed this with the execution of Christians during the next eight years. The first main phase of Christian expansion ended with the Edict of Milan in AD 313, when the joint Emperors Constantine and Licinius gave Christianity legal recognition.

In granting recognition to Christianity, Constantine hoped that Christianity would unite all his subjects in a common faith and help withstand the barbarian incursions into the Roman Empire. In AD 331, Constantine moved the capital of the Empire from Rome to Constantinople (Istanbul), the new city he had built to command the sea passage from the Mediterranean to the Black Sea. As the western parts of the Empire crumbled, so the cultural differences between the eastern, Greek-speaking Christians and the western Latin-speakers became more obvious. The uncertainties of intermittent persecution and tolerance had helped unite Christians but the new official recognition brought differences into the open.

Freedom from fear of official interference allowed resentments to surface against Christians who had submitted to the Roman laws against Christianity, even though a Church synod ruled that there should be no rejection of the lapsed who wished to return. A more serious split among Christians developed from Alexandria, where a controversy raged about the exact status of Jesus Christ as God and spread throughout the eastern churches. Constantine convened a council at Nicea in AD 325, which set out the basic beliefs of Christianity in a creed for universal acceptance. Nicea was followed by six more ecumenical councils during the following four and a half centuries to try to settle further controversies and establish a form of Christianity agreed by all Christians. They met at Constantinople (AD 381), Ephesus (AD 431), Chalcedon (AD 451), Constantinople again (AD 553 and 680) and Nicea (AD 787).

Inevitably, the Christians adopted much of the Roman Empire's administrative organization, if only because it provided convenient and natural geographical division

'I am the true vine, and my Father is the husbandman. Every branch in me that beareth not fruit he taketh away: and every branch that beareth fruit, he purgeth it, that it may bring forth more fruit. Now ye are clean through the word which I have spoken unto you. Abide in me, and I in you. As the branch cannot bear fruit of itself, except it abide in the vine; no more can ye, except ye abide in me. I am the vine, ye are the branches: He that abideth in me, and I in him, the same bringeth forth much fruit: for without me ye can do nothing.'

John 15:1–5

and symbols of authority. A diocese was originally a larger administrative region of secular government within the Roman Empire, containing a number of provinces. In time the term was applied to the larger areas of ecclesiastical jurisdiction, containing a number of bishoprics, and finally to the smaller area ruled by each bishop. An important stage in the recognition of special influence by the Bishop of Rome was reached at the time of the Council of Chalcedon, when the Bishop of Constantinople appealed to Leo, Bishop of Rome, for help and received a summary of the Christian faith, the 'Tome of Leo', which was given official status by the Council.

Even before the recognition of Christianity by Constantinople, a new movement developed first in Egypt and then in other places that was to have lasting effects on the spread of Christianity. Christian hermits who had withdrawn to the desert in Egypt became so numerous that they organized themselves into communities with a common rule, which recognized the individualism of the hermits' ideals but provided for shared worship. The movement, monasticism, spread in modified forms to Arabia, Asia Minor, north Africa, Spain, Britain and Ireland, where Patrick made it the means of consolidating Christianity in that land. In the following century, Columba

TOMB OF STONE

Jesus's body was taken down from the cross and laid in an empty rock tomb similar to this one. The rolled-back circular stone door was the first sign of Jesus's Resurrection from the dead.

took monasticism from Ireland to Scotland, establishing a monastery at what was then a centre of communications on the island of Iona, and consolidated the work begun by Ninian nearly two centuries earlier.

The form of monasticism most familiar in the West stems from Benedict, who transformed the hermit type of monasticism in Italy into a thoroughly integrated and organized form of community life controlled by his famous Rule. Benedict's twin principles of 'stability' – commitment to the community and to the Rule – quickly gained followers. The Benedictine form of monasticism spread rapidly within Italy and was introduced into Britain by Augustine of Canterbury in AD 597. Eventually, it became the normal form of monasticism in the West and one of the main means of extending the influence of Rome within Christianity.

With the collapse of the western parts of the Roman Empire under barbarian attacks and the gradual conversion of the invading peoples, it might have seemed that Christianity would prove to be a unifying force to replace the old military might of Rome. However, an important setback to such an ideal came from an unexpected area in the Arabian Desert to the east of the Red Sea.

The main religion of the nomads of the Arabian Desert and the people of the isolated towns on the main caravan routes was a polytheism of many gods, associated with particular localities or various aspects of nature and of human need. All that was changed dramatically by Muhammad, who was born into a prominent family in Mecca about AD 570. The first 40 years of his life were in no way extraordinary. Muhammad travelled with the caravans from Mecca as far as Syria as a merchant, and married. His call as a prophet came to him at the age of 40, and he began his preaching some three years later in Mecca, now in modern-day Saudi Arabia.

Both Judaism and Christianity had penetrated into Arabia, and the caravans came into contact with them at the great trading centres in Syria and Mesopotamia. However, Muhammad preached a monotheism that identified Allah, the chief god of Mecca, as the sole God of the universe, who alone must be worshipped. The main practical consequence for believers was acceptance of the equality of all people before God, and the duty of all to care for the less fortunate. Muhammad claimed that he was only the last of a line of prophets sent by God, which included Abraham, Moses and Jesus, but to

Muhammad God dictated a sacred book through an angel that contains all that is needed for belief, the regulation of personal life and the organization of society. This book, the Koran (or Qur'an), is written in Arabic and is divided into 114 chapters or suras. It is so sacred for Islam that strict Muslims will not recognize any translation of it. The pattern of life derived from the Koran is expressed in five 'pillars of faith' – belief in Allah as the only God, and Muhammad, as his prophet; prayer five times each day; alms-giving; fasting during daylight hours in the month of Ramadan; and a pilgrimage to Mecca.

From the beginning, Muhammad had to assert the supremacy of his teaching by force to overcome the antagonism of the families that controlled western Arabia, particularly Mecca. War remained a legitimate means of spreading God's revelation if people would not accept it peacefully. But the religion preached by Muhammad, and perpetuated through the Koran, would never have achieved such remarkable success if it had not been so attractive. To the believer, it provides a simple, systematic and coherent way of life.

With remarkable speed, the new religion embarked on a great campaign of conquest, first within Arabia itself and then into the surrounding areas of Syria, Palestine, Mesopotamia, Egypt and North Africa. By the middle of the 8th Century it had expanded into India and had control of most of Spain. Much of this was achieved within 20 years of the death of Muhammad in AD 632. Breathtakingly beautiful shrines were erected, such as the Dome of the Rock in Jerusalem. It was built in AD 691 over the place where Muslims believe that Muhammad began his 'night journey', in which the glories of heaven were revealed to him. Traditionally, this is also the place where Abraham was prepared to sacrifice Isaac (Genesis 22) and the site of the Hebrew Temple before its destruction by the Romans in AD 70.

THE DOME OF THE ROCK

Seen from the Mount of Olives, the Temple area dominates Jerusalem. The main feature is the great stone platform for the Temple courtyards, built by Herod the Great. The Temple itself stood on the site of the domed building, a Muslim shrine that protects the bare rock of the hill sacred to Jews and Muslims. The Jerusalem of King David's time lay to the left of the present Temple area and the city spread beyond the Temple, where modern Jerusalem has continued to expand.

Glossary

Altar A place of sacrifice, usually a heap of earth or stones, a single stone, or a stone table, standing before a temple.

Akkadian An ancient language spoken in Mesopotamia from c. 3000 BC until the time of Christ. Assyrian and Babylonian were two dialect forms. The Akkadians adopted the cuneiform system of writing. *See Cuneiform.*

Amalekites A nomadic shepherd tribe of southern Palestine and the Sinai Peninsula.

Ammonites An Aramaean tribe that settled east of the Jordan Valley.

Anoint To pour oil on people or objects to show they are dedicated to sacred purposes, particularly kings or priests. *See Christ and Messiah.*

Apostle From Greek, the word means 'one who is sent with authority'. In the New Testament it usually refers to one of Jesus's 12 disciples.

Aramaeans Nomadic tribes of Syria and Mesopotamia, related to the Hebrews.

Aramaic The Semitic language of the Aramaeans, widely used for 1,000 years from the time of the Persian Empire. This was the native language of Jesus.

Ark of the Covenant The small, sacred box, containing the Ten Commandments, carried to Canaan by the Hebrews, for which the Temple in Jerusalem was built by Solomon.

Assyrians The Mesopotamians who conquered the Near and Middle East early in the 1st Millennium BC. Their main capital was Nineveh on the River Tigris.

Baal Literally 'overlord' in Hebrew; the title of the main Canaanite fertility god.

Babylonians The Mesopotamians of the River Euphrates, who overthrew the Assyrians and took the Hebrews into exile.

Bronze An alloy of copper and tin, strong and easily worked, in common use before iron. The Bronze Age was c. 3000–1200 BC.

Canaan The older, 2nd Millennium BC name for the general region of Palestine.

Cataract One of a stretch of rapids interrupting the flow of the River Nile. There are six main cataracts and they have sometimes been used to mark political frontiers.

Chaldeans A Semitic tribe of southern Mesopotamia.

Christ Literally 'the anointed one' in Greek, and thus God's chosen servant. *See Messiah.*

City-state A self-governing city that was also a state and often had dependencies – mainly in ancient Greece.

Council The supreme Jewish religious council during New Testament times.

Covenant The solemn agreement with God in which the Hebrews believed he had chosen them.

Crucifixion Execution by nailing or tying to a wooden cross.

Cuneiform From the Latin word for 'wedge', Mesopotamian writing with wedge-shaped letters. It was written on clay tablets using a pointed stylus.

Diaspora Jewish communities outside Palestine.

Edomites People living in an area from the Dead Sea south to the Gulf of Aqaba.

Egyptians People of the Nile Valley from the First Cataract to the Mediterranean Sea.

Essenes An unorthodox Jewish monastic movement of New Testament times, who wrote the Dead Sea Scrolls. *See Scroll.*

Ethiopians People of the Nile Valley above the First Cataract living in Cush (modern Sudan). They were also called Nubians.

Eucharist Literally 'thanksgiving' in Greek. *See Last Supper.*

Evangelist A teacher of the 'gospel'; more usually the author of a Gospel.

Exile The deportation of Hebrews to Babylonia in 598 BC and 587–539 BC.

Exodus The escape of the Hebrews from slavery in Egypt in c. 1250 BC.

Fertile Crescent The agricultural area from Upper Egypt, through Palestine and Syria, to Mesopotamia and the Persian Gulf.

Gentile Anyone who is not Jewish.

Gnosticism Derived from the Greek meaning 'pertaining to knowledge'; a religious movement that offered salvation by secret knowledge.

Gospel Literally 'good news'; the message of salvation associated with Jesus Christ.

Hebrew language A Canaanite dialect, replaced by Aramaic but surviving in sacred writings and worship.

Hebrews The descendants of Abraham. The origins of the word are obscure and may have designated a mercenary warrior class associated with nomadic Semitic tribesmen.

Hellenism The culture that spread from the Greek mainland and its colonies.

Herod Usually Herod the Great, King of Judaea under the Romans 37–34 BC, but also several of his descendants.

Hittites A people who ruled Syria from Turkey before the time of the Israelites and Aramaeans. They narrowly lost the Battle of Kadesh against the Egyptians in 1285 BC.

Hurrians A group of people who formed part of the Hittite Empire. They date from 2500 BC and were settled throughout the Fertile Crescent.

Hyksos The Asiatic people who invaded Egypt in the Second Intermediate Period between the Middle Kingdom and the New Kingdom. It is likely that the Israelites settled in Egypt during the Hyksos period.

Incense Aromatic gums, burned in worship, especially during sacrifices.

Iron The most common metal from c. 1200 BC, hence 'Iron Age'.

Islam The main religion of much of Asia, in which Muhammad is the prophet. Followers of the Islamic faith are called Muslims. They are devoted to the Koran, a book written in Arabic, which is believed to be the revelation of God to Muhammad.

Israelites Confusingly, all Hebrews, or members of the northern Hebrew kingdom, from the split into two kingdoms (931 BC) until its destruction in 721 BC. Their capital was Samaria.

Jehovah *See Yahweh.*

Jew Strictly a member of the tribe of Judah, but, after the exile, any Hebrew.

Judaea Southern Palestine in Greek and Roman times.

Judah One of the 12 tribes, and the southern Hebrew kingdom after the split of 931 BC until its destruction in 587 BC. The capital was Jerusalem.

Kassites A people who ruled in Babylon from the 18th

Century until the 20th Century BC. They were probably Indo-Europeans.

Last Supper Also called the Lord's Supper, the final meal of Jesus and the disciples before his arrest. The Eucharist, the Christian sacrament commemorating it, is derived from the meal. *See Eucharist.*

Maccabee Literally 'hammer' in Hebrew; the nickname of the leaders of the Jewish rebellion against Greek rule in 165 BC.

Magi Persian priests.

Marduk The chief god of Babylon.

Mesopotamia The land area from the Persian Gulf northwards, drained by the Tigris and Euphrates rivers.

Messiah Literally 'the anointed one' in Hebrew.

Midianites A nomadic tribe closely associated with the Israelites, who lived along the coast of the Red Sea to the south of Edom. Moses married a Midianite woman.

Millennium A period of 1,000 years.

Mitanni The name of a state in Mesopotamia, powerful between 1500 and 1370 BC. It supported a large Hurrian population. Mitanni was conquered by the Hittites early in the 14th Century BC.

Moabites A people who lived to the east of the Dead Sea on the River Arnon. Although they were related to them through Lot, they frequently fought against the Israelites during the Old Testament period.

Nomads Tented tribes who herd sheep and goats across sparse pastures.

Obelisk A four-sided tapering shaft of stone with a small pyramid at the top. Obelisks were associated with sun worship and were often placed in pairs outside the entrances of Egyptian temples and tombs.

Oil Invariably olive oil, used in cooking, medicine, cosmetics, lamps and religious rites. *See Ancint.*

Palestine Strictly the coastal strip north-east of Egypt, settled by Philistines but extenced to refer to the land from Lebanon to the Sinai Desert.

Parthians A people famous for their archers and horsemen, whose empire was at its height in the 1st Century BC. It extended from the River Euphrates as far as the Indus and the Indian Ocean. The empire fell into decline when the Persians conquered the Parthians in AD 226.

Passover The oldest Hebrew festival, which commemorates the Exodus from Egypt.

Patriarchs The main Hebrew ancestors, from Adam to Joseph.

Pentateuch Literally 'five books' in Greek; the first five books of the Old Testament.

Pentecost From the Greek meaning 50th; a harvest festival 50 days after that of Unleavened Bread.

Persians A people east of the Persian Gulf who overthrew the Babylonians in 540 BC; conquered by Alexander the Great in 331 BC.

Pharisees A lay Jewish group committed to a strict interpretation of the law.

Philistines The people who occupied the Palestinian coastal plain between the Mediterranean (the Great Sea) and the Shephelah. The name 'Palestine' is a derivative of Philistine. Some of the Sea Peoples who invaded Egypt in the late 19th and early 20th dynasties were Philistines.

Polytheism The belief in many or more than one god.

Priest The class responsible for oracles, law and performing sacrifices. It eventually became exclusive and hereditary.

Procurator A Roman official directly responsible to the Emperor.

Prophet A person claiming to speak in God's name.

Psalm A song used in worship.

Puppet kingdom A kingdom that is more or less completely governed by and answerable to a more powerful kingdom or state.

Qumran Site of an Essene community near the north-west shore of the Dead Sea.

Rabbi Literally 'my master' in Aramaic; a teacher, especially a scribe.

Satrap A governor of a province (or satrapy) in ancient Persia.

Scroll A rolled book usually written on a long strip of papyrus or sheepskin. The Dead Sea Scrolls are the recently discovered Essene library from Qumran.

Sea Peoples *See Philistines.*

Semites A people from the Arabian Desert, including Hebrews, with related languages.

Septuagint The ancient translation of the Old Testament into Greek.

Sumerians A people controlling southern Mesopotamia in the 3rd Millennium BC.

Synagogue Literally 'assembly place', derived from Greek; a Jewish meeting place for worship, teaching and discussion.

Tabernacle The tent-shrine of the Ark of the Covenant before the Temple was built.

Tabernacles The third harvest festival, named after the tents that harvesters used in the fields

Temple A building dedicated to gods and associated with their presence. In this book, temple with a capital 'T' refers to the one in Jerusalem.

Testament Another translation of the words for 'covenant'. *See Covenant.*

Tetrarchy In the Roman Empire, a fourth part of a country or province. Each part was ruled by a tetrarch.

Theocracy A form of government in which a god is recognized as supreme ruler and his laws are carried out by priests.

Unleavened bread Bread made without yeast, offered as a pure harvest sacrifice, hence the name of the first harvest festival attached to the Passover.

Vulgate The ancient Latin translation of the Bible.

Wadi A watercourse, found in places such as Egypt, that is dry except during periods of rainfall.

Yahweh The modern transliteration of the Hebrew personal name of God.

Zealots A fanatical Jewish sect who rebelled against the Romans and were not accepted by other Jews. They carried out many assassinations and were responsible for numerous revolts. They were the main initiators of the Jewish-Roman war in AD 66.

Zeus The chief god of the ancient Greeks, identified as Jupiter by the Romans.

Ziggurat A Mesopotamian tower-like temple.

Zion The ancient Davidic citadel of Jerusalem. The exact location is not certain.

INDEX

Page numbers in **bold** refer to maps; page numbers in *italic* refer to illustrations.

Acknowledgements

For Cartographica Press
Design, Maps and Typesetting: Jeanne Radford, PAB Smith, Alexander Swanston, Malcolm Swanston and Jonathan Young

Biblical advice: Reverend Roland Jones

Picture credits
19 shutterstock.com/360b; 20 shutterstock.com/mountainpix; 22 shutterstock.com/ChameleonsEye; 27 shutterstock.com/Nathan Holland; 33 shutterstock.com/Kamira; 44 shutterstock.com/Nicku; 45 shutterstock.com/ChameleonsEye; 48-49 shutterstock.com/Idan Ben Haim; 68 shutterstock.com/bumihills; 94 shutterstock.com/Nickolay Vinokurov; 109 shutterstock.com/Waj; 112 shutterstock.com/Nitr; 117 shutterstock.com/Nicku; 125 shutterstock.com/mtsyri; 127 shutterstock.com/Kamira; 149 shutterstock.com/JPRichard; 153 shutterstock.com/k45025 Rita K; 154 shutterstock.com/Nicku; 159 shutterstock.com/mountainpix; 169 shutterstock.com/Dimitrios; 171 shutterstock.com/Nicku; 175 shutterstock.com/Anton_Ivanov; 177 shutterstock.com/gilya; 183 shutterstock.com/Pavel Bernshtam; 184 shutterstock.com/Boris Diakovsky; 195 shutterstock.com/Renata Sedmakova; 213 shutterstock.com/Motordigitaal; 215 shutterstock.com/FXEGS Javier Espuny; 216 shutterstock.com/Jeff Dalton; 217 shutterstock.com/Ryan Simpson; 220 shutterstock.com/Phish Photography; 225 shutterstock.com/SERHAT AKAVCI; 231 shutterstock.com/Evgeny Eremeev; 232 shutterstock.com/ChameleonsEye; 239 shutterstock.com/Bill McKelvie; 241 shutterstock.com/EvrenKalinbacak; 248-9 shutterstock.com/photo.ua

Quarto Publishing Group 21, 39, 85, 89, 131, 144, 157, 182, 187, 200–1, 203, 247

Wikipedia 7, 30, 41, 51, 56, 64, 71, 73, 74, 77, 82, 91, 97, 119, 128-9, 139, 192, 196, 205, 235, 243

While every effort has been made to credit contributors, Quantum would like to apologize should there have been any omissions or errors.